Distributed Cloud

Reference Architecture Design

Weiqi Tian

Distributed Cloud Reference Architecture Design 1st Edition

Weiqi Tian

Hong Lin

From the public cloud to private cloud, hybrid cloud, and multi-cloud, each step can bring certain special futures to users. However, some problems still exist, for example, even a hybrid cloud with edge and multi-cloud cannot solve the problem of interoperability, portability and inconsistency. Today, enterprise businesses are diverse and constantly changing. No single size fits all. Any system with certain unique features will not be able to meet all requirements.

Although Gartner proposed a Distributed Cloud: "Distributed Cloud is the distribution of public cloud services to different physical locations, while the operation, governance, updates, and evolution of the services are the responsibility of the originating public cloud provider.", this cloud architecture emphasizes that it uses one of the public cloud providers as an entrance controller to manage all distributed on-premises and public cloud infrastructures, this approach will bring at least two problems: One is using third-party public cloud provider to host the entrance controller can not resolve the vender-locking issue, another one is any public cloud provider cannot be 100% neutral, it is inevitable to be biased and selective when integrating to other public cloud providers.

This book proposes a different architecture that takes the central control point, OneCenter, living anywhere, is independent and not fixed to any cloud provider including on-premise; OneCenter manages global resources from all providers in a neutral, consistent, and unified method. Distributed Cloud leverages edge computing, telco edge, public cloud, private cloud, hybrid cloud, multi-cloud benefits, and beyond all of those clouds. This book mainly provides a general framework, basic ideas, core points, and essential technologies. It does not cover every aspect of Distributed Cloud products.

Why I Wrote This Book

Some cloud vendors claim that they can provide distributed cloud products. However, the products they mentioned are only the traditional CDN or conventional edge cloud; such a system can not yet resolve the vendor-locking issue. Besides, even the hybrid or multi-cloud, cannot solve the problem of operational and management inconsistency. This book proposes a different innovative architecture with four essential layers, the design of architecture includes elaborating a versatile OneCenter, discussing the concept of an elastic distributed site, expanding the scope of intelligent resource scheduling and provisioning of computing, networking, and storage to cloud, on-premises and Telco edge computing all over the world.

In addition, this book designs a new native modern big data platform and a scalable distributed conference edge computing platform based on the Distributed Cloud architecture natively. At the same time, finally, this book also presents some new innovative points of cloud architecture of the talent VDC and GVPC. Those are essential features that all current clouds lack and are also the future trend of cloud computing.

What's Inside

Chapter 1 and Chapter 2 give the definition, top-view design architecture, application model, and ultra scaling of the Distributed Cloud.

Chapter 3 to Chapter 5 introduces the critical creative supporting technologies and architecture design of the networking, computing, and storage in the Distributed Cloud.

Chapter 6 explains the site-related key concepts of Distributed Cloud and the site's architecture elaborate design regarding computing, networking, and storage.

Chapter 7 describes the 'Single Pane of Glass' Manager and Controller, OneCenter, and the general architecture, abstraction, and virtualization of the uneven heterogeneous underlying infrastructures for the Distributed Cloud.

Chapter 8 offers the architecture design of Hybrid, Multi-cloud, WANaaS, and Disaster Recovery as primary capacities in the Distributed Cloud.

Chapter 9 presents 3GPP edge computing integration to empower the Distributed Cloud.

Chapter 10 to Chapter 11 brings both the telco edge computing and modern data architecture design as the typical user cases leveraging the benefits of the Distributed Cloud's innovative architecture characteristics.

Who and How to Read This Book

This book assumes you have basic computer science, cloud computing, big data, networks, and telecommunications knowledge. If you are a teacher, student, or staff engaged in those related areas, this book will be of great value to you.

This book does not cover everything because Distributed Cloud involve many technical points and design details. If you have any comments or mistaken findings regarding how I can improve the quality of this book or otherwise alter it to suit your needs better, you can contact me by e-mail at onedux@gmail.com. I greatly appreciate your advice and assistance.

TABLE OF CONTENTS

Chapter 1   Introduction

After 2000, the Hypervisor virtualization software launched by VMWare no longer relies on a parent operating system, allowing users to divide hardware and network resources into multiple units, thereby realizing the pooling, sharing, and on-demand scheduling of computing resources. In 2006, Amazon launched the S3 object storage service and simple queue service(SQS), creating a precedent for Public Cloud Computing services.

In 2009, to help explain the excitement around cloud computing, "The Berkeley View on Cloud Computing" identified six potential features and advantages of cloud computing:

1. The appearance of infinite computing resources on demand.

2. The elimination of an up-front commitment by cloud users.

3. The ability to pay for the use of computing resources on a short-term basis as needed.

4. Economies of scale that significantly reduced cost due to many, very large data centers.

5. Simplifying operation and increasing utilization via resource virtualization.

6. Higher hardware utilization by multiplexing workloads from different organizations.

AWS's success in cloud computing proves that cloud computing is the core technology of future technology infrastructure. Microsoft, IBM, and Google have successively joined the public cloud service market, and the services provided have also expanded from essential computing resources to databases, artificial intelligence Intelligent, the Internet of Things, edge computing, private 5G, and other technical fields.

In 2016, Microsoft launched the first private cloud platform, Azure Stack. In 2019, Amazon, which has always believed that the public cloud is the direction and end point of cloud computing, also launched its private cloud platform, Outposts.

Private cloud solves customer pain points to a certain extent, such as security issues, but private cloud will never be able to take advantage of elastic resource utilization (large or small) and real economies of scale.

For most customers, organizations may have public cloud resources, private cloud, or even on-premises infrastructure at the same time. In this case, connecting all cloud and local infrastructure will inevitably become a mandatory requirement. That is, the hybrid cloud emerges. The hybrid cloud solves the problem of security compliance. Long-term and stable resources are invested in and maintained by the enterprise itself. Backup, disaster recovery, or short-term burst capacity can be obtained from the public cloud provider (standard cloud region/zone and substation), which improves the overall system reliability and enables compliance and investment. And business needs are optimized and balanced.

The development of the public cloud is very fast, and now, many cloud players are involved. The cloud services provided by each vendor are diversified and differentiated in terms of price, region distribution, and special field advantages. If the company's hybrid cloud is connected to only one public cloud platform, a single cloud provider may not be able to meet all needs. More importantly, a single provider is easily vendor-locking, so enterprises need to be unbound to any cloud vendors and connect to multiple suitable vendors simultaneously. Cloud computing come to the multi-cloud era.

With Hybrid and multi-cloud, new issues arise, such as complex heterogeneous resource management, differentiated inter-cloud connection and communication, cross-cloud resource scheduling and migration, multi-cloud security issues, which location should be taken as the central control point, interoperability, portability and inconsistency, and so on.

In addition, in a centralized cloud computing environment, hyper-scale public cloud providers mainly address some disadvantages of the on-premise environment when organizations migrate their applications onto the cloud progressively. With the development of AI, big data, IoT, and 5G technology, enterprises encounter some new challenges and requirements, such as data regulation, latency, scalability, flexibility, mobility, sovereignty, heterogeneity, etc.

Moreover, traditional cloud computing mainly delivers IT resources and services on demand, including servers, storage, and databases, to name a few. These services are typically provided over the public internet or private network connection from one of many hyper-scale cloud providers. Cloud services can be categorized as public cloud, private cloud (based on on-premises data centers using a mini version of the public cloud platform), hybrid cloud (the combination of public and private through dedicated links), and multi-cloud (including multiple public cloud providers at the same time).

For enterprises, in order to address these challenges, a cloud platform with a new architecture is needed to enable enterprises to manage any location, any type of infrastructure, and resources, including the public cloud, on a single portal, with self-control in management and optimal cost in a neutral, unified approach. And security is controllable, flexible, and scalable.

1.1   The Distributed Cloud Definition

The Distributed Cloud is a scalable software-defined enterprise cloud that uses an organization-owned single point of central control plane, OneCenter, to build, orchestrate, operate, and govern any dispersed, geographically distributed locations of underlying workload infrastructures worldwide. With global end-to-end network connection and integration, those infrastructures cater to unified computing, networking, storage, and data of Distributed Cloud. They are provided by the heterogeneous physical locations of cloud, on-premises, edge, and other third-party bare metal data center or colocation locations, etc.

As shown in Figure 1-1, typically, in this book, the cloud provider can be a traditional regional available zone of public hyper-scale clouds like AWS and Azure, substations, or the bare metal cloud, etc. On-premises provider here is a general umbrella term including data center, headquarters, branch, and campus; and the edge provider mainly refers to the 3GPP Edge, including 3GPP Non-Public Network (NPN) site, and 3GPP Public Network Integration (PNI)-MEC site, and non-3GPP Edge such as LoraWAN server/gateway, etc.

The control plane, OneCenter, is the Distributed Cloud core brain that mainly consists of OneZone, OneX, and the underlying drivers; the OneX includes Marketplace, OneContainer, OneData, OneStorage, and so on.

In essence, OneCenter is built by the enterprise itself on an on-premises (such as data center, branch, campus) infrastructure or based on a third-party infrastructure provider like public cloud, whereas an enterprise Distributed Cloud services run in multiple geo-distributed locations, multiple providers, and worldwide, including:

- The public cloud provider's infrastructure and resources worldwide and neutrally (including the large-scale regions, available zones and the substations).

- Enterprise on-premises at end customer locations in the data centers, branch, etc.

- The enterprise 3GPP (5G or new 6G) Non-Public Network (NPN) location such as an industrial 4.0 factory.

- The radio access network (RAN) edge data center, aggregate data center, regional data center or central data center in carrier infrastructure where the Telco Multiple Edge Computing (MEC) is provided for the Distributed Cloud by Communications Service Provider (CSP).

- The non-3GPP IoT edge sites.

- On third-party colocation data center or bare metal hardware.

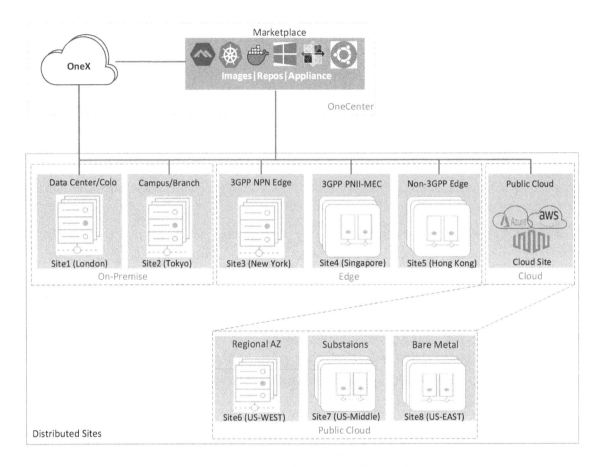

Figure 1-1 The Distributed Cloud Top View

Although there are multiple locations, multiple providers, and distributed geographies involved, all of the cloud infrastructure and services are managed from a single central control plane that handles the differences and inconsistencies in such an on-premises, hybrid, multi-cloud, telco 3GPP edge or non-3GPP edge environment.

This distribution of infrastructures with services enables an organization to meet very specific requirements for response time and performance, regulatory or governance compliance mandate, or other demands requiring cloud infrastructure to be located anywhere other than the public cloud provider's typical stationary regions and availability zones.

Distributed Cloud Computing does not and does not aim to substitute any cloud (edge cloud, telco edge, public cloud, private cloud, hybrid cloud, or even not multi-cloud), but it utilizes all of those cloud infrastructures fully. An independent management and orchestration controller all equally manage these various cloud platforms (we name this controller as OneCenter).

OneCenter can be deployed anywhere, whether in the public cloud, on-premise infrastructures, edge, or colocation place. These global infrastructures are all managed as one by OneCenter and consumed by the customer like a single cloud platform. OneCenter will not be bound to and rely on any edge, data center, or cloud provider, while any other type of cloud (hybrid and multi-cloud, etc.) architecture cannot.

In general, the Distributed Cloud is a software-defined cloud that aims to be in any geo-location, on any infrastructure, host any application, and run at any time for any organizations in a flexible and unified approach.

NOTE: Gartner suggests selecting one originating public cloud provider in charge of the function of the single point of the central controller. This approach brings at least two problems: First, the central controller is bound to a public cloud provider and it incurs the vendor-locking issue, and another is any public cloud provider cannot be 100% neutral; it is inevitable to be biased and selective when integrating with other cloud providers. This book proposes a different architecture and takes the central control point, OneCenter, independent and not fixed to any third-party cloud provider, including on-premise; OneCenter manages geo-distributed infrastructures from any cloud providers in an equal, neutral, consistent, and unified method all over the world.

1.2   Key Features and Benefits

Single pane of glass management - Adopting a Distributed Cloud approach enhances visibility into an on-premises, hybrid, multi-cloud, and edge deployment, including the ability to manage all the infrastructure as a single cloud from a single console with a single set of tools. This centralized control plane reduces operational complexity, optimizes application performance, and increases the security efficacy of your application by observing end-to-end application traffic and events.

Dynamic Scaling - The Distributed Cloud enables expansion to all kinds of existing locations without the need to build out additional infrastructure. As needs grow, the cloud can grow along seamlessly, supporting the organization's burst and changing needs. When the business scale or resource requirements shrink, the Distributed Cloud can release some resources to save money automatically.

Flexibility - The Distributed Cloud simplifies the installation, deployment, monitoring, and debugging of new infrastructure and services. It gives the infrastructure provider a wide range of candidates for deploying their resources, depending on special needs. They may only need a single node to run a far-edge Lite-type site or a handful of nodes for high-availability applications with a Mini site, or they may need larger-scale infrastructure to construct a Pro or Max-type site at a given location to meet the enterprise business need. About the new terminology and concepts of site catalogs in the Distributed Cloud, you can refer to [Chapter 6 The Distributed Cloud Site Architecture] for details.

Security and Regulation - Almost all countries or regions have regulations that stipulate that data must not go out of the country/region. The Distributed Cloud meets in such cases need. To make sure that an enterprise has the ability to retain specific data and processes in its private environment within its integrated public cloud.

Low Latency - Current 5G or future new 6G and edge use cases depend heavily on low-latency response times. Delivering low latency is a key driver for pushing computing to the edge. Distributed Cloud provides Non-public Networking (NPN), Public Networking Integration-MEC(PNI-MEC) sites, and non-3GPP edge sites to meet the low latency requirement.

Any Location - Distributed Cloud applications can be scattered in any geo-location with the heterogenous infrastructures in the public cloud, data center, branch, campus, SoHo,3GPP NPN edge site,3GPP PNI-MEC edge site, non-3GPP edge site, or even colocation.

Any Infrastructure - Integrate bare metal and multiple types of hypervisor virtualization technologies to meet workload needs, such as Vmware vSphere, Kernel-based Virtual Machine (KVM) virtual machines for fully virtualized clouds, and Firecracker microVMs for serverless deployments. The Distributed Cloud also provides the necessary tools for running containerized applications from the Kubernetes and Docker repositories while ensuring enterprise requirements for DevOps practices. It helps organizations to easily embrace the private cloud, hybrid cloud, multi-cloud, edge computing, and telco edge, allowing them to grow their Enterprise Cloud on demand with infrastructure from third-party Public Cloud and bare-metal providers such as AWS, Azure, etc.

Any Time - With the control plane of the Distributed Cloud, automatically add, augment, release, or decrease resources in order to in close proximity to end users, meet bursting peaks in demand or to implement fault-tolerant strategies or latency requirements.

Any Application - Combine bare metal server, containerized applications from Kubernetes and Docker ecosystems, and Virtual Machine workloads in a common shared environment to offer the best of all worlds: bare metal server, mature virtualization technology, and orchestration of application containers.

Open Source - For easy understanding, universality, and neutrality, some open course software and typical systems are adopted to elaborate the architecture principle of the Distributed Cloud, as examples in this book.

Chapter 2   The Distributed Cloud Architecture

The Distributed Cloud brings absolute freedom to Enterprise Cloud; the Distributed Cloud is a powerful but easy-to-use, optimized solution to build and manage enterprise clouds. It combines bare metal, hypervisor virtualization, firecracker, and container technologies with multi-tenancy, automatic provision, and elasticity to offer on-demand applications and services in public, on-premises, hybrid, and edge environments. This chapter presents the overview architecture, innovation features with Any Location, Any Infrastructure, Any Time, and Any Application features, and the particular application operation (and execution with ultra global scaling) model of the Distributed Cloud.

2.1   Top View Architecture

In the Distributed Cloud, users have only a single pane of glass. Organizations manage their global assets and provide resources from a single view to application, and the Application operator looks at the Distributed Cloud as a unique flattened plane even though the actual underlying infrastructure is uneven. For archiving this, the Distributed Cloud needs an abstraction layer between the underlying heterogeneous infrastructure and the virtual resource layer, which is thought of as a resource layer. Although the underlying heterogeneous infrastructures have diversities in location (public cloud, data center, branch, campus, SoHo,3GPP NPN edge site,3GPP PNI-MEC edge site, non-3GPP edge site, or even the colocation.) and resource types (physical machine, bare metal node, standard virtual machine, light virtual machine, or containers).

From the top view of the Distributed Cloud, all kinds of infrastructures are orchestrated by the Unified Resource Manager in the OneCenter, and we can think all kinds of those heterogeneous infrastructures and resources are controlled by the Unified Resource Manager as Underlay Infrastructure. Unified Resource Manager normalizes those heterogeneous infrastructures and resources. After that, you can take unified resources as a single virtual infrastructure plane. Thus, you can use unique methods and tools to manipulate all unified virtual resources.

The fundamental components of a Distributed Cloud architecture consist of four essential layers: The infrastructure layer, abstraction layer, resource layer and the workload/consuming layer. They will be introduced in the following section respectively.

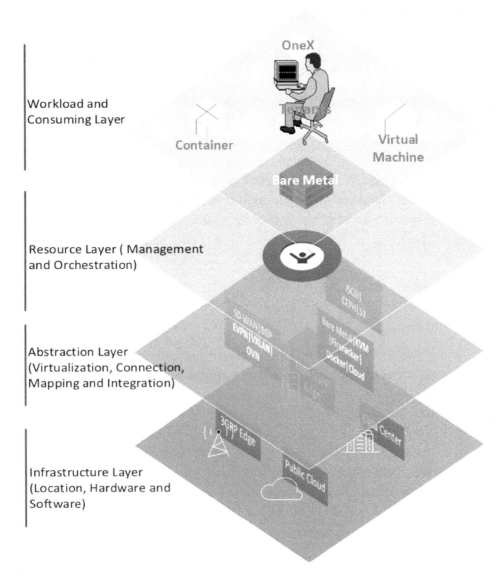

Figure 2-1 Top View Architecture of The Distributed Cloud

2.1.1   Infrastructure Layer - Location, Hardware and Software

Geographically Dispersed Distributed Locations

One of the critical features of the Distributed Cloud is it supports geographically dispersed heterogeneous locations, public cloud, data centers, branches, campuses, SoHo,3GPP NPN edge sites,3GPP PNI-MEC edge sites, non-3GPP edge sites, or even the colocation locations.

Heterogeneous Cloud Infrastructures

Various infrastructure resources are the heterogeneous, inconsistent, dispersed underlying computing, storage, networking, data, and security elements. For more information about the Heterogeneous Cloud Infrastructures in the Infrastructure Layer, refer to section [7.3 Infrastructure Layer - Location, Hardware and Software].

2.1.2   Abstraction Layer-Virtualization, Connection, Mapping and Integration

For the Distributed Cloud, in addition to integrating hybrid cloud and multi-cloud resources, edge (3GPP edge and non-3GPP edge) and telecommunications infrastructure (enterprise-owned and integrated with the Communications Service Providers CORD data center) are also its most important concerns. The computing, storage, and especially network scenarios are very diverse, connected, and integrated. It is extremely complex. The abstraction layer needs to connect, map, and integrate these geographically distributed, diverse, inconsistent, heterogeneous, and dynamic resources to form a unified and consistent global view, thereby making it look like a single cloud platform for tenants, applications, and end users. For more information about the Abstraction Layer, you can refer to the section [7.4 Abstraction Layer - Unified Resource Manager].

NOTE: *In this book, there are three kinds of virtualizations. The first is Distributed Cloud virtualization, which refers to the abstraction of underlying geo-distributed heterogeneous infrastructures through connection, mapping, and integration to form a unified normalized cloud resource pane. The second one is hypervisor virtualization, such as KVM/QEMU or XEN, for building and managing the virtual machine in the cloud environment. The third one is data virtualization that is an ideal data integration strategy that provides an actual-time view of the consolidated data, leaving the source data exactly* *where it is when the data is processed or operated. Refer to section [11.2.3.1 Data Virtualization] for more information about data virtualization.*

2.1.3   Resources Layer - Management and Orchestration

Global End-to-End Network is for the Abstraction Layer. With the abstraction by a unified resource manager, we can obtain a virtual resource layer, in this layer, a universal distributed logical Router and Switch can be applied, and a global end-to-end network over the underlay for tenant can be stitched.

Unified Resources Manager Is a transform layer between the Infrastructure Layer and Resource Layer in the Distributed Cloud that enables the management of heterogeneous components of the IT and CT infrastructure as a single, consistent set of resources, regardless of infrastructure catalog and the physical location and provider of these resources. It is all about operational functionality rather than technological infrastructure. Thus, the Distributed Cloud is much more than "multiple clouds.", A Distributed Cloud environment is characterized by the unification and abstraction of private cloud, public, and hybrid clouds built on and off-premises along with enterprise data centers, branches, campus, 3GPP NPN, 3GPP PNI-MEC and non-3GPP edge infrastructure.

The 'Single Pane of Glass' Management enables real-time orchestration and automatic provisioning of compute, storage, security, and network resources while abstracting the complexity of the underlying infrastructure, application, and other stacks.

Any Infrastructure integrates multiple types of technologies to meet workload needs, such as Physical Servers, VMware vSphere clusters, and KVM virtual machines for virtualized clouds, Firecracker microVMs for serverless deployments. Distributed Cloud also provides the necessary tools for running containerized applications from Kubernetes and Docker repositories while ensuring enterprise requirements for DevOps practices.

OneData is a unified global big data platform that is presented by Data Fabric with Hybrid Data Mesh and is placed in OneCenter location. For more information on OneData, please read [Chapter 11 The Distributed Cloud Based Data Platform Architecture].

OneStorage provides a unified storage space and is also placed in OneCenter location. For more information on OneStorage, please read section [4.3 Object Storage with Multi-Site Gateway].

2.1.4   Workload and Consuming Layer - Multi-Tenants

The Organizational Perspective – Virtual Distributed Cloud

Users can be organized into Groups (like Projects or Tenants concepts in other Cloud platforms). A Group is an authorization boundary that can be thought of as a business unit or a company if you are considering it as part of a Distributed Cloud. While a site is used to group physical resources according to common characteristics, such as networking topology or physical location, Virtual Distributed Cloud (VDC) allow the Distributed Cloud admins to define "logical" pools of physical resources (which can belong to different edge hosts, clusters and zones) and allocate them to specific groups of users.

A VDC is a fully isolated virtual infrastructure environment where a group of users (or, sometimes, several Groups of users), under the control of a group admin, can create and manage virtual computing, networking, and storage resources. The users in the Group, including the Group admin, would only see these virtual resources and not the underlying physical infrastructure by default. The physical resources allocated to the group are managed by the cloud administrator through the VDC. The resources grouped in the VDCs can be dedicated exclusively by default to the group, providing isolation at the physical level too.

Cloud also can be configured for the privileges of the group users and the admin regarding the operations over the virtual resources created by other users. for instance, the privileges of the group users and the admin regarding the operations over the virtual resources created by other users in the group.

Users can access their resources through any of the existing the Distributed Cloud interfaces, such as the OneCenter WebUI, the CLI, the Cloud API, or the Public Cloud (such as AWS) APIs. Group admins can manage their groups through the CLI or via the Group Admin View in the WebUI of OneCenter. Cloud administrators can manage the groups through the CLI or GUI of OneCenter.

The Distributed Cloud provisioning model based on VDCs enables an integrated, comprehensive framework to dynamically provision the infrastructure resources in multi-site or large multi-data center environments to different organizations, business units, or groups. This brings some following benefits:

- Effective partitioning of physical resources between groups of users.

- Complete isolation of users, organizations, or workloads.

- Allocation of sites with different levels of security, performance, or high availability.

- Containers for the execution of software-defined zones and sites.

- Way of hiding underlying physical infrastructure from group members.

- Simple federation, scalability, and cloud bursting of cloud infrastructures beyond a single cloud instance, data center and edge.

- Reusing the whole scope of underlying heterogeneous infrastructure can bring cost expense savings.

Provisioning Scenarios – Distributed Cloud Multi Tenants

The distributed cloud introduced in this book is enterprise-level, and its tenants are mainly organizations. The Family and Personal Edition of Distributed Cloud will be introduced in other books.

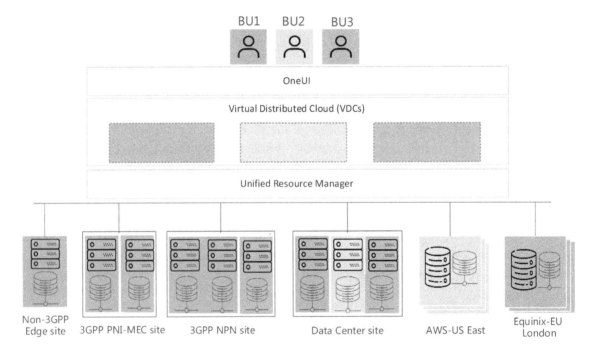

Figure 2-2 Example of Virtual Distributed Cloud Organization

The Figure 2-2 is the case that an enterprise in large cloud computing deployments. In this kind of large enterprise, it is assumed that there are three Business Unit (BU): BU1, BU2, BU3. Mapping to the Distributed Cloud architecture, you can think of Telco, Public, and IT as those three business units respectively represented by Groups, allocate them resources from some of your on-premises data centers, branch, campus, 3GPP NPN, 3GPP PNI-MEC, non-3GPP edge site, and public clouds to create three different VDCs:

- VDC Pink for the Business Unit 1 (BU1), with 1 site in the on-premises non-3GPP edge site, 1 Cluster in on-premises 3GPP PNI-MEC site, 2 Clusters in on-premises 3GPP NPN site and 1 Cluster in on-premises Data Center.

- VDC Yellow Business Unit 2 (BU2), with 1 Cluster in on-premises Data Center and 1 Cluster in AWS-US East.

- VDC Gray for Business Unit 3 (BU3), with 1 Cluster in on-premises 3GPP PNI-MEC site, 1 Cluster in on-premises 3GPP NPN site, 1 Cluster in on-premises Data Center and 1 Cluster in Equinix-EU-London.

Global End-to-End Virtual Private Cloud

Traditional Virtual Private Cloud (VPN) is mainly used to isolate physical resources on public cloud (AWS or Azure) platforms to achieve multi-tenant sharing of public cloud resource infrastructure. Each VPC is limited to a cloud region. Under the same account, between regions, communication can only be done through special means to manually create links between different cloud regions (using different VPCs).

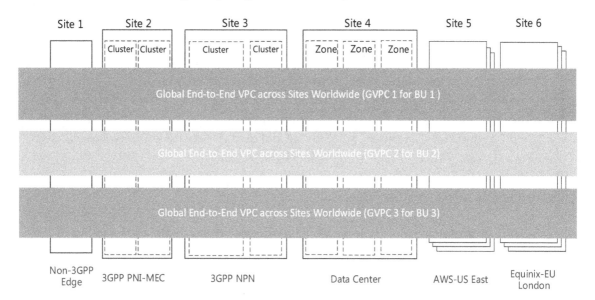

Figure 2-3 Global End-to-End Virtual Private Cloud

In the Distributed Cloud environment, with the central point controller, OneCenter, to leverages SD-WAN, VXLAN, EVPN, and OVN's special advanced capacities to implement the Global End-to-End Virtual Private Cloud (GVPC) to communications, stitch, routing, and transfer of internal node, inter-node, internal site, and inter-sites talk over WAN.

NOTE: *In this book, the term VPC refers to the conventional Virtual Private Cloud in the classic cloud like aws, while the GVPC refers to the Global End-to-End Virtual Private Cloud in the Distributed Cloud environment. When the Distributed Cloud entend to the Public Cloud, the VPC domain is integrated into the GVPC.*

Cloud Access Roles

A key management task in the Distributed Cloud Infrastructure environment has to do with determining who can use the cloud resources and, what actions those users can operate and tasks those users are authorized to perform. The person with the role of cloud service administrator is authorized to assign the appropriate rights required by other users. In most cases, very few people should be granted administrator privileges. In this section, we will describe the concept of several roles and introduce you to the default type of user roles:

Cloud Users - End Users

A Distributed Cloud can offer VDC on-demand to groups of users (projects, organizations, or business units). In these cases, each group can define one or multiple users as group Admins. Users with group Admin privileges can also create new users in the group, operate on the resources such as the group's VM and disk images, share pre-built templates with the members of the group, and check group usage and quotas. Group Admins typically access the cloud by using the CLI or the group admin view in OneUI.

Cloud Service Administrators - Operators

Cloud Administrators typically access the cloud using the CLI, the Admin view in the GUI of the provisioning tool. Cloud operators use provisioning tool for the automatic deployment and setup of a site on on-premises data centers, remote clouds, and edge providers and often provide support to cloud users in any aspect related to the cloud service.

Cloud Infrastructure Administrators - Cloud Admin

Cloud infrastructure administrators typically Install and configure the Distributed Cloud Control Plane OneCenter services; Deploy and configure the sites and resources (Hosts, Network, and Datastores) and their integration with the underlying infrastructure services (computing, networking fabric, storage servers); Monitor the status and health of the cloud services and the infrastructure resources.

2.2   Distributed Infrastructure Architecture

Leverage Upcoming Ecosystem of All Kinds Site Providers

A site provider catalog allows organizations building the Distributed Cloud to choose all kinds of (cloud, on-premises, and edge) right combination of geographically distributed site locations to efficiently execute their workloads, meet their enterprise requirement, and mitigate vendor locking-in.

Combine Centralized Cloud Resources with Edge Resources

A powerful resource provisioning tool allows organizations to automatically allocate and configure the physical resources needed to build their Distributed Cloud with the sites on-demand.

Run any workload, bare-metal, virtual machine, micro virtual machine and containers with Kubernetes, on any infrastructure, anywhere, edge, on-premises, or on a public cloud provider:

- Automatic deployment of public cloud nodes worldwide at site locations in close proximity to end-users, public cloud can provide both region/zone and the substations resources as the edge.

- Fast cloud site node configuration and deployment.

- On-demand, pay-per-use allocation, and provision of site resources from bare-metal cloud providers.

- Dynamic addition and removal of resources with ease at a given specific site location.

- Highly scalable building tens of thousands of site resources.

- Hybrid Multi-Cloud interoperability at the unified virtualized infrastructure layer; an application can be deployed anywhere on the site without any additional setup operations.

- Embracing the 3GPP NPN edge, 3GPP PNI-MEC (like AWS Wavelength) edge and non-3GPP IoT edge such as LoRa WAN Gateway, WIFI edge. etc.

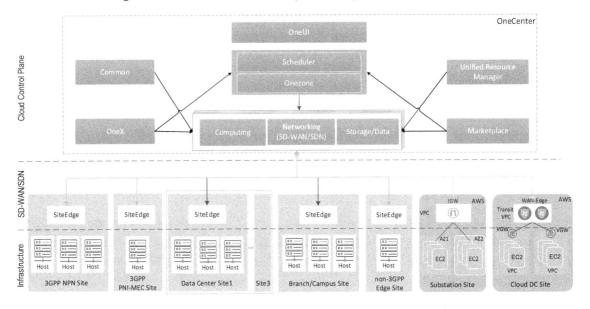

Figure 2-4 Distributed Infrastructure Architecture

2.2.1   The Infrastructure Perspective

A standard Distributed Cloud architecture consists of a Cloud Management Cluster (comprising the OneCenter nodes), the Distributed Cloud networking (SDN with OVN and SD-WAN), and the Cloud Infrastructure (made of one or multiple workload sites with the computing nodes and the storage system), which can be located at multiple distributed international geographical locations, all interconnected with multiple networks for internal storage and node management, and for private and public guest (bare metal, VM, micro-VM or container) communication.

Those workload sites can present different architectures and software/hardware execution environments to fulfill the needs of different workload profiles. Moreover, many organizations have access to external public clouds through which they can build true hybrid and edge computing scenarios where the private capacity of their data centers is expanded with resources from external providers so that they can address peaks of demand, increase service availability, or meet data location (and data regulation) or low latency requirements.

There are several types of site models that can be used with the Distributed Cloud: Max site, Pro site, Mini site, Lite site, access site, edge site, Data Center site, and Cloud site. For detailed information on the Distributed Cloud site terminology and concepts, refer to section [6.2 Sites Taxonomy].

Large companies with multiple sites running multiple data centers can run different Distributed Cloud Zone instances (termed "OneZone"). For example, a company can have two sites in different geographic locations, the US West Coast and Europe, and an agreement with a public cloud provider such as AWS, Azure, or Equinix. The site can be managed by a separate remote OneZone instance, which is placed in the OneCenter location (in this way, a OneZone instance can control multiple sites) or, alternatively, each site can run its own local zone instance. Multiple Distributed Cloud zones can be configured as a federation, and in this case, they will share the same user accounts, groups, and permissions across sites. A multi-zone deployment is used when sites are in different network administrative domains or when the connectivity across sites does not meet latency and bandwidth requirements or only for high availability.

2.2.2   The True Hybrid and Edge Computing

The Distributed Cloud sites can be deployed on on-premises data centers, branches, campuses, 3GPP NPN, 3GPP PNI-MEC, and non-3GPP edge infrastructures as well as on bare-metal and virtualized cloud providers to enable powerful hybrid, multi-cloud, and edge computing. Infrastructure teams can choose their appropriate hardware platform and cloud provider and deliver an exceptional Distributed Cloud experience. Similarly, Administration teams can seamlessly manage applications across clouds, on-premises, and edge providers and leverage the growing ecosystem of hyperscale and edge clouds.

NOTE: *In a Distributed Cloud environment, a vendor usually refers to third-party companies that sell public cloud services and resources, like, for instance, AWS, Azure, Equinix, etc. The Provider typically refers to any underlying infrastructure giver, where resources such as hosts (bare metal or virtual machine), networks (VPN and IP, etc.), or storage are allocated to implement a provision. It not only includes the third-party infrastructure provider but also refers to any the on-premises infrastructure owner such as data center, branch, campus, SoHo, 3GPP NPN site, 3GPP PNI-MEC site, non-3GPP edge site, or even a colocation, etc.*

A Resource Provider Catalog that will maintain a list of site resource providers that are certified to work with the Distributed Cloud. This catalog will allow users to easily select which providers, locations, and instances are better suited for their edge applications in terms of performance, cost, capacity, latency, bandwidth, etc. This process should be automatic for mainstream public cloud providers.

The Cloud Computing field is growing at an accelerated pace. Hence, new infrastructure providers are publishing their offerings continuously. The following types of infrastructure providers can be included in the Resource Provider Catalog based on the latency they are able to deliver to end-users.

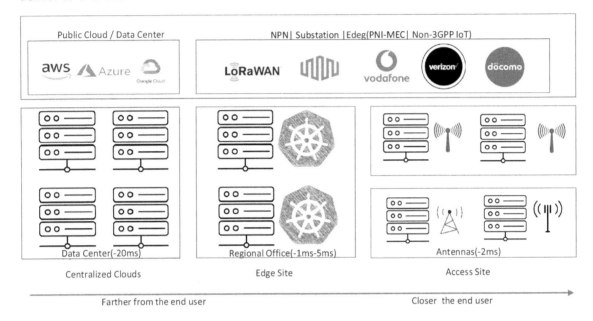

Figure 2-5 Different Types of Infrastructure Resource Providers by Proximity to End-users

Centralized Cloud Provider: Public Clouds

This offering refers to public cloud providers with a bare-metal server offering. As opposed to their classic cloud provider offering (i.e., the ability to manage Virtual Machines), the bare metal offering opens the possibility to define different site architectures. For Distributed Cloud, this means being able to offer a common site architecture across different public cloud providers. They can typically offer a latency for services above 20 ms.

Examples of public cloud providers with bare metal offerings include classic public cloud providers like famous AWS, Google Cloud Engine, and Azure Cloud, as well as smaller infrastructure providers like Equinix, Linode, and many others.

Centralized Cloud Provider: Data Centers

Enterprise-owned on-premises Datacenter-like providers such as a data center, branch, campus, or even a colocation place can also provide similar resources (bare metal nodes) and features (latency above 20 ms) to the public cloud.

Edge Site Provider: 3GPP NPN Edge

This type of provider has greater proximity to the end-user (compared with the previous public cloud and Data Center site case), enabling a lower latency for the edge application, in the order of 1-5 ms.

A typical case is the 3GPP NPN edge described in section [9.3.2   Non-Public Network (NPN)], which provides specific infrastructure deployments that embed the Distributed Cloud computing and storage services right within the data centers at the edge of the growing 3GPP network of communication services provider.

Edge Site Provider: Cloud Substations

Cloud substations evoke the image of subsidiary stations, for instance, branch post offices, where people gather to use services. The public cloud substations are the responsibility of the originating public cloud provider for Distributed Cloud. The critical cloud value propositions of productivity, innovation, and support remain intact. The Distributed Cloud will work based on the assumption that cloud substations are everywhere - much like Wi-Fi hot spots.

Access Site Providers

This provider with specialized antennas is able to house computing resources. This renders the closest computation to the end-user and can deliver latencies in the order of about 2ms.

The typical case of 3GPP PNI-MEC providers is traditional telecommunication companies leverage the CORD infrastructure (Central Office Re-architected as a Data Center) like, for instance, DoCoMo, AT&T, Verizon, and so on. In this case, the Distributed Cloud extends its computing and storage services to the CORD in close proximity to the users.

About how the Distributed Cloud integrates into the Telco Data Center infrastructure, you can refer to section [9.3.3   3GPP Public Network Integrated MEC - 3GPP PNI-MEC] and [10.3.2 3GPP Edge Computing - Containerized PNI-MEC Site].

Another scenario is the non-3GPP IoT edge site, such as Wi-Fi 6 AP, Lora WAN gateway, and so on, it also can provide renders the closest computation to the end-user and can deliver latencies.

NOTE: *The main advantage of the Distributed Cloud architecture is the ability to deploy sites anywhere, which can be a host, a cluster, or a zone. This provides application mobility and true Distributed Cloud computing in the most literal sense. Clusters can be deployed on edge, on-premises, colocation infrastructure, on public cloud bare-metal providers, and on virtualized cloud environments to enable powerful edge, hybrid, and multi-cloud computing. Infrastructure teams have the flexibility to choose their preferred location, hardware platform, and cloud provider and deliver an outstanding Distributed Cloud experience.*

2.3 Execution and Operation Architecture

The goal of the Distributed Cloud is to enable the startup of OneCenter, create sites, and deploy and orchestrate the applications on geo-Distributed Cloud infrastructure. The Architecture introduced in this section describes the main steps and workflow that the Distributed Cloud will follow in order to meet the Cloud and Application Administrator's requirement of being able to deliver the application at the site to provide low latency, regulation, traits, and other requirements to the user.

This Architecture is designed to achieve the lowest possible friction between the different components involved. Each step hides the complexity of the underlying components and resources that are created, using pre-defined architectures for the Distributed Cloud so the knowledge of the actual infrastructure details can be kept to a minimum.

Distributed Cloud deploys and provisions resources at the site and offers a simplified, efficient way to execute workloads (bare metal, virtual machine, or containers) with minimum input from the user.

The execution and operation in Distributed-Clou include the following different phases:

- The first phase is about the operations needed to perform in order to build a OneCenter on an appropriate location. These actions are performed by the Infrastructure Administrator and the phase is shown as ① in Figure 2-6.

- The second phase is about the operations needed to be performed in order to create a distributed site on a desired location or set of locations. These actions are performed by the Infrastructure Administrator and the phase is shown as ② in Figure 2-6.

- The third phase refers to the set of operations needed to deploy any applications (hosted by bare metal, standard virtual machine, micro-VM, and container) or services in the site built in the previous phase. These actions are performed by the Application Administrator and this step is termed Any Application Deployment Phase shown as ③in Figure 2-6.

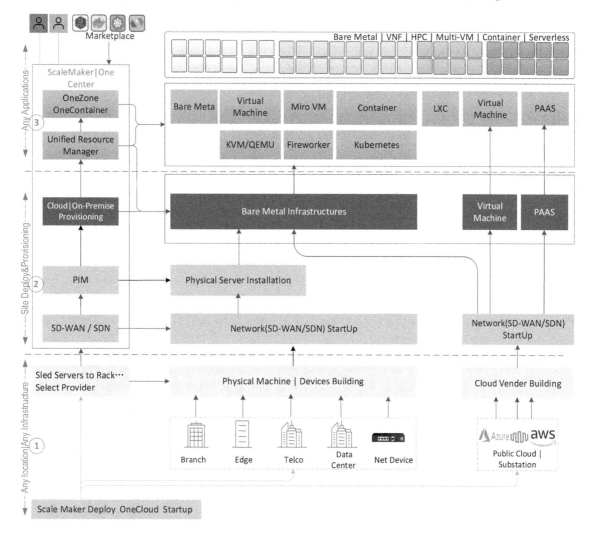

Figure 2-6 The Distributed Cloud Execution and Operation Architecture

2.3.1   Setup OneCenter with Any Location

Before the Distributed Cloud platform startup, the organization needs to consider the business analysis, the location distribution of users, the site location dispersion, the residency of OneCenter, and the global deployment architecture.

After that, OneCenter needs to be set up. In Distributed Cloud, OneCenter is the central controller that manages the whole cloud infrastructure and resources across the globe. This controller is deployed in a meticulously planned location, which is the center point of enterprise business and workload. The OneCenter instance is not bound to any third-party, public cloud provider (such as AWS or Azure), which means it can be placed not only on the public cloud (AWS or Azure, for example) but also can be in the enterprise's any on-premises infrastructure place, for example, data center or edge site.

At the OneCenter location, an organization can deploy the OneCenter instance with solely a control plane role. Except for the control place of OneCenter, users can also expand it to deploy a workload infrastructure of a single host, cluster, or even a zone, depending on the business needs and the resource capacity of the OneCenter location. In the case of workload, the control plane and the workload resource are in a separate logical space within the same location. From the OneCenter point of view, the extended workload infrastructure is looked at as a normal Distributed Site.

The Scale Maker is an essential component that is also mandatory for the startup of the Distributed Cloud platform in OneCenter. With the Scale Maker, the Distributed Cloud Administrator can scale, operate, and monitor the site, node, and application automatically with the DevOps function based on security capacities. For the detail of Scale Maker information, you can refer to section [7.2 ScaleMaker].

After the rest of the main components of the OneCenter instance are started and initialized, the Administrator can deploy the distributed sites and applications through the OneUI or CLI through the OneCenter.

2.3.2   Site Deployment

After the startup of OneCenter, the administrator needs access to a OneCenter instance before building a Distributed Cloud infrastructure at the site. The OneCenter is the single central point of the Distributed Cloud. It resides in an arbitrary public cloud provider set up by the Infrastructure Administrator in case there is no on-premises cloud infrastructure, or other scenarios are also possible, the most common being the existence of a private infrastructure on the company's premises. In the premise case, OneCenter would extend its native private cloud orchestration capabilities to those resources deployed at the remote edge sites.

The first step to deploy a Distributed Cloud site is, therefore, logging into OneCenter using the Infrastructure Administrator credentials. The OneUI of OneCenter presents the Infrastructure Administrator view, which follows a wizard-like approach. To select the best site location, OneUI will present a list of site locations pulled from the SiteCatalog module, along with information useful to make a decision: prices, availability, capacity, regulation, compatibility, special characters, latencies, etc. This is coupled with tools and hints to aid and simplify the decision-making process to choose the best provider and location for the application that meets the special requirement to be deployed on the site.

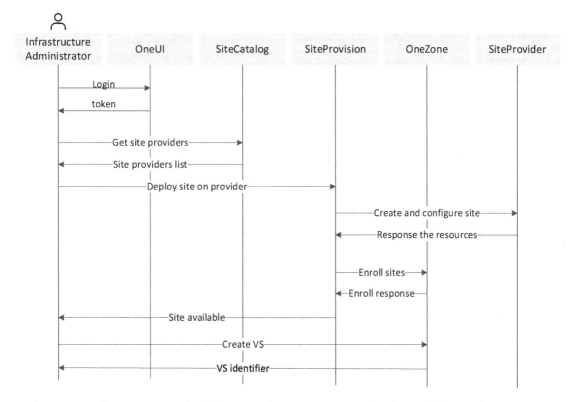

Figure 2-7 Infrastructure Administrator Flow to Create a Distributed Cloud Infrastructure

Once a Site Provider is (or Site Providers are) selected, the SiteProvision component offers an easy-to-consume functionality (through the OneCenter API or even the CLI) to set up the credentials of those providers and allocate the physical resources needed to build the desired Distributed Cloud. Tools for the life cycle management of these site resources are also provided, as well as monitoring. Once the site infrastructure is created, its services are enrolled in the OneZone in a transparent way.

Ultimately, create a Virtual Global End-to-End Distributed Cloud (GVDC) on the OneCenter component that gives access to the new dedicated virtual cloud. With this GVDC along the global VPC, the Application Administrator can deploy the application in a GVDC across the sites.

2.3.3   Application Models

Bare Metal Applications

In the cloud era, although virtualized and containerized infrastructure have been widely used, there still remain some scenarios that need the bare metal (physical server) for performance or isolation requirements. Here are some scenarios for bare metal in Distributed Cloud:

- Special computing application for performance, security, dependability, and other special regulatory requirements.

- Computing tasks that require access to hardware devices that can't be virtualized.

- Big Data platform and Database hosting (big data process and some databases run poorly in a virtual machine or container).

Virtualized (Virtual Machine) Applications

Besides orchestrating Virtual Machines, according to the different types of hypervisors, Distributed Cloud can be deployed on top of your VMware vCenter infrastructure, but it can also manage KVM-based workloads as well as LXC system containers and lightweight Firecracker micro-VMs (this kind of virtual machine can conveniently run application containers).

VM-based applications are created from images and templates that are available from the Distributed Cloud Marketplace (global marketplace or local marketplace) but can also be created by the users themselves and shared by the cloud administrator using a local corporate marketplace.

Containerized Applications

The Distributed Cloud offers a new, native approach for running containerized applications and workflows by directly using the official Docker images available from the Docker Hub mirror and running them as LXC system containers or as lightweight AWS powered Firecracker microVMs (shown in Figure 2-8), this method can provide an extra level of efficiency and security. This solution combines all the benefits of containers with the security, orchestration, and multi-tenant features without adding extra components of management, thus reducing the cloud complexity and costs.

For those cases where Kubernetes is required or is the best fit, the Distributed Cloud should also bring support for the deployment of Kubernetes clusters through a CNCF-certified virtual appliance available from the Distributed Cloud Global Marketplace or through the k3s Lightweight Kubernetes for resource-constrained and lightweight edge locations.

Distributed Cloud enables the quick instantiation of applications and complex services, and the Distributed Cloud also integrates with popular open-source technologies like Docker, Kubernetes, and Kubernetes Clusters Manager (about the Kubernetes Clusters Manager, you can refer to section [5.4.3 Dispersed Heterogeneous Kubernetes Clusters]).

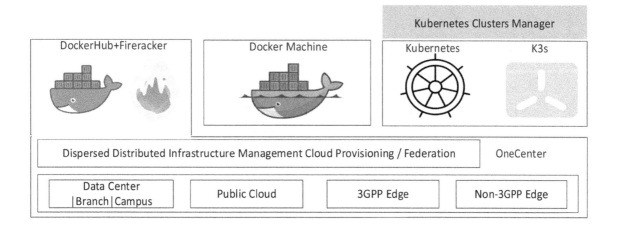

Figure 2-8 Containerized Applications

2.3.4   Application Deployment

Distributed Cloud supports at least two main types of Applications: the single Instance application (with access to an external IP) and the multi-instance application (with access to an external IP and optionally single or multiple private virtual networks). A multi-Instance application represents a multi-tiered application composed of interconnected Virtual Machines or Containers with deployment dependencies between them. The application (regardless of being single or multiple instances) is deployed and managed as a single entity, and elasticity rules based on hypervisor and/or application metrics can be defined (about the multi-instance application elastic scaling, refers to section [2.3.5 Ultra Global Scaling]). Site applications can be backed by Bare Metal, Virtual Machines, or system containers. These site applications can, in turn, be application container orchestration tools Kubernetes. The final application is deployed through using, for instance, a Helm Chart.

NOTE: *The external IP can be the public IP (for example, elastic Ip - EIP in AWS) or Floating IP in case of an on-premises environment.*

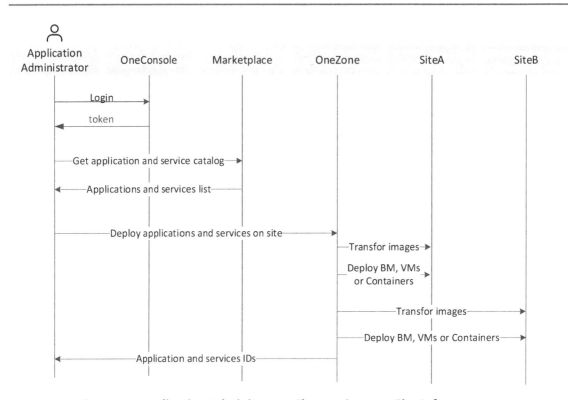

Figure 2-9 Application Administrator Flow to Create a Site Infrastructure

After receiving the VDC identifier (and login credentials if needed) from the Infrastructure Administrator, the application administrator logs into the OneCenter to deploy the desired application on the Distributed Cloud site created in the previous phase. The application administrator is presented with a catalog of applications (pulled from the Marketplace). She has then to decide which one of these pre-packaged applications is going to be used to deploy the desired application. For instance, they can select a Kubernetes service to later deploy a Kubernetes pod on top if the final application is, for instance, defined by a helm chart. One will then automatically download the site application.

Once an application is selected, the OneCenter component is instructed to deploy the application on top of the Distributed Cloud site residing in a specific site provider location selected by the application administrator. OneCenter then contacts this Distributed Cloud site location for:

- Transfer the images that the application needs.

- Create the needed networks and address ranges within those Virtual Networks.

- Create the needed workload entity (bare metal nodes, Virtual Machines, or containers) for the application (this can be one workload entity in the single instance case or multiple workload entities modeled as a Flow Template in the multi-tier application case).

- Initialize the workload entity to configure the application.

Once the application is deployed, OneCenter offers the functionality to control the lifecycle of the application as a whole.

2.3.5   Ultra Global Scaling

As the new innovative cloud platform, the Distributed Cloud executes and operates the applications in modern ways which is unified, global, and geo-distributed, letting the tenants and consumer agnostic for the dispersed location and resource heterogeneous. This section introduces some application types in the Distributed Cloud and the creative elastic scaling Mode in the Distributed Cloud based on distributed sites and global resources.

Now assume that an instance of a site application not only can execute on one single site location but also multiple instances of the same application can be executed on multiple site locations simultaneously.

The instances can be auto-scaled both within a site scope and across the distributed sites. Figure 2-10 depicts how the two tiers auto-scaling works. The simplest site application consists of one single component, as follows:

- **Application Image** contains the application runtime and the needed support for the operating system (OS). The OS pieces may depend on the compute node used by the site location of the provider.

- **Public Internet IP** address.

- **Capacity Specification** is about CPU, Memory, and Disk.

- **Hardware** requirements are additional requirements to run the application, e.g., a specific processor layout or access to specific hardware like single root I/O virtualization (SR-IOV) or graphics processing units (GPUs).

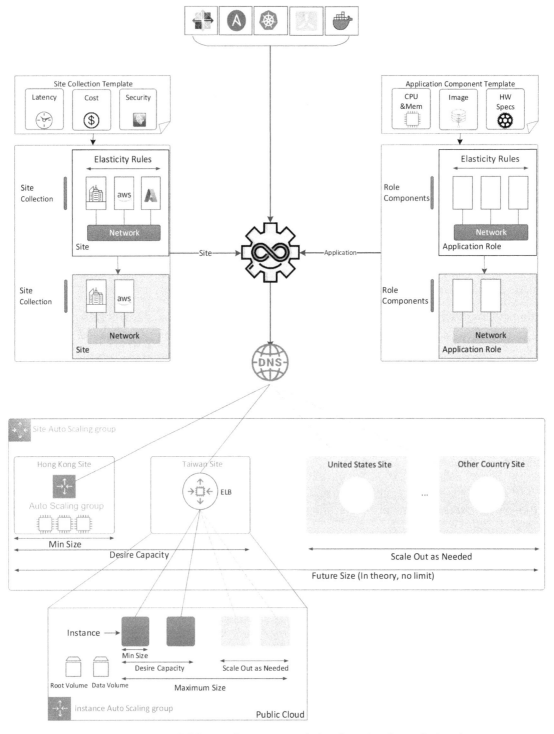

Figure 2-10 Scalable Application Mode in The Distributed Cloud

Typically, an application component is implemented by a single virtual machine or system container, and sometimes also needs bare metal nodes.

In general, a site application will consist of more than one component as the one described above. In these multi-virtual machine, multi bare metal node and multi-container applications, the application components are structured in tiers or roles. An application role is a set of application components (for example virtual machine) that implement a specific functional aspect of the application, and consist of:

- **A Component Template** contains the image, network connections, capacity specification, and hardware requirements.

- **Deployment Dependencies** for the role, for example, the roles that need to be running before deploying this role.

- **Auto-scaling or Elasticity Rules** that determine the default initial, maximum, and minimum number of components in the role over time.

Finally, in addition to the roles, a multi-Instance application may also include one internal private network to interconnect the components of the application. Figure 2-10 represents the concepts introduced in this section for a single application and a classical two-tier multi-instances application. Distributed Cloud's global SD-WAN with VPN make policy-driven routing and networking at the application level a breeze. Instantly connect every component seamlessly and securely, no matter which cloud, edge, or the environment is on-premises.

Global Site Auto Scaling

There are many use cases with such typical requirements, such as video conferencing. As the locations of clients and participants change, the distribution of the Distributed Cloud dynamic sites will also change to other different locations.

Another user case is a technical or consulting service company, and their clients may be distributed worldwide. Thus, their office and staff move to different locations from time to time.

When the above event occurs, the Distributed Cloud will trigger the cloud site to scale up and down automatically and worldwide, as shown in Figure 2-10.

Generally speaking, the target site of this kind of site auto scaling chooses the public cloud provider, so before executing site auto scaling, it is necessary to ensure that there are enough candidate public cloud provider locations with reasonable location allocation. Of course, the provider also includes public substations. In this way, when users are emerging, increasing, or decreasing in a certain area of the earth, the distributed cloud central scheduler will perform corresponding actions at that location, including creating a new site, expanding the site, or deleting the site.

Application Instance Auto Scaling

The Auto Scaling Group within a site contains several instances (can be a virtual machine, Micro virtual machine, bare metal server, or containers) that combine to form a group. It allows you to configure a minimum number of instances to create a group individually. So that Auto Scaling would ensure your group should not go below the minimum size of your group limit. Similarly, you can also configure a maximum number of instances to create a group and Auto Scaling would ensure that your group should not exceed above this size limit.

Distributed Cloud Instances Auto Scaling helps to explore your infrastructure with the help of scaling group and launch configuration. It discovers what can be scaled within your application by automatic and periodic health checkups and metrics.

Distributed Cloud compute resources are basically scaled based on a set of instructions termed Scaling Plans. There is another important concept called Scaling Strategy which tells Auto Scaling to optimize the utilization of the resources in a scaling plan in Dynamic Scaling, it adjusts resources capacity based on live changes to the resource utilization. It mainly provides enough capacity to maintain the utilization of the target value mentioned in the scaling strategy.

Furthermore, Predictive Scaling uses machine learning to analyze the historical workload of cloud resources and also helps in workload forecasting for the future.

Chapter 3   The Distributed Cloud Enterprise Networking

In the Distributed Cloud, networking is the most important and plays a fundamental role; it is the base for users' communication, site distribution, infrastructure connection, and resource movement. This chapter mainly introduces the Distributed Cloud related networking technology foundation such as VLAN and VXLAN protocol and some innovative network technologies and solutions such as MP-BGP EVPN, Multi-site with EVPN VXLAN, SDN, SD-WAN, and OVN/OVS components that are critical components and beneficial for the Distributed Cloud.

This chapter also discusses the inside networking of cloud nodes, including the EVPN with OVN/OVS for the Bare Metal, Hypervisor, and Kubernetes.

3.1   Network Fundamental

VLAN, and VXLAN are the foundation of network systems that must be mastered to understand the cloud, especially in the cloud data center.

3.1.1   VLAN

Overview

Early Ethernet was a data network communication technology based on a Carrier Sense Multiple Access/Collision Detection (CSMA/CD) shared communication medium. When the number of hosts is large, it will lead to serious conflicts, flooding of broadcasts, significant performance degradation, and even network unavailability. Although LAN interconnection through Layer 2 devices can solve the problem of serious conflicts, it still cannot isolate broadcast packets and improve network quality.

In this case, VLAN technology appeared. This technology can divide a LAN into multiple logical VLANs. Each VLAN is a broadcast domain. The communication between hosts in a VLAN is the same as in a LAN. Restricted within a VLAN.

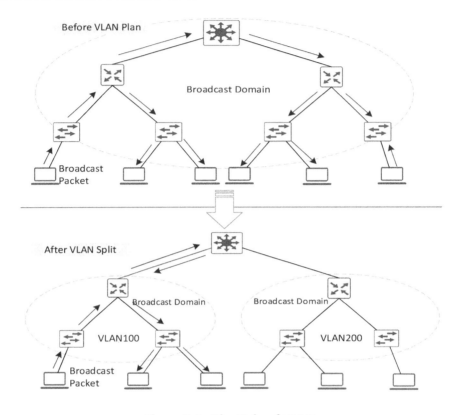

Figure 3-1 The Role of VLAN

VLAN Tag and VLAN ID

To enable the switch to distinguish packets of different VLANs, a field identifying VLAN information needs to be added to the packets. The IEEE 802.1Q protocol stipulates that a 4-byte VLAN tag (also known as VLAN Tag, or Tag for short) is added to an Ethernet data frame to identify VLAN information.

VLAN Interface Type and VLAN Tag Processing Mechanism

Users belonging to the same VLAN in the live network may be connected to different switches, and there may be more than one VLAN across switches. If intercommunication between users is required, the interfaces between switches must be able to identify and send multiple VLANs 's

Data Frames at the same time. According to the connection object of the interface and the processing method of data frames sent and received, there are currently multiple interface types of VLAN to adapt to different connections and networking. Generally, there are three common types of VLAN interfaces, including Access, Trunk, and Hybrid interfaces:

Access Interface is generally used to connect to user terminals (such as user hosts and servers) that cannot recognize tags or when different VLAN members do not need to be distinguished.

Trunk Interface is generally used to connect switches, routers, and access points that can send and receive tagged and untagged frames at the same time. It can allow frames of multiple VLANs to pass through with tags but only allow frames belonging to the default VLAN to be sent out from this type of interface without tags (that is, to strip tags).

Hybrid Interface can be used not only to connect user terminals and network devices that cannot recognize tags but also to connect switches, routers, voice terminals, and access points that can send and receive tagged and untagged frames at the same time. It can allow frames of multiple VLANs to pass through with tags and allow frames sent from this type of interface to be configured with frames of some VLANs with tags and frames of some VLANs without tags.

3.1.2   VXLAN

Overview

VXLAN runs over the existing networking infrastructure and provides a method to spread a Layer 2 network. That means VXLAN is a Layer 2 overlay scheme on a Layer 3 network. Each overlay is termed a VXLAN network segment. Only devices within the same VXLAN segment can communicate with each other by default. Each VXLAN segment is identified through a 24-bit segment ID, termed the "VXLAN Network Identifier (VNI)". This allows up to 16 million VXLAN segments to coexist within the same VXLAN administrative domain.

The VNI identifies the scope of the inner MAC frame originated by the individual endpoint. In two different VXLAN segments, the MAC addresses can be overlapped, but the traffic cannot cross over between the two VXLAN segment because the VNI isolate the traffic from each other.

Due to encapsulation, VXLAN can also be called a tunneling scheme to overlay Layer 2 networks on top of Layer 3 networks. The tunnels are stateless, so each frame is encapsulated according to a set of rules. In the case when the end point of the tunnel (VXLAN Tunnel End Point or VTEP) is located within the hypervisor on the server that hosts the VM. Thus, the VNI and VXLAN-related tunnel / outer header encapsulation/decapsulation take place at the VTEP and are known only to the VTEP - the VM never knows and sees it. Note that it is often that VTEPs can also be resident in a physical switch or physical server and can be implemented in software or hardware.

In a VXLAN environment, using one type of control plane - data plane learning. In this scheme, the association of the endpoint's MAC to VTEP's IP address is discovered by source-address learning. That use multicast carries unknown, broadcast, and multicast (BUM) destination frames.

Of course, except for a learning-based control plane, there are other methods possible for the distribution of the VTEP IP to Terminal MAC mapping information. For example, a central authority-/directory-based lookup by the individual VTEPs, distribution of this mapping information to the VTEPs by the central authority, and so on. In the later of this book, a popularly used VXLAN control plane Multiprotocol BGP(MP-BGP) EVPN (Ethernet Virtual Private Network) will be emphasized and introduced.

VXLAN Encapsulation and Packet Format

VXLAN implements the Layer 2 overlay scheme over a Layer 3 network. It encapsulates a MAC Address into the User Datagram Protocol (MAC-in-UDP) to extend Layer 2 segments across the data center network. This solution is designed to support a flexible, large-scale, multi-tenant environment over a shared common physical infrastructure.

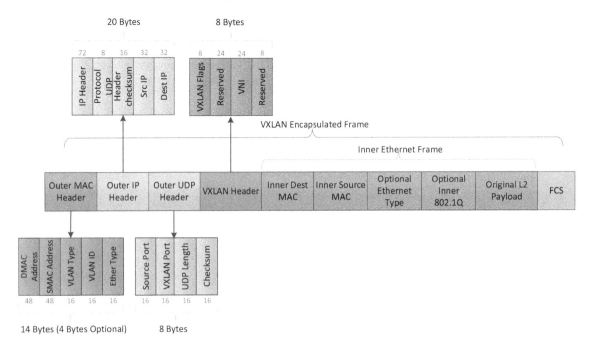

Figure 3-2 VXLAN Packet Format

In this MAC-in-UDP encapsulation scheme, a VXLAN header is inserted before the original Layer 2 frame and then wrapped into a UDP-IP packet. That is, the VXLAN header, together with the original Ethernet frame, goes inside the UDP payload with this MAC-in-UDP encapsulation, VXLAN tunnels Layer 2 network over Layer 3 network.

VXLAN header total 8-byte length with a 24-bit VNI ID, VXLAN Flags, and reserved bits. The 24-bit VNI ID is used to identify Layer 2 segments and to maintain Layer 2 isolation between the segments. The 24-bit VNI ID can accommodate 16 million LAN segments. The above Figure 3-2 shows the VXLAN packet format contents.

3.1.2.1 Virtual Tunnel End Point

A VXLAN tunnel end point (VTEP) is a device that performs VXLAN encapsulation when a packet goes out forward to a peer end point and de-capsulation when a packet arrives at a destination end point. VTEPs terminate VXLAN tunnels at the pair end point where VTEPs reside in it.

Each VTEP has two switch interfaces. One is a Layer 2 interface on the local LAN segment to support a local endpoint communication through bridging. The other is a Layer 3 IP interface to interact with the transport IP network.

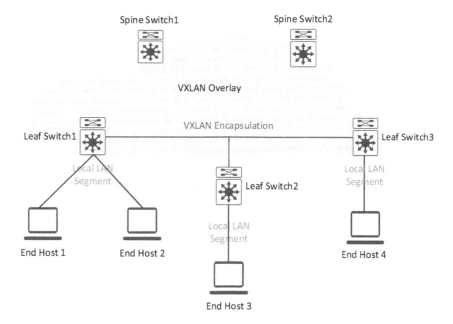

Figure 3-3 Overlay VXLAN Network

The VTEP device has an IP interface with a unique address in the transport network. This IP address can be used to encapsulate Ethernet frames and transmit the packets in the transport network. A VTEP discovers other VTEP devices that share the same VNIs it has locally connected. It advertises the locally connected MAC addresses to its peers. It also learns remote MAC Address-to-VTEP mapping information from its IP interface.

The above Figure 3-3 demonstrates the working of an overlay VXLAN network connecting various VTEPs:

3.1.2.2   VXLAN Tunnel

A VXLAN encapsulated communication between two VTEP devices where they encapsulate and decapsulate an inner original Ethernet frame, is called a VXLAN tunnel. VXLAN tunnels are stateless because they use UDP protocol to encapsulate.

3.1.2.3   Layer 2 Virtual Network Instance

The creation of a VXLAN overlay network allows the end host connected to various leaf or Top of Rack (ToR) nodes, that are separated by multiple Layer 3 networks, to interact as if they were connected to a single Layer 2 network, which is the VXLAN segment. This logical Layer 2 segment is called Layer 2 VNI. The traffic that passes through a Layer 2 VNI between two 802.1Q VLANs within the same subnet is known as bridged traffic.

A VLAN that is locally defined on a VTEP can be mapped to a Layer 2 VNI. In order to allow the end host to connect to a Layer 2 VNI, the connected VLAN must be mapped to the Layer 2 VNI, and then the Layer 2 VNI is associated with the Network Virtualization Edge (NVE) logical interface on the VTEP device.

3.1.2.4   Layer 3 Virtual Network Instance

When the end host connected to a Layer 2 VNI needs to communicate with the end host belonging to other different IP subnets, they send the traffic to their self-default gateway first. Communication between end hosts belonging to different Layer 2 VNIs is possible only through a Layer 3 routing function. In a Border Gateway Protocol (BGP) EVPN VXLAN environment, the various Layer 2 segments that are defined by combining the local VLANs and the global Layer 2 VNIs can be associated with an IP Virtual routing and forwarding (VRF) in order to communicate.

A Layer 3 VNI facilitates Layer 3 segmentation for every VRF on a VTEP. This is done by associating each VRF instance to a unique Layer 3 VNI in the network and mapping the various Layer 2 VNIs for a VTEP to the same VRF. This allows inter-VXLAN communication throughout the Layer 3 VNI within a particular VRF instance. The use of VRFs to enable a logical Layer 3 isolation implement multi-tenancy. The traffic that flows through a Layer 3 VNI between two VLANs with different subnets is known as routed traffic.

The Figure 3-4 show the communication between end host in the same and different subnets through Layer 2 and Layer 3 VNIs respectively:

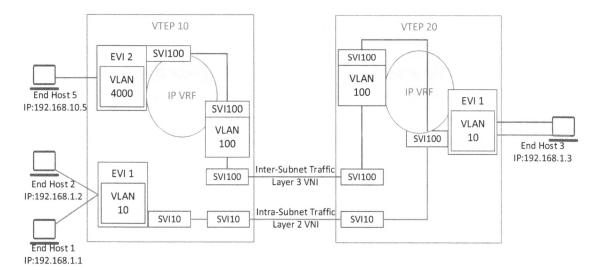

Figure 3-4 Traffic through Layer 2 and Layer 3 VNIs

3.1.2.5 VXLAN Network Identifier

Each VXLAN segment is identified by a 24-bit segment ID, it also be termed as the VXLAN network identifier. This means that an administrative domain can accommodate up to 16 million VXLAN segments in it.

3.1.2.6 Underlay

A virtual overlay network is established over a pre-existing physical network which be termed as an underlay network. The overlay network is defined along with the data-plane encapsulation and a method of transporting the data.

BGP EVPN provides reachability information between the source and destination VTEPs, the underlay Layer 3 network encapsulates and transports packets to the destination VTEP according to reachability information. The VXLAN overlay and the underlying layer 3 IP network between the VTEPs are independent of each other. The following Figure 3-5 illustrates an underlay network.

The main purpose of the underlay in the VXLAN fabric is to advertise the reachability of the Virtual Tunnel Endpoints (VTEPs) and provide a fast and reliable transport for the VXLAN traffic.

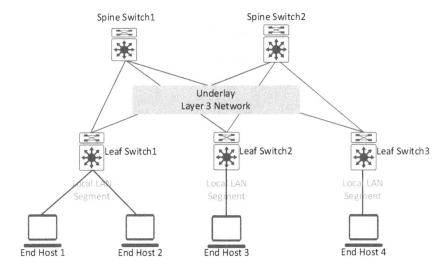

Figure 3-5 Underlay Layer 3 Network in BGP EVPN VXLAN

3.1.2.7 Overlay

An overlay network is a logical/virtual network that is built at the top of an existing Layer 2 or Layer 3 network by establishing a static or dynamic tunnel that runs over the physical underlying network infrastructure termed as underlay.

When a data packet is sent through an overlay network, the original packet or frame is packaged or encapsulated at a source edge device where the VTEP instance is placed with an outer header and dispatched toward the outer header destination IP address indicated target edge device. The intermediate network devices forward the packet according to the outer header without any awareness of the data in the original packet. At the destination edge device (VTEP), the packet is decapsulated by stripping off the overlay outer header and then forwarded based on the Inner dest address in the inner ethernet header (see Figure 3-2) indicated destination.

In the BGP EVPN VXLAN environment, VXLAN is used as the overlay technology to encapsulate the data packets and tunnel the traffic over a Layer 2 network or Layer 3 network. VXLAN builds a Layer 2 overlay network by encapsulating the final actual MAC address in a UDP packet. A VXLAN header is added to the original Layer 2 frame, and it is then placed within a UDP-IP packet. A VXLAN overlay network is also termed a VXLAN segment. Only end hosts and virtual machines within the same VXLAN segment can communicate with each other without routing.

3.1.2.8 Overlay Multicast

Overlay multicast is the method by which an overlay network forwards multicast traffic across various VTEPs present in the network. Tenant Routed Multicast (TRM) provides a mechanism to efficiently forward multicast traffic in a VXLAN overlay network. TRM is a BGP-EVPN based solution that enables multicast routing between sources and receivers connected on VTEPs in VXLAN fabric.

If without TRM, the multicast traffic is sent as part of the underlay network in the form of BUM traffic either using underlay multicast or ingress replication (IR) methods. This does not allow sources and receivers that are present between different subnets to communicate with each other. With TRM, multicast communication does not use the BUM underlay traffic. This achieves an efficient multicast communication in the overlay network irrespective of the subnet in which the source or the receiver resides. The detailed information on BUM traffic replication is omitted in this book.

3.1.2.9 Integrated Routing and Bridging

VXLAN with MBGP EVPN control plane can support Integrated Routing and Bridging (IRB) functionality, which allows the VTEPs in a VXLAN network to forward both Layer 2 and Layer 3 traffic. The Layer 2 forwarding process is termed bridging, and the Layer 3 forwarding process is termed routing. The traffic between different subnets is forwarded through the VXLAN gateways. IRB can be implemented in Asymmetric IRB and Symmetric IRB.

VXLAN Gateways

A VXLAN Gateway is an entity in the network that forwards traffic between VXLAN segments or stitches a VXLAN environment with a non-VXLAN environment. There are two types of VXLAN gateways: Layer 2 VXLAN gateways and Layer 3 VXLAN gateways.

Layer 2 VXLAN gateways forward traffic within the same subnet. The gateway can map between the VXLAN segment and VLAN segment by VNI and VLAN ID.

Layer 3 VXLAN gateways forward traffic to a different subnet. The gateway allows both VXLAN to VXLAN routing as well as VXLAN to VLAN routing. VXLAN to VXLAN routing provides Layer 3 connectivity between two VNIs, as VXLAN to VLAN routing provides connectivity between a VNI and a VLAN.

Layer 3 VXLAN gateways function can be offloaded to the leaf node from the spine node. Consequently, the leaf switches in a VXLAN network can function as both Layer 2 and Layer 3 VXLAN gateways. Such a Gateway is termed a Distributed VXLAN Gateway.

Distributed Anycast Gateway

Distributed Anycast Gateway use default gateway addressing that uses the same IP and MAC address (single virtual IP (VIP) address) across all the leaves or border that are a part of a VNI. In this way, every leaf or border can function as the default gateway for the workloads directly connected to it. The distributed Anycast Gateway feature can be applied in the BGP EVPN Multi-site architecture to facilitate flexible workload placement and optimal traffic forwarding across the VXLAN fabric.

The virtual IP address is represented by a dedicated loopback interface associated with the Network Virtualization Endpoint (NVE) interface.

3.1.3   MP-BGP

MP-BGP EVPN utilizes the MP-BGP feature and mechanism. MP-BGP is an enhanced version of BGP-4. This section will present the BGP-4 and how the MP-BGP extends the BGP-4.

BGP-4

Before understanding the fundamentals of MP-BGP, we first understand the traditional BGP. As in following Figure 3-6, original BGP-4 peers exchange routing information by sending Update messages. An Update message can advertise reachable routes with the same path attribute. These routes are carried in the Network Layer Reachability Information (NLRI) field. BGP-4 mainly be used to support IPv4 unicast routing.

❶NLRI (Network Layer Reachability Information)

This field is resident paralleled with path attributes.

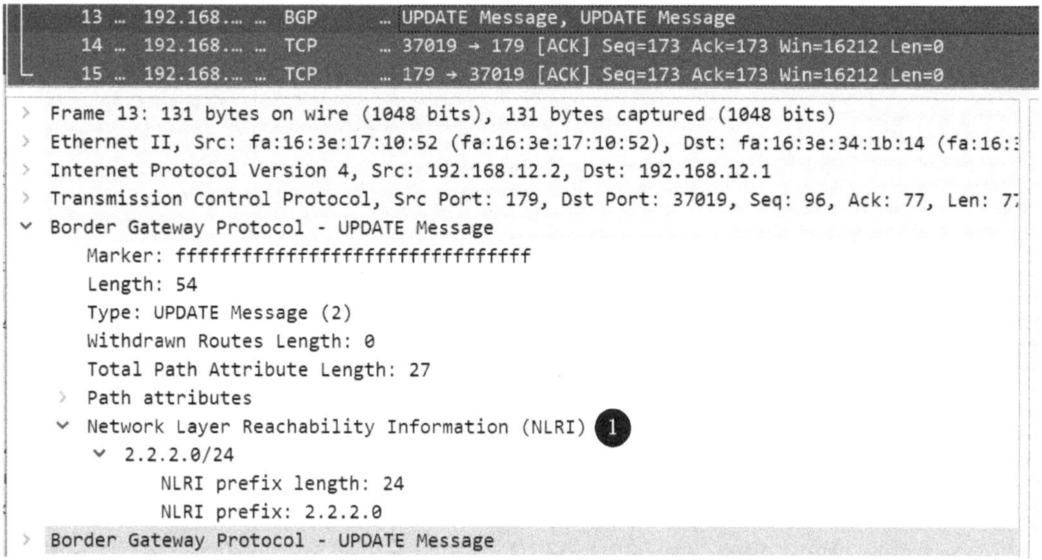

```
 13 …  192.168.… …  BGP       … UPDATE Message, UPDATE Message
 14 …  192.168.… …  TCP       … 37019 → 179 [ACK] Seq=173 Ack=173 Win=16212 Len=0
 15 …  192.168.… …  TCP       … 179 → 37019 [ACK] Seq=173 Ack=173 Win=16212 Len=0
```

```
>  Frame 13: 131 bytes on wire (1048 bits), 131 bytes captured (1048 bits)
>  Ethernet II, Src: fa:16:3e:17:10:52 (fa:16:3e:17:10:52), Dst: fa:16:3e:34:1b:14 (fa:16:3
>  Internet Protocol Version 4, Src: 192.168.12.2, Dst: 192.168.12.1
>  Transmission Control Protocol, Src Port: 179, Dst Port: 37019, Seq: 96, Ack: 77, Len: 7
v  Border Gateway Protocol - UPDATE Message
       Marker: ffffffffffffffffffffffffffffffff
       Length: 54
       Type: UPDATE Message (2)
       Withdrawn Routes Length: 0
       Total Path Attribute Length: 27
    >  Path attributes
    v  Network Layer Reachability Information (NLRI) ❶
       v  2.2.2.0/24
              NLRI prefix length: 24
              NLRI prefix: 2.2.2.0
>  Border Gateway Protocol - UPDATE Message
```

Figure 3-6   NLRI in BGP-4 Update Message

MP-BGP

The following Figure 3-7 presents the detailed information of the MP-BGP Update Message that advertises the routing information.

❶ - Path Attributes

This field is the same as in BGP-4 with IPv4 unicast routing information, it includes ORIGIN, AS_PATH, LOCAL_PREF, EXTENDED_COMMUNITES, ORIGNATER_ID, CLUSTER_LIST Path attribute.

❷ - MP_REACH_NLRI

Conventional BGP-4 manages only IPv4 unicast routing information, and inter-AS (Autonomous System) transmission of packets of other network layer protocols, such as multicast, is limited.

To support multiple network layer protocols, BGP-4 be extended to forward compatible MP-BGP (Multiprotocol Border Gateway Protocol). Whether the routers support BGP extension or not, they can communicate with each other.

MP_REACH_NLRI indicates the multiprotocol reachable NLRI. It in is charge of advertising a reachable route and its next hop.

MP_UNREACH_NLRI indicates the multiprotocol unreachable NLRI. It is used for deleting an unreachable route.

NLRI Field is within the path attributes; this is different from BGP-4.

❸, ❹ - Address Family

BGP-4 can manage only IPv4 unicast routing information, whereas MP-BGP was developed to support multiple network layer protocols, such as IPv6 and multicast. MP-BGP uses address families to distinguish different these network layer protocols.

MP-BGP extends NLRI based on BGP-4. After extension, the description of the address family is added to NLRI to differentiate network layer protocols, such as the IPv6 unicast address family and VPN instance address family.

The Address Family Information field consists of a 2-byte Address Family Identifier (AFI) and a 1-byte Subsequent Address Family Identifier (SAFI).

The new EVPN NLRI is carried in BGP using Multi-protocol BGP Extensions with a newly defined Address Family Identifier (AFI) and Subsequent Address Family Identifier (SAFI).in the BGP-EVPN Address Family, AFI=25 and SAFI =70 as shown in Figure 3-7.

❺ - Route Type

As illustrated in Figure 3-6, the original Multiprotocol Label Switching (MPLS) RFC (7348) and subsequent IP prefix draft introduce five unique EVPN route types.

Following is the list of the five types of EVPN routes defined in EVPN NLRI. Type 1 to Type 4 routes are defined in RFC 7432, and Type 5 route is defined in a draft-ietf-bess-evpn-prefix-advertisement draft.

EVPN Type 1 and Type 4 routes are used in EVPN Ethernet Segment Identifier (ESI) all-active scenarios. The EVPN ESI all-active function allows multi-homing and all-active VXLAN gateways to be deployed based on RFC standards, effectively improving the reliability on the VXLAN access side.

EVPN Type 2 Route, also termed as MAC/IP advertisement routes, are used by VTEPs to advertise host IP and MAC address information to each other.

EVPN Type 3 Route be used by VTEPs to advertise L2VNIs and VTEP IP addresses to each other for creating an ingress replication list. That is, Type 3 routes are used for automatic VTEP discovery and dynamic VXLAN tunnel establishment. If there is a reachable route to the peer VTEP's IP address, a VXLAN tunnel is established from the local VTEP to the peer VTEP. Additionally, if the local and remote VNIs are the same, an ingress replication list is created for BUM packet forwarding.

EVPN Type 4 Route, also be termed Ethernet Segment Routes that are needed in multi-homing scenarios and used for Designated Forwarder Election. Designated Forwarder is responsible for sending broadcast, unknown multicast and multicast (BUM) traffic.

EVPN Type 5 Route, also termed as IP prefix routes, are used to transmit network segment routes. Different from Type 2 routes that transmit only 32-bit (IPv4) or 128-bit (IPv6) host routes, Type 5 routes can transmit network segment routes with mask lengths ranging from 0 to 32 or 0 to 128 bits.

❻- RD and RT

Route Distinguisher (RD) distinguishes the advertised address with a unique number in the VRF, ensuring without causing IPs and MACs conflicts across different tenants.

Route Target (RT) controls the import and export of routes across VRFs, EVPN routes are advertised with RT, and RT is BGP extended communities which can be thought of as the tag of a route. The purpose of marking this tag is to associate the route with the peer VRF instance or those, and the receiver will import the route into the VRF marked by the tag according to this tag. The RT can be auto derived based on the AS number and the VNI of the MAC-VRF

❼Advertised MAC/IP Address

EVPN uses the MP-BGP mechanism and defines a new sub-address family, the EVPN address family, in the L2VPN address family. In the EVPN address family, a new type of NLRI is added, that is, EVPN NLRI. EVPN NLRI defines several types of BGP EVPN routes, which can carry information such as the host IP address, MAC address, VNI, and VRF. After a VTEP learns the IP address and MAC address of the connected hosts, the VTEP can send the information to other VTEPs through an MP-BGP update message. In this way, learning of host IP address and MAC address information can be implemented on the control plane, by this approach, traffic flooding on the data plane has been suppressed.

17	33.897934	120.0.1.1	120.0.2.1	BGP	336 UPDATE Message
18	34.101345	120.0.2.2	120.0.1.1	BGP	334 UPDATE Message

```
    Total Path Attribute Length: 73
  ∨ Path attributes
    > Path Attribute - ORIGIN: IGP
①  > Path Attribute - AS_PATH: empty
    > Path Attribute - LOCAL_PREF: 100
    > Path Attribute - EXTENDED_COMMUNITIES
    ∨ Path Attribute - MP_REACH_NLRI ②
       > Flags: 0x90, Optional, Extended-Length, Non-transitive, Complete
         Type Code: MP_REACH_NLRI (14)
         Length: 44
③      Address family identifier (AFI): Layer-2 VPN (25)
④      Subsequent address family identifier (SAFI): EVPN (70)
         Next hop: 120.0.2.1
         Number of Subnetwork points of attachment (SNPA): 0
       ∨ Network Layer Reachability Information (NLRI)
          ∨ EVPN NLRI: MAC Advertisement Route
⑤            Route Type: MAC Advertisement Route (2)
                Length: 33
⑥            Route Distinguisher: 0001780002010064 (120.0.2.1:100)
             > ESI: 00:00:00:00:00:00:10:00:00:05
                Ethernet Tag ID: 100
                MAC Address Length: 48
⑦            MAC Address: JuniperN_70:19:80 (4c:96:14:70:19:80)
                IP Address Length: 0
⑦          IP Address: NOT INCLUDED
                > [Expert Info (Note/Protocol): IP Address: NOT INCLUDED]
                0100 1001 0011 0101 0000 .... = MPLS Label 1: 299856
> Border Gateway Protocol - UPDATE Message
∨ Border Gateway Protocol - UPDATE Message
    Marker: ffffffffffffffffffffffffffffffff
    Length: 30
    Type: UPDATE Message (2)
    Withdrawn Routes Length: 0
    Total Path Attribute Length: 7
  ∨ Path attributes
    ∨ Path Attribute - MP_UNREACH_NLRI ②
       > Flags: 0x90, Optional, Extended-Length, Non-transitive, Complete
         Type Code: MP_UNREACH_NLRI (15)
         Length: 3
         Address family identifier (AFI): Layer-2 VPN (25)
         Subsequent address family identifier (SAFI): EVPN (70)
         Withdrawn Routes
```

EVPN Route Types
Type-1: Ethernet A-D Route
Type-2: MAC Advertisement Route
Type-3: Inclusive Multicast Route
Type-4: Ethernet Segment Route
Type-5: IP Prefix Route

Figure 3-7 MP-BGP Update Message

3.1.4   VXLAN Control Plane

This section introduces two control planes that are always implemented with VXLAN. The first one is simple, basic, and can usually be manually applied, whereas the second is widely used in most cases and can be implemented in many popular network hardware devices and software products.

1. Flood and Learn Multicast-Based Learning

In order to configure a VXLAN to use a multicast-based control plane, a specific VXLAN VNI should be joined in the same multicast group when configuring the VTEP. Each VNI belongs to a private multicast group or shares a multicast group with other VNI. The multicast group is in charge of forwarding broadcast, unknown unicast, and multicast (BUM) traffic for a VNI and must be configured to support BUM traffic for a VNI.

At the local, the VTEP Initially learns the MAC addresses of end hosts that are directly connected to them, while the remote MAC address to VTEP mappings is learned via conversational learning.

2. VXLAN MP-BGP EVPN

The previous section described the Flood and Learn method. It can work, but this book focuses on considering using the better enhanced MP-BGP Ethernet VPN (EVPN) control plane, which leverages a distributed Anycast Gateway with Layer 2 and Layer 3 VXLAN overlay networks.

MP-BGP EVPN separates the control plane and data plane. It provides a unified control plane for both Layer-2 and Layer-3 forwarding in a VXLAN overlay network.

In a data-center-like environment, an MP-BGP EVPN control plane can offer:

- The MP-BGP EVPN protocol is based on industry standards to provide inter vendor interoperability.

- It provides a mechanism and control plane to learn end-host Layer-2 and Layer-3 reachability information, enabling organizations to build more robust and scalable VXLAN overlay networks.

- It utilizes the traditional MP-BGP VPN facilities and technology to support scalable multitenant VXLAN overlay Elimination.

- Eliminating or minimizing network flooding through protocol-based host MAC/IP route distribution and ARP suppression on the local VTEPs.

- Providing optimal forwarding for east-west and north-south traffic and supporting workload mobility with the distributed anycast features.

- Providing VTEP peer discovery and authentication, enhancing the security of VTEP in the VXLAN overlay network.

- Supporting active-active multihoming at Layer-2.

3.1.5   VXLAN Multitenancy

Multitenancy is a mode of operation in which multiple independent logical instances (tenants) operate in a shared environment. This section introduces the Layer 2 and Layer 3 Multi-tenancy. The VXLAN Multitenancy technology with EVPN provides a mechanism and capacity for global GVPC and end-to-end communication of hosts in the Distributed Cloud environment.

3.1.5.1 Bridge Domains

The Bridge Domain is a broadcast domain that represents the scope of the Layer 2 network. In the VXLAN network, the bridge domain extends up to two to 24th power about 16 million segments of VNI. So, there are two types of encapsulation exits to allow mapping from VLAN to VNI and vice versa. This mapping configuration is always operated on an edge device or VTEP.

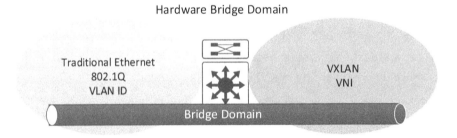

Figure 3-8 Bridge Domain

Generally, the bridge domain mainly contains three components:

- The standard Ethernet domain with the traditional VLAN namespace.

- VXLAN domain with the VNI namespace.

- Network switch with hardware or software bridge domain resource.

3.1.5.2 Multi-tenancy Overview

In a VXLAN environment, multi-tenancy is a mode of operation where multiple independent instances (Layer-3 VRFs, Layer-2 VLANs) of a tenant (such as business entity, user group, applications, or security) operate in a shared VXLAN environment (VXLAN BGP EVPN fabric) while ensuring logical segmentation between the instances. The different tenant instances, such as VRF and VLANs, are logically isolated but physically operate on the same fabric.

3.1.5.2.1 Layer-3 and Layer-2 VNIs

In a VXLAN BGP EVPN fabric, a Layer-3 Virtual Network Identifier (VNI) maps to a tenant. Each tenant has a VRF instance.

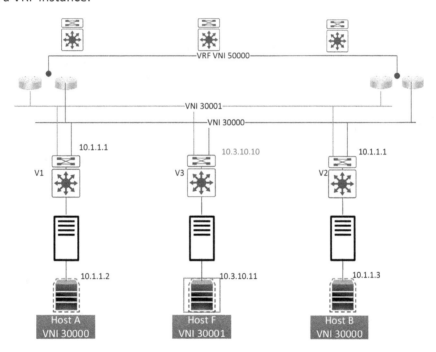

Figure 3-9   Physical Representation of Server Traffic and Segregation Across the VXLAN BGP EVPN Fabric

As a pendant to Layer-3, Layer-2 virtual networks (VLANs) can carry a unique Layer-2 Virtual Network Identifier (VNI) in the fabric. Separate Layer-2 and Layer-3 networks can be created to achieve Layer-2 and Layer-3 segmentation, like for business units, user groups, applications, etc. Typically, a Layer-2 virtual network is associated with a single IP subnet, while a VRF can contain multiple Layer-2 networks.

From a global VXLAN BGP EVPN fabric perspective, the VNI is the important identifier that is used across the fabric. When we design a networking architecture, this identifier is the most valuable aspect to consider.

Endpoints belonging to a Layer-2 virtual network can be spread across the fabric and might be associated with different ToR or Leaf switches depending on the networking environment. When the endpoints are under the same Layer-2 virtual network, they communicate with each other by bridging, otherwise by routing.

Across the VXLAN BGP EVPN fabric, the L2 and L3 VNIs are unique and play a global significance. All the Layer-2 virtual networks of a tenant or VRF are associated with a common, unique Layer-3 VRF VNI. Pay attention that The L2 and L3 VNI use the same VNI field in the VXLAN encapsulation and avoid overlapping.

In the above topology, Host A and Host B belong to the same Layer-2 virtual network (VNI 30000, in blue color), so the traffic between them is bridged. Host A and Host F belong to different VNI, which means they belong to different Host A to Host F, so the Traffic from Host A to Host F (VNI 30001, in red color) is routed through the VRF VNI (50000).

3.1.5.2.2 Routing between Layer-2 Virtual Networks

In the VXLAN BGP EVPN fabric, each Layer-2 virtual network needs to be configured with a first-hop gateway. This first hop gateway will allow it to pass through the Layer-3 boundary and send traffic to an end host in another Layer-2 virtual network (another segment). Since a Layer-2 virtual network might have a presence across the fabric with its end hosts attached to multiple border leaf or ToRs switches, the same default first hop gateway IP address should be configured on those border leaf or ToR switches where it has a presence. This method is known as Distributed Anycast Gateway. About Distributed Anycast Gateway, section [3.2.3 Border Gateway Placement] is described in some more detail.

In Figure 3-9, to route traffic from Host A (Layer-2 VNI 30000) to Host F (Layer-2 VNI 30001), a first hop gateway IP address be configured (say 10.1.1.1/24) on the attached ToR switch V1. To route Host B traffic to Host F, the same first hop gateway (10.1.1.1/24) should be enabled on the attached ToR switch V2. This is because Host A and B belong to the same Layer-2 network (VNI 30000). When using the Distributed Anycast Gateway as a first hop gateway, the IP address, as well as the MAC address for the gateway itself, will be the same across all borer Leaf or ToR switches. This IP address represents all border leaf or ToR switches and is known as Virtual IP.

3.1.5.3 Layer-2 Multi-tenancy

Same Parent VLAN and VLAN on the Wire

In Figure 3-10, on ToR switch VTEP V1, VLAN 43 is mapped to L2 VNI 30000. All end host ports that have servers of this network should be associated with VLAN 43.

Host B on V2 belongs to the same Layer-2 virtual network (30000). On ToR switch VTEP V2, Host B is mapped to VLAN 43, and VLAN 43 is mapped to VNI 30000.

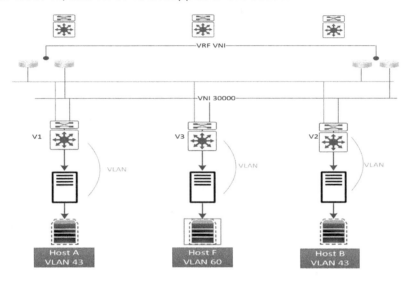

Figure 3-10   Same Parent VLAN and VLAN on The Wire

Since VLANs only have ToR/Leaf switch significance, different switches connected to different VTEPs can have different VLAN IDs to represent a Layer 2 segment. However, using the same VLAN ID across switches can bring convenience without complex mapping. The Layer 2 VNI binds the Layer-2 virtual network and extends Layer-2 reachability across the fabric.

From a ToR or leaf switch's perspective, a Layer-2 virtual network is represented by a VNI on the VXLAN BGP EVPN fabric side (VNI 30000 in Figure 3-11) and a unique VLAN (43) on the tenant side. On the ToR switch, the one-to-one mapping should be configured between the parent VLAN and the VNI. A ToR switch can traditionally only accommodate 4096 (12-bit) VLAN namespace. However, the VLAN limitation at the network level is eliminated due to the introduction of VNIs or segments in the fabric.

VLAN 43 and VNI 30000 are mapped with each other. You should configure an access port to enable Layer 2 to traffic on the interface.

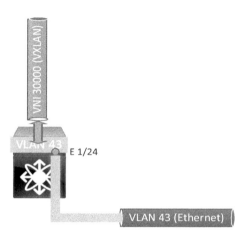

Figure 3-11   Same Parent VLAN and VLAN on the Wire - ToR Switch VTEP

Multiple VLANs on The Wire Mapped to a Parent VLAN

1. Parent VLAN

In this use case, VNI 30000 represents a Layer-2 virtual network on the fabric side. VLAN 40 is the parent VLAN on the ToR switch that represents the Layer-2 virtual network of the tenant side. VLAN 40 should be mapped to VNI 30000 for Layer-2 stitching or extension.

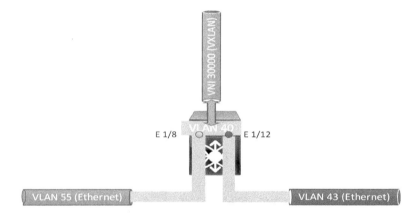

Figure 3-12   Same VLAN Translation Different Multiple VLANs Mapped to a Parent VLAN

2. VLANs on The Wire

VLANs 55 and 43 are on the wire, and end hosts are mapped to these VLANs. They also represent the Layer-2 virtual network 30000, but only through VLAN 40, the parent VLAN. A Parent VLAN

40 and map to a Layer 2 VNI 30000, a trunk port to enable Layer-2 to traffic across VLANs—Ethernet interface 1/8, VLAN 55 is local and significant only to the port on which it is configured (Ethernet interface 1/8 in Figure 3-12). VLAN 55 is mapped to parent VLAN 40. a trunk port to enable Layer-2 to traffic across VLANs - Ethernet interface 1/12, VLAN 43 is local and significant only to the port on which it is configured (Ethernet 1/12 in above Figure 3-12 this case). VLAN 43 is also mapped to parent VLAN 40.

3.1.5.4 Layer-3 Multi-tenancy

When Layer 2 virtual networks need to communicate with each other, an L3 virtual interface (that is, switch virtual interface [SVI]) should be created for each Layer 2 virtual network on a ToR or leaf switch. Each SVI should be associated with the tenant VRF, thereby adding it to the VRF table. A sample scenario is depicted as the following Figure 3-13.

Tenant VRF A is tied to Layer-3 VNI 50000. On this Leaf switch/ToR VTEP, this tenant has two Layer 2 virtual networks with Layer 2 VNI 30000 and 30006, respectively. VLAN 2500 is created for L3 VNI 50000. An SVI, interface VLAN 2500, is created for the tenant VRF.

Similarly, SVIs are created for Layer 2 VNI 30000 (VLAN 55), and Layer 2 VNI 30006 (VLAN 75). The SVIs are interface VLAN 55 and interface VLAN 75. An IP address is assigned to each SVI.

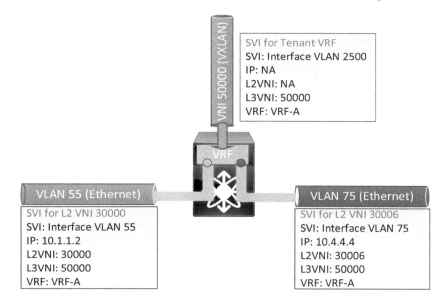

Figure 3-13 Same Layer-3 Multi-Tenancy

3.2 MBGP-EVPN VXLAN Multi-Site

In the Multi-Site model, every site with a data center is deployed and managed as an independent domain. This model increases the resiliency of the overall design by deploying each site as an independent availability zone, and it is often used to address the disaster recovery use case, although it can be extended to the deployment of active-active data centers. MP-BGP EVPN and VXLAN are used to extend Layer 2 and Layer 3 connectivity across separate sites. This approach is also often considered in migration scenarios in which a new VXLAN fabric must be connected to an existing data center network.

Using MP-BGP EVPN VXLAN Multi-pod can archive the scalability from room to room or metropolitan-area distances from each other, but this method has some limitations, such as deployment distance and connection bandwidth. A true Multi-site solution is still the best option for providing separate zones across site locations.

NOTE: *In the case of a site with a single Data Center as a Distributed Cloud zone, the terms Site and Data Center have the same scope and are equivalent.*

3.2.1 Multi-Site Topology

The main advantage of the EVPN Multi-site approach is that it not only can support fabric scalability but also can be deployed for site or data center interconnection for providing separate availability zones across site locations.

Interconnect for Site (Data Center)

EVPN Multi-Site architecture can be used for site Interconnect scenarios (Figure 3-14). This architecture was built with DCI in mind. The overall architecture allows the interconnection between two or more sites remotely, and each site contains one or multiple VXLAN fabrics (which can correspond to data centers). In VXLAN Multi-site architecture, with seamless and controlled Layer 2 and Layer 3 extension through the use of VXLAN BGP EVPN within and between sites, the capabilities of VXLAN BGP EVPN itself have been increased. Network control, VTEP masking, and BUM traffic are the new functions that help make EVPN Multi-Site architecture the most efficient DCI technology.

BGW-to-Cloud Model (DCI)

A preferred choice is to deploy the Border Gateways (BGWs) at the border of the fabric with the border leaf and DCI node functions. The BGW-to-cloud model (Figure 3 16) has a redundant Layer 3 cloud between the different sites. In this deployment model, the Layer 3 cloud provides to each site redundant connectivity points to which the BGWs can connect. Assuming four BGWs in site 2 (London) and two BGWs in the other two public cloud sites (Los Angeles and Tokyo) respectively. Each site connects to two devices in the Layer 3 network core. Full-mesh connectivity can be established among them all, using the basic principle of building triangles, not squares. Similar connectivity can be achieved by the other sites. In this way, every BGW has redundant connectivity to the Layer 3 cloud, which also reduces the convergence time in a link-failure scenario.

The only specific requirements for the Layer 3 network are that it provides IP connectivity between the Virtual IP and Private IP (PIP) addresses of the BGWs and accommodates the MTU for the VXLAN-encapsulated traffic across the Layer 3 network. The Layer 3 network can be any routed service, such as a flat Layer 3 routed network, an MPLS Layer 3 VPN, or other provider routed services. When a VPN-like service is provided in the Layer 3 network, the physical interfaces on the BGW site must remain in the default VRF instance. Since MP-BGP peering with VPN address families is supported only as part of the default VRF instance.

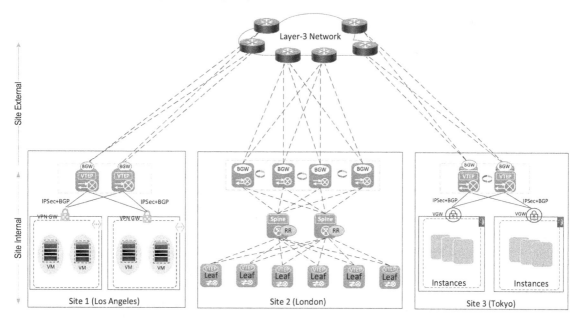

Figure 3-14   BGW-to-Cloud Model

When a solution with a massive scale of fabric sites and BGWs, the need for full-mesh external Border Gateway Protocol (eBGP) peering between any BGWs for the overlay control plane may become dramatically complex. At this time, bringing a Route Server (RS) can simplify the design and reduce the burden of having so many BGP peering. This route server is basically an eBGP route reflector, which does not exist in the BGP world. An eBGP route server does the same work as an Internal Border Gateway Protocol (iBGP) route reflector. Both type of reflector never works in the data path to perform this function. Such a route server can be placed in the Layer 3 network cloud or in another separate location reachable from every BGW. The route server will act as a star point for all the control-plane peering for all the BGWs and will help ensure the reflection of BGP updates. For resiliency, a pair of route servers is recommended.

This mode can be used in a Zone group with multiple zones in a Max site, each EVPN VXLAN site can be mapped to a Distributed Cloud zone. Figure 3-24 in [3.2.6.2 External WAN Edge Router - Zonegroup with Multiple Zones] depicts some points of this mode.

Model with BGWs Between Spine and Superspine for Scaling a Single Large Fabric

When you scale up a network, one device or component easily reaches the scale ceiling. The scale-out approach offers an improvement for data center fabrics. Nevertheless, a single data center fabric also has scale limits, and thus, the scale-out approach for a single large data center fabric is necessary.

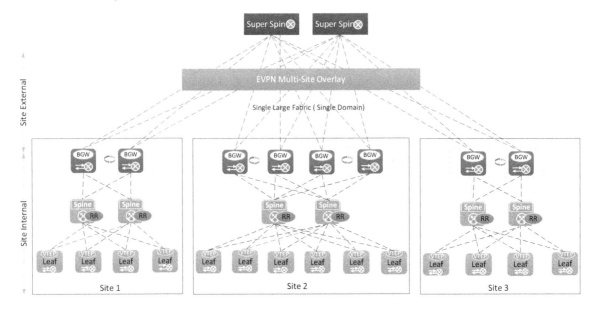

Figure 3-15   Model with BGWs Between Spine and Superspine

Except to scale out within a single fabric, with EVPN Multi-Site architecture, you can scale out in the higher level of the hierarchy. As you add more leaf or ToR nodes for expanding capacity within a data center fabric, you can add fabrics (sites) to horizontally scale the overall environment for scaling in EVPN Multi-Site architecture. In this way, in addition to increasing the scale, you can contain the full-mesh adjacencies of VXLAN between the VXLAN Tunnel Endpoints (VTEPs) in a fabric.

BGWs are placed between the spine and external super spine (on the top of Figure 3-15). the site-internal network uses a spine-and-leaf folded clos model, and the BGWs are located on top of the internal spine. All the BGWs of the various sites connect to the super spine together. In this way, this topology has the same network layers as in the previous BGW-to-cloud model. The critical difference is in the geographical radius of such a topology. In comparison, the BGW-to-cloud approach considers the Layer 3 cloud to be extended across a long distance, such as between different cities. The super spine likely exists within a site with different VXLAN fabrics (VXLAN sites). This approach creates a high-speed backbone within a site.

The Model with BGWs between the spine and super spine presents a deployment use case different from the DCI use case. With this model, VXLAN fabrics are scaled by interconnecting them in a hierarchical fashion. In addition to the extension of connectivity across fabrics, this approach also leverages the masking that EVPN Multi-Site architecture uses to reduce the amount of peering between all VTEPs and thus increase scale capacity. Using BGP EVPN Multi-Site architecture with the BGWs, you can compartmentalize functional building blocks. The easy interconnection of these compartments is achieved through the integrated Layer 2 and Layer 3 extensions offered by BGP EVPN Multi-Site architecture. By using selective control-plane advertisement and the enforcement of BUM traffic at the BGWs, you can achieve more control over extension between fabrics.

As the BGW-to-cloud method, the use of a BGP route server can also be beneficial when you deploy BGWs between the spine and the super spine. When many sites and many BGWs per site exist, the number of peering can easily grow dramatically. The route-server approach can offer control-plane exchanges between all the BGWs across sites with a simplified peering model.

This model can be used in a Distributed Cloud zone that contains multiple Data Centers. For example, each EVPN VXLAN site maps to a data center. Note that the EVPN VXLAN site is greatly different from the Distributed Cloud site. One Distributed Cloud site can contain a single or multiple EVPN VXLAN sites. Figure 3-25 in [3.2.6.3 External WAN Edge Router - Zone with Multiple Data Centers] depicts some points of this model; you can see it.

3.2.2   Border Gateway

The main functional component of the EVPN Multi-Site architecture is the border gateway or BGW. BGWs separate the fabric side (site-internal fabric) from the network that interconnects the sites (site-external DCI) and mask the site-internal VTEPs.

Just as its name implies, an EVPN Multi-Site deployment consists of two or more sites, which are interconnected through a VXLAN BGP EVPN Layer 2 and Layer 3 overlay (Figure 3-16). typically, the BGW is connected to the site-internal VTEPs through spine nodes and to a site-external transport network that allows traffic to reach the BGWs at other, remote sites. The BGWs at the remote sites have site internal VTEPs behind them. Only the underlay IP addresses of the BGWs are seen inside the transport network between the BGWs. The site's internal VTEPs are always masked behind the BGWs.

From the point of view of the BGW, the role of the site-internal VTEPs is to share the common VXLAN and BGP-EVPN functions. To interoperate with a BGW, the following functions are mandatory for a site-internal node:

- VXLAN with Protocol-Independent Multicast (PIM) Any-Source Multicast (ASM) or ingress replication (BGP EVPN Route Type 3) in the underlay network.

- With BGP EVPN Route Type 2 and Route Type 5 for the overlay control plan.

- Provide a Route reflector for exchanging BGP EVPN Route Type 4.

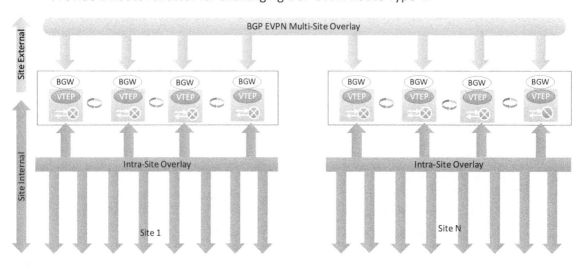

Figure 3-16   BGP EVPN Multi-Site Deployment

From the site-external network perspective, no specific requirements are demanded apart from IP transport reachability between the BGWs and accommodation of an increased packet MTU size. The BGWs always preclude the use of Ingress Replication for Layer 2 BUM traffic across BGWs in different sites, but they can use either PIM ASM or ingress replication within a given site. This capability archives flexibility for existing deployments and transport independence for the site-external network.

The BGW provides the capacity to perform the internal-to-external site-separation procedure on its own side. Therefore, the BGW doesn't require a neighboring device to achieve this function. Just as a traditional VTEP can connect from a site-internal network to a BGW, a traditional VTEP can also connect to a BGW from a site-external network. That means a BGW at the source site doesn't require a neighboring BGW at the destination site; a normal classic VTEP will suffice. Such flexibility built into the BGW allows deployments beyond the traditional BGP EVPN Multi-Site pairings.

3.2.3 Border Gateway Placement

In an EVPN Multi-Site architecture deployment, you can place the dedicated set of BGW at the leaf layer or let BGW co-located on the spine of the fabric. In the leaf layer case, the spine is just like any other VTEP in the fabric (site internal VTEPs). If the BGW is on the spine, multiple functions are overloaded together, such as route-reflector, Rendezvous-Point (RP), east-west traffic, and external connectivity functions. In the latter case, additional factors related to scale, configuration, and failure scenarios should be considered.

Anycast border gateway

The Anycast BGW (A-BGW) performs the BGW function and offers a capacity to scale out the BGWs horizontally and does not need the sharing of inter-device dependencies.

"A-BGW" refers to the sharing of a common Virtual IP address or anycast IP address between the BGWs in a normal site. Usually, the virtual IP address refers also to the EVPN Multi-Site anycast IP address.

The virtual IP address on the BGW is responsible for all data-plane communication leaving the site and between sites when the EVPN Multi-Site extension is used to reach the remote sites. The single virtual IP address is used both within the site to reach an exit point and across the sites, with the BGWs always using the virtual IP address to communicate with each other. Typically, the single virtual IP address is represented by a dedicated loopback interface associated with the Network Virtualization Endpoint (NVE) interface.

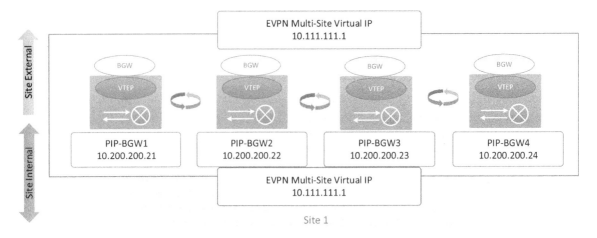

Figure 3-17 Anycast Border Gateway

By this approach, and with an Equal-Cost Multipath (ECMP) network, all BGWs are always equally reachable and active for data-traffic forwarding. The underlay transport network within or between the sites is responsible for hashing the VXLAN traffic among the available equal-cost paths. This approach avoids skewness, given the entropy of VXLAN, and it enhances resiliency. When one or more BGWs fail, the remaining BGWs still advertise the virtual IP address and, hence, are immediately available to take over all the ongoing data traffic. The use of anycast IP addresses or virtual IP addresses offers network-based resiliency instead of resiliency that depends on device hellos or similar state notification protocols.

Besides anycast IP address or the virtual IP address, every BGW has its own individual private represented primary VTEP IP (PIP) address that is responsible for handling BUM traffic in the BGW. Every BGW leverages its PIP address to perform BUM replication, either in the multicast underlay or when advertising BGP EVPN Route Type 3, used for ingress replication. Therefore, every BGW of sites has an active role in BUM traffic forwarding. As the virtual IP address, the PIP address is advertised to both the site-internal network and the site-external network.

If the BGW is providing external connectivity with VRF-lite next to the EVPN Multi-Site deployment, routing prefixes that are learned from the external Layer 3 network devices are advertised inside the VXLAN fabric using the PIP address as the next-hop address. From the BGW's point of view, these externally learned IP prefixes are considered to originate locally from a BGW with the BGP EVPN address family. This process creates an individual BGP EVPN Route Type 5 (IP prefix route) from every BGW that learns a relevant IP prefix externally. Under ideal conditions, the site-internal network has an ECMP route to reach non-EVPN Multi-Site networks.

Externally learned IP prefixes can be redistributed to BGP EVPN from any BGP IPv4/IPv6 unicast, Open Shortest Path First (OSPF), or other dynamic or static routing protocol that allows redistribution to BGP EVPN.

Designated forwarder

As introduced before, every A-BGW actively participates in the BUM traffic forwarding, Specifically, the Designated-Forwarder (DF) function for BUM traffic is distributed on a Per-Layer 2 VXLAN Network Identifier (VNI) basis. To synchronize the DF, BGP EVPN Route Type 4 (Ethernet segment route) updating messages be exchanged between the BGWs within the same site.

3.2.4   BGP-EVPN Control Plane

BGW devices are the main functional component of the EVPN Multi-Site architecture. The deployment of BGW affects the way that the overlay network performs its Layer 2 and Layer 3 services. Overlay is the most important for stability and the proper design of underlay is also critical.

There are many options when designing the underlay and overlay of MP-BGP EVPN with VXLAN, the most popular two options are I-E-I and E-E-E:

In the **I-E-I** option, for Intra-Site, the underlay control plane uses Interior Gateway Protocol (IGP) such as OSPF and IS-IS. And overlay control plane uses iBGP, while eBGP is for both underlay and overlay for Inter-Sites.

In the **E-E-E** option, eBGP be used as both the underlay and overlay control plane for both Intra-Site and Inter-Sites.

The two models can be mixed in the sense that one site can run on "E" (eBGP-eBGP for both the underlay and overlay), and the other remote site can run on "I" (IGP-iBGP, underlay use IGP, and overlay use iBGP). From an inter-site underlay, eBGP can be replaced with any routing protocol as long as a clean separation exists between the site-internal and site-external routing domains. The "E" (eBGP) portion for the overlay is mandatory for inter-sites.

Not only choosing the underlay routing protocols, but you also need to separate the site-internal and site-external routing domains. When using the I-E-I option, the underlays will not likely be redistributed between the "I" (IGP) and the "E" (eBGP) domains. Furthermore, you must actively separate the site-internal underlay from the site-external underlay in the E-E-E scenario since, by default, BGP automatically exchanges information between the underlay domains. Do not join site-internal and site-external underlays, or you will incur some unanticipated forwarding and failures.

3.2.4.1 Underlay Control Plane

You can use a full mesh of MP-eBGP EVPN adjacencies across sites, but deploying a couple of eBGP Route Servers in a separate AS to perform control plane functions is recommended in case there are more than three sites in your environment.

eBGP Route-Servers can provide EVPN route reflection, next-hop-unchanged, and route-target rewrite capacities. For detailed information on eBGP Route-Reflectors, please refer to Internet Engineering Task Force (IETF) RFC 7947.

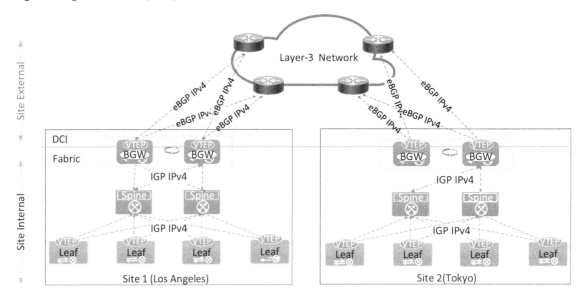

Figure 3-18 Multi-site Unerlay Control Plane

Site-internal Underlay (Fabric)

The site-internal underlay can be deployed in various forms. Most commonly, an IGP is used to provide reachability between the intra-site VTEP (Leaf), the spine, and the BGWs. BGP (with dual- and multiple-autonomous systems.) also can be used for underlay unicast reachability.

EVPN Multi-Site architecture allows both multicast (PIM ASM) and ingress replication to be configured for BUM replication. It also allows different BUM replication modes to be used at different sites. Thus, the local site-internal network can be configured with ingress replication while the remote site-internal network can be configured with a multicast-based underlay.

BGP EVPN allows BUM replication based on either ingress replication or multicast (PIM ASM). When using EVPN, network-based BUM replication mechanism such as multicast is still available.

The Figure 3-19 shows the BGW with a site-internal topology. The loopback interface used for the router ID and BGP peering must be advertised to the site-internal underlay as well as to the site-external underlay. If deemed beneficial, separate loopback interfaces can be used for site-internal and site-external purposes or for various routing protocols.

In the site-internal underlay, point-to-point IP addressing or IP unnumbered addressing can also be used.

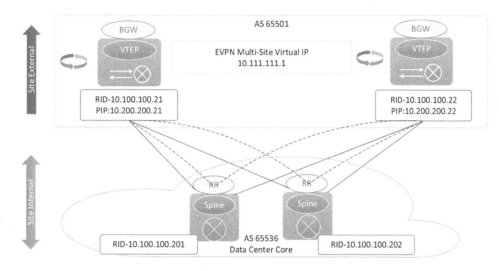

Figure 3-19 BGW with Site-internal Topology

Site-External Underlay for DCI

The site-external underlay is the network that interconnects multiple VXLAN BGP EVPN fabrics and traditional external VTEPs. It is a transport network that allows reachability across all the EVPN Multi-Site BGWs and traditional external VTEPs. Organizations can use an additional spine tier - super spine, and other deployments have a routed Layer 3 network.

The site-external underlay network routing protocols have multiple options, while the eBGP always has its interdomain nature benefits for providing reachability between the BGWs of multiple sites.

For BUM replication across sites, EVPN Multi-Site architecture only uses ingress replication to simplify the goals of the site-external underlay network.

Although the site-external network between sites exclusively uses Ingress replication to handle BUM replication, the site-internal network has no such limit. That means the site-internal network can use ingress replication or multicast (PIM ASM), and the site-internal network in different sites need not consistently use the same BUM replication method.

BGW-Site-external eBGP Underlay

In Muti-site architecture, a Point-to-Point IP address is used for site-external underlay routing; point-to-point IP addressing with /30 is shown in Figure 3-20. In site-external underlay, EVPN Multi-Site interface tracking can be used.

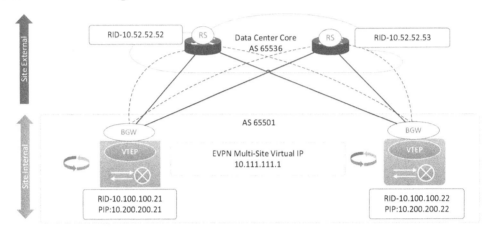

Figure 3-20 BGW with Site-external Topology

3.2.4.2 Overlay Control Plane

For the single-autonomous-system VXLAN BGP EVPN site-internal overlay, iBGP deployment is always used. Although dual- and multiple-autonomous-system can be configured, this section focuses on EVPN Multi-Site architecture; dual- and multiple-autonomous-system are omitted.

If BGP EVPN control-plane communication across BGWs through a site-internal BGP route reflector, the route reflector must support BGP EVPN Route Type 4. If not, direct BGW-to-BGW full-mesh iBGP peering must be configured. BGP EVPN Route Type 4 is used for EVPN Multi-Site designated-forwarder election.

For the site-external overlay, the VXLAN BGP EVPN exclusively uses eBGP, because the eBGP next-hop behavior is used for VXLAN tunnel origination and termination.

In the EVPN Multi-Site architecture, the MAC address or IP prefix advertisement to site-internal originates from the local BGWs with their anycast VTEPs as the next hop. Likewise, the BGWs of the local site receive a MAC address or IP prefix advertised from remote BGWs with their anycast VTEPs as the next hop. This behavior is in accordance with eBGP's well-known and proven process of changing the next hop at the autonomous system boundary. Using eBGP in EVPN Multi-Site architecture not only for VXLAN tunnel termination and re-origination but also for its loop prevention mechanism offered through the as-path attribute. With this approach, on the control plane, prefixes originating at one site will never be imported back into the same site. This can prevent routing loops. On the data plane, designated-forwarder election and split-horizon rules complement the control-plane loop-prevention functions.

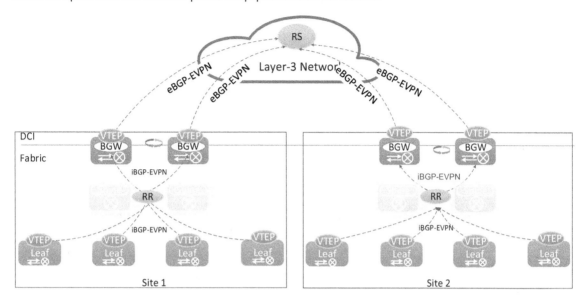

Figure 3-21 Overlay Control Plane

BGP EVPN control-plane communication across BGWs at different sites can be implemented using either a full mesh or a route server, also termed an eBGP route reflector. About when to use full mesh or eBGP Route Reflector, please refer to section [3.2.5 Route Server - eBGP Route Reflector].

3.2.5 Route Server - eBGP Route Reflector

Given the various failure scenarios that are possible in a large scale of deployment with many more sites and BGW to each site, the number of full mesh BGP peering becomes difficult to manage and creates a burden on the control plane.

In the iBGP environments, using a star point to broker the site-external overlay control plane (Figure 3-22) to a scale-out EVPN Multi-Site is the more elegant approach. Such nodes are well known in iBGP environments as route reflectors, which are present to reflect routes that are being sent from their clients that don't require a full mesh anymore.

This approach allows the environment to scale efficiently from control-plane peering, and it also reduces the management burden of configuration and operation. BGP route reflectors are limited to providing their services to iBGP-based peering. In the case of eBGP networks, no route-reflector function exists.

However, for eBGP networks, a function similar to the route-reflector function is offered by the Route Server, as described in IETF RFC 7947: Internet Exchange BGP Route Server.

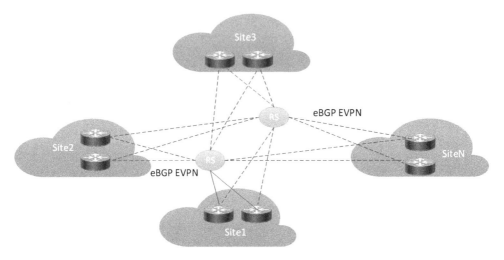

Figure 3-22 EVPN Multi-Site with Route Server

Like an iBGP route reflector, a eBGP Route Server performs a pure control-plane function and does not bear any user data traffic from any of the BGWs. To help ensure that the route-server deployment provides resiliency for the EVPN Multi-Site control-plane exchange in any failure scenario, connectivity or device redundancy is required. The Route Server must be able to support the EVPN address family, reflect VPN routes, and manipulate the next-hop behavior.

3.2.6   Internet and WAN Connectivity among Sites

In an EVPN Multi-Site environment, the requirement for external connectivity is as relevant as the requirement for extension across sites. External connectivity includes the connection of the site (or data center if the site exists only a single data center) to the Internet, the Wide Area Network (WAN), 3GPP NPN site, 3GPP PNI-MEC site, non-3GPP edge site or the branch/campus site through the SD-WAN fabric. Note that all options provided for external connectivity are multitenant aware and focus on Layer 3 network transport to the external network domains.

There are two models for providing external connectivity to EVPN Multi-Site architecture:

- By placing the BGWs at the border between the site-internal and site-external domains, a set of nodes is already available at each site that can provide encapsulation and decapsulation for transit traffic. In addition to the EVPN Multi-Site functions, the BGW allows the coexistence of VRF-aware connectivity with VRF-lite.

- Besides per-BGW or per-site external connectivity, connectivity can be provided through a WAN edge Router. In this case, a dedicated set of border nodes is placed at the site-external portion of multiple sites. All these sites connect through BGP EVPN VXLAN to this WAN Edge Router set, which then provides external connectivity. The WAN-Edge-Router approach also allows MPLS L3VPN, or VRF-lite hand-off to multiple sites.

3.2.6.1 VXLAN BGP EVPN-VRF-lite

In the following Figure 3-23, left is the VXLAN BGP EVPN fabrics. Routes within the fabric are exchanged between all edge devices (VTEPs) as well as Route-Reflectors; the control plane used is MP-BGP with EVPN address family. The edge devices (VTEPs) acting as border nodes are configured to pass on prefixes to the external router (ER). This is achieved by exporting prefixes from MP-BGP EVPN to IPv4 per-VRF peering. Multiple routing protocols can be used for the per-VRF peering. In most cases, eBGP is the protocol of preferred choice, IGPs like OSPF also can be leveraged but with some redistributions.

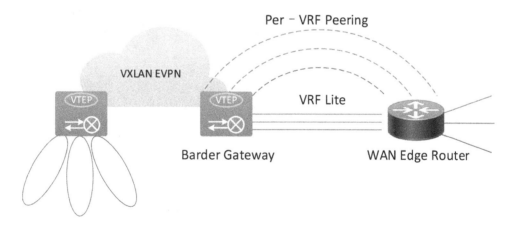

Figure 3-23 External Layer-3 Connectivity - VRF-lite

3.2.6.2 External WAN Edge Router – Single Zonegroup with Multiple Zones

The WAN Edge Router acts as an external connectivity point for VXLAN BGP EVPN fabrics that are interconnected with EVPN Multi-Site architecture. The WAN Edge Routers can be Internet / WAN gateways shared between sites or per site Internet/WAN gateways.

The WAN Edge Router is completely independent of any VXLAN EVPN Multi-Site software or hardware; it is solely a border node with VTEP function and topologically outside of single or multiple sites. The WAN Edge Router operates like a traditional VTEP, but unlike the site-internal VTEPs discussed previously, the WAN Edge Router is a site-external VTEP. In the case of external connectivity, the WAN Edge Router operates only in Layer 3 mode, and hence, BUM replication between the BGW and WAN Edge Router nodes is not necessary. What you must configure on the WAN Edge Router is the VXLAN BGP EVPN VTEP and its presence in a different autonomous system than the one that includes the BGWs.

For an EVPN Multi-Site BGW to connect with a WAN Edge Router, it requires a configuration similar to that for connecting the gateway to the BGW of a remote site. Existing different with the EVPN Multi-Site site-external underlay configuration, interface tracking is not needed when configuring the interface facing the WAN Edge Router nodes.

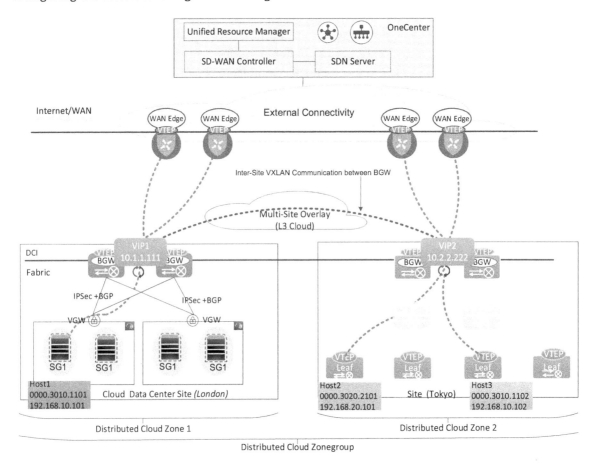

Figure 3-24 EVPN Multi-Site WAN Edge Router for Single Zonegroup with Multiple Zones

This design architecture is based on BGW-to-Cloud Model shown in Figure 3-24. In this architecture, the London site is on the public cloud, whereas the Tokyo site can be on-premises far away from the London site (Distributed Cloud also supports the two sites both on-premise and located within the same city for low latency). You can design the site as an EVPN VXLAN fabric to implement a Distributed Cloud zone. Each zone of London and Tokyo has a respective connection to the external network with self WAN Edge Routers.

3.2.6.3 External WAN Edge Router – Single Zone with Multiple Data Centers

This section presents another approach to connect the Distributed Cloud Zone to external world compared to previous approach.

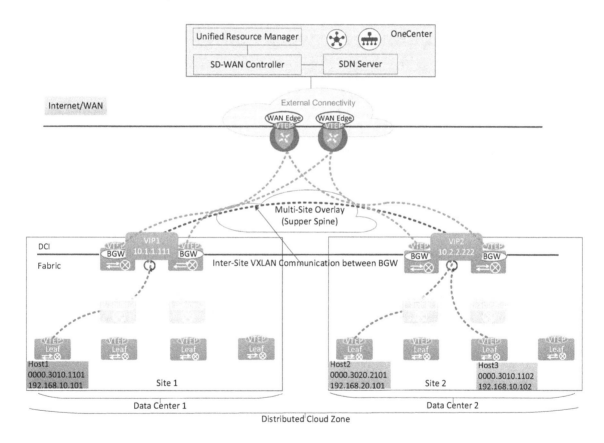

Figure 3-25 EVPN Multi-Site WAN Edge Router for Single Zone with Multiple Date Centers

This design architecture is based on the Model with BGWs between the Spine and Super Spine for Scaling a Single Large Fabric shown in Figure 3-25 and is similar to the previous architecture in Figure 3-24, except for the following differential:

In this architecture, each VXLAN site can correspond to a data center in a Distributed Cloud zone. These multiple sites with multiple EVPN-VXLAN fabrics share a single pair of WAN Edge Routers for the external connections.

Site 1 is and site 2 both be on-premises; those two sites located within the same physical location for low latency. These multiple sites typically build a single Distributed Cloud zone.

The super spine likely exists within a physical location. With the super spine model, all BGWs of all sites connect to all super spines. This approach creates a high-speed backbone within a zone of this site.

3.3   Software-Defined Network - SDN

There are several SDN solutions that can be chosen for organizations. Opendaylight is a popular and mature SDN solution, but it mainly aims at physical network devices not suitable for cloud circumstances. Neutron is cloudy, but it has performance problems and is tightly bonded with OpenStack, so this book introduces an Open Virtual Network (OVN) with an SDN Server module in OneCenter as the Distributed Cloud SDN solution.

OVN is a system that supports logical network abstraction in virtual machine and container environments. OVN with the existing capabilities of Open vSwitch (OVS) to add extra native support for logical network abstractions, such as logical L2 and L3 overlays and security groups. Other services such as DHCP and DNS are also desirable features. OVN provides a production-quality implementation that can operate at hyperscale and in a Distributed Cloud environment.

3.3.1   OVN Architecture

In the OneCenter, the SDN Server is the interface between OneCenter and the OVN System, which routes and forwards the OneCenter configuration and user command to the OVN Adaptor. The OVN Adaptor converts the configuration and command into OVN format and writes it to the OVN Northbound Database through the Open vSwitch Database (OVSDB). All networking information is registered to the Unified Resource Manager.

The following main components and features are important for us to understand how the OVN system works.

OVN Northbound Database stores the logical network configuration passed by the SDN Server. The OVN Northbound Database has the logical network configuration passed down to it by OneCenter and contains the current desired state of the network, presented as a collection of logical ports, logical switches, logical routers, an Access Control List (ACL), and more.

OVN-northd is the intermediary client between OVN-Northbound Database and OVN-Southbound Database. It translates the logical network configuration in terms of conventional network concepts, taken from the OVN-Northbound database, into logical data path flows in the OVN-Southbound database below it.

OVN Southbound Database has physical and logical representations of the network and binding tables that bind them together. Every chassis in the cluster is represented in the OVN Southbound Database, and you can see the ports that are connected to it. It also contains all the logic flows that are shared with the OVN-Controller that runs on each chassis and turns those into OpenFlow rules to program OVS.

OVN-Controller is the agent in the OVN environment, running on each chassis (hypervisor or gateway). Northbound, OVN-Controller connects to the OVN Southbound Database to learn about OVN configuration and status and to populate the physical network table and the Chassis column in a binding table with the hypervisor's status. Southbound, the OVN-Controller connects to ovs–vswitchd as an OpenFlow controller for control over network traffic and to the local ovsdb–server to allow it to monitor and control OVS configuration.

OVS-vSwitchd and OVSDB-Server are two conventional components of Open vSwitch.

OVN Metadata Agent creates the haproxy instances for managing the OVS interfaces, network namespaces and haproxy processes used to proxy metadata API requests. The agent runs on all compute and gateway nodes.

OVN Supported Features

Current OVN offers at least the following virtual network services:

Layer-2 (Switching) - Native implementation to support software-based L2 gateways and ToR based L2 gateways that implement the hardware VTEP schema.

Layer-3 (Routing) - Native implementation that supports distributed routing and L3 gateways from logical to physical networks.

DHCP - Native distributed implementation.

DPDK (Data Plane Development Kit) - Works with any OVS Datapath (such as the default Linux kernel Datapath) that supports all required features (namely Geneve tunnels and OVS connection tracking).

VLAN Tenant Networks - The OVN does support VLAN tenant networks.

DNS - A native built-in DNS implementation.

Port Forwarding - The OVN supports port forwarding as an extension of floating IPs.

Packet Logging - The packet logging service is designed as an SDN Adapter that captures network packets for relevant resources when the registered events occur. OVN supports this feature based on security groups.

Routed Provider Networks - Allows for multiple localnet ports to be attached to a single Logical Switch entry. This work also assumes that only a single localnet port (of the same Logical Switch) is actually mapped to a given hypervisor.

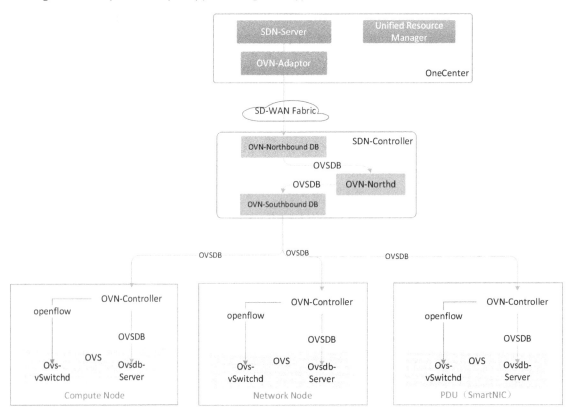

Figure 3-26   OVN Architecture

3.3.2 OVN Components

This section introduces the key components and their primary feathers. It is impossible to cover every detail of the OVN solution. For more information, you can refer to https://www.ovn.org/en.

3.3.2.1 OVN Chassis

Chassis is a special concept of OVN, and it is a Hypervisor node or VTEP gateway. Chassis information is stored in Southbound DB, which is maintained by OVN-controller or OVN-controller-VTEP.

When a chassis is set up, it automatically sets up an Open vSwitch bridge, called the integration bridge, to be used for OVN dedicatedly. If this bridge does not exist when ovn-controller starts, it will be created automatically with the default configuration. The ports on the integration bridge contain the following:

Any chassis has tunnel ports that OVN uses for maintaining logical network connectivity. OVN-Controller on chassis response for adding, updating, and deleting these tunnel ports.

On a hypervisor, any VIFs that are to be attached to logical networks. For instance, connected through kernel virtual network ports such as TUN/TAP or VETH pairs, the hypervisor itself will normally create ports and plug them into the integration bridge. For instances connected through representor ports, typically used with hardware offloading, the ONV-Controller may, on SDN-Server direction, consult a VIF plug provider for representor port lookup and plug them into the integration bridge.

On a gateway, the physical port is used for logical network connectivity. This port can be added using system startup scripts to the bridge prior to starting the OVN-Controller. This can be a patch port to another bridge instead of a physical port in more sophisticated setups.

Any other ports cannot be attached to the integration bridge.

3.3.2.2 OVN Ports

Logical Switch Ports (LSPs) are points of connectivity into and out of logical switches.

VIF is the most ordinary logical switch port, which is an attachment point for VMs or containers. A VIF logical port is associated with the physical location of its VM, which might change as the VM migrates. (A VIF logical port can be associated with a VM that is powered down or suspended. Such a logical port has no location and no connectivity.).

Router Logical Switch Port connects a logical switch to a logical router, designating a particular LRP as its peer.

A Localnet Logical Switch Port is a special port that bridges a logical switch to a physical VLAN. A logical switch may have single or multiple localnet ports.

Localport Logical Switch Port is a special kind of VIF logical switch port that is present in every chassis without binding to any particular one. Traffic forward to such a port will never be forwarded through a tunnel, and traffic from such a port is expected to be destined only to the same chassis, typically in response to a request it received. This kind of port can be used to serve metadata to VMs. It is attached to the metadata proxy process, and all VMs within the same network will reach it at the same IP/MAC address without any traffic being sent over a tunnel.

Distributed Gateway Ports are designed mainly to allow as much traffic as possible to be handled locally on the hypervisor where a VM or container resides. Whenever possible, packets from the VM or container to the external should be processed completely on that VM's or container's hypervisor, eventually traversing a localnet port instance or a tunnel to the physical network or a different other OVN deployment. Vise versa, whenever possible, packets from the outside world to a VM or container should be directed through the physical network directly traverse to the hypervisor VM or container.

In order to process the distributed packets, distributed gateway ports need to be logical patch ports that reside on each hypervisor, instead of l3gateway ports that are bound to a particular gateway chassis. However, the flows associated with distributed gateway ports often need to connect to a physical network.

OVN–northd creates two southbound Port_Binding records to represent a distributed gateway port rather than the usual only one. Figure 3-35 in section [3.5 OVN-Kubernetes] describes more about two ports. You can read it for detailed information.

Chassisredirect Logical Port is simply a way to indicate that although the packet is destined for the distributed gateway port, it needs to be redirected to a different other chassis. For each distributed gateway port, there is one type chassisredirect port, and the other distributed logical patch port represents the distributed gateway port.

Logical router ports (LRPs) are points of connectivity into and out of logical routers. A LRP connects a logical router either to a logical switch or to another logical router. Any VMs, containers, and other network nodes that can not connect to a logical router directly must go through Logical switches.

Port bindings with types VTEP, l2gateway port and l3gateway port are all used for gateways. See section 3.3.2.4 for more information about OVN Gateways

3.3.2.3 OVN Logical Switch and Router

Logical network concepts in OVN include logical switches and logical routers, the logical version of ethernet switches (the equivalent of a Subnet, enables L2 forwarding for all attached ports.), and IP routers (provides distributed routing between directly connected subnets), respectively. Like their physical cousins, logical switches and routers can be connected into sophisticated topologies. Logical switches and routers are ordinarily purely logical entities. That is, they are not associated or bound to any physical location directly, and they are implemented in a distributed manner at each hypervisor in the OVN environment.

Logical switches and logical routers have distinct kinds of logical ports, so properly speaking, one should usually talk about logical switch ports or logical router ports. But when we say "logical port," however, it usually means a logical switch port.

Logical routers and logical patch ports are not for the physical connection (without a physical location) and effectively reside on every hypervisor. This is the case for logical patch ports between logical routers and logical switches behind those logical routers, to which VMs and VIFs attach.

3.3.2.4 OVN Gateways

OVN gateways provide limited connectivity between logical networks and physical ones. They can also provide connectivity between different OVN deployments. This book will mainly present the former, the latter will be omitted in this book. OVN supports the following several kinds of gateways:

VTEP Gateways

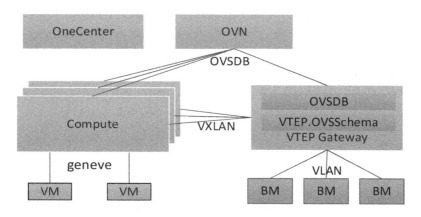

Figure 3-27 OVN VTEP Gateways

A "VTEP gateway" connects an OVN logical network to a physical (or virtual) switch that implements the OVSDB VTEP schema that accompanies Open vSwitch.

The main intended use case for VTEP gateways is to attach physical servers to an OVN logical network using a physical Top-of-Rack (ToR) switch that supports the OVSDB VTEP schema.

L2 Gateways

An OVN Layer 2 gateway simply attaches a designated physical L2 segment available on the chassis to a logical network. The physical network effectively becomes part of the logical network.

L2 Gateway ports have features in common with localnet ports. However, with a localnet port, the physical network becomes the transport between hypervisors. With the L2 Gateway, the traffic between hypervisors can still be transported over GENEVE Tunnels, but the traffic goes out to the external network (physical network) using the l2gateway port.

The application of L2 gateways is similar to that for VTEP gateways, e.g., to add physical machines to a logical network, but L2 Gateways do not require special support from Top-of-Rack (TOR) physical hardware switches.

L3 Gateway Routers

Unlike ordinary OVN logical routers which are distributed, the logical routers are not implemented in a single place but rather in every hypervisor chassis. Distributed Routers (DR) have a problem with stateful services such as Source Network Address Translation (SNAT) and Destination Network Address Translation (DNAT), which need to be implemented in a centralized manner.

To support this kind of functionality, OVN implements L3 gateway routers, which are OVN logical routers that are implemented in a designated chassis. Gateway routers are normally located between distributed logical routers and physical networks. The distributed logical router and the logical switches behind it, to which VMs and containers attach, effectively reside on each hypervisor. The distributed router and the gateway router are connected by another logical switch, say a "join" logical switch. On the other side, the gateway router connects to another logical switch which has a localnet port connecting to the physical network.

3.3.2.5 OVN Tunnel

There are three tunnel types supported by OVN, namely Geneve, Stateless Transport Tunneling (STT), and VXLAN. The traffic between Hypervisor and Hypervisor can only use Geneve and STT.

The traffic between Hypervisor and VTEP gateways can use VXLAN in addition to Geneve and STT. This is for compatibility with hardware VTEP gateways because most hardware gateway with VTEP only supports VXLAN. Although VXLAN is a tunnel technology commonly used in data centers, the length of the VXLAN header is fixed, and only one VNI can be transmitted. VXLAN cannot transmit more other information in the tunnel. Hence OVN chose Geneve and STT for the tunnel. The header of Geneve has an option field, which supports the type-length-value (TLV) format. Users can expand it according to their own needs, and the header of STT can transmit 64-bit data, which is larger than the 24-bit of VXLAN a lot of.

3.3.3 OVN Traffic

With OVN, all the East/West traffic, which traverses a virtual router, is completely distributed, going from compute to compute node without passing through the gateway nodes. When the traffic has no floating IPs, the N/S traffic needs an SNAT process and always passes through the centralized gateway nodes. When multiple gateway nodes exist, the OVN will leverage its High Availability (HA) capabilities.

3.3.3.1 North/South Traffic

Centralized Floating IPs

In this centralized floating IP scenario, all the North/Southern routers traffic through an SNAT process with floating IPs going through the gateway nodes. Maybe the compute nodes don't need to connect to the external network, although the connection can easily be provided if we want to have direct connectivity to such a network from some internal instances.

For external connectivity (for instance, going to the internet), gateway nodes have to set ovn-cms-options with enable-chassis-as-gw in the Open_vSwitch tables external_ids column.

Distributed Floating IPs

In this distributed floating IP case (termed as DVR [Distributed virtual router] or DLR [Distributed logical router] on OVN environment), the floating IP N/S traffic can flows directly from/to the compute nodes through the specific provider network bridge. In this case, compute nodes need connectivity to the external network. Each compute node includes the network components.

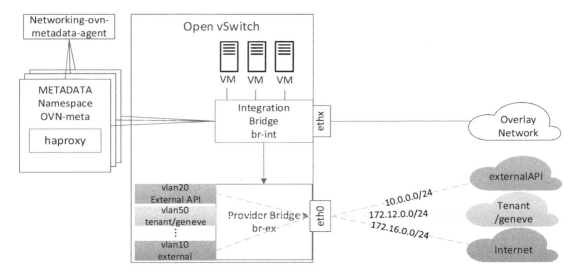

Figure 3-28   Distributed Floating Ips

Several external connections can be optionally created via the provider bridges. Those can be used for direct virtual machine connectivity to the specific networks or the use of distributed floating IPs.

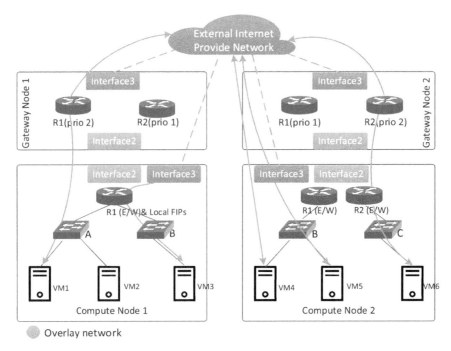

Figure 3-29   North/South Traffic

In the above Figure 3-29, it is assumed that the VM1 and VM6 have no floating IP with it. They still communicate through the gateway nodes using the SNAT process on the gateway nodes R1 and R2.

Because the VM3, VM4, and VM5 have an assigned floating IP, its traffic flows directly through the local provider bridge and interface to the external network.

3.3.3.2 East/West Traffic

In the OVN environment, East/West traffic is completely distributed, which means that routing will happen internally on the compute nodes without the need to go through the gateway.

Traffic Going Through a Logical Router and Different Subnets

Traffic going through a logical router and going from a virtual network/subnet to another will flow directly from the compute-to-compute node encapsulated as usual, while all the routing operations like decreasing TTL or switching MAC addresses will be handled in OpenFlow at the source node of the packet.

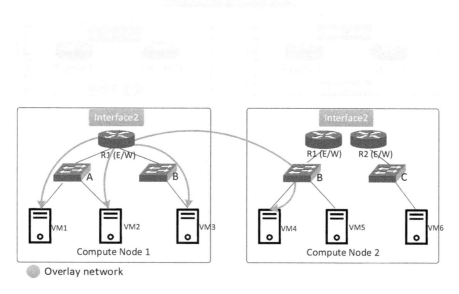

Figure 3-30 Traffic Going Through a Logical Router and Different Subnets

Traffic Across the Same Subnet

The Figure 3-31 demonstrates the traffic across a subnet through just encapsulation. Although this kind of communication does not need routing at all, it has been included for completeness.

Traffic goes directly from instance to instance through an integration bridge (also termed as br-int) in the case of both instances residing in the same compute node (VM1 and VM2 in Figure 3-31) or via encapsulation when living on different compute node (VM3 and VM4 in Figure 3-31).

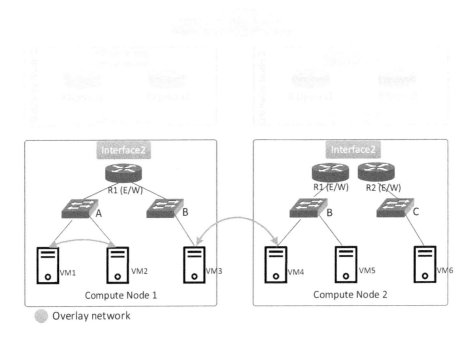

Figure 3-31   Traffic Across the Same Subnet

3.4   Software-Defined WAN - SD-WAN

Due to historical reasons, the construction of traditional Wide-Area Network (WAN) facilities is time-based, heterogeneous, and not unified. For an enterprise, in the face of traditional WAN, there are many obstacles when using these WAN resources:

- The business of the enterprise is constantly developing, and these facilities cannot meet the requirements. For example, enterprises have mobile devices and IoT devices traffic.

- The cost for enterprises to acquire this traditional infrastructure is very high. For example, if an enterprise builds a private network in two places, it needs to build a dedicated connection and pay high bandwidth fees.

- It takes a long time to build an enterprise network using traditional WAN, from design to network design, deployment, testing, and verification, and the construction period is too long.

- It is inconvenient to change the expansion of the enterprise network, and the operator needs to implement multiple procedures.

- It is difficult to guarantee the security of enterprise networks based on traditional WAN.

In recent years, software-defined wide-area networking (SD-WAN) solutions have evolved to address the above challenges. In fact, some ideas of SDN can be brought to SD-WAN. SDN is a centralized approach to network management that abstracts away the underlying network infrastructure from its applications. This de-coupling of data plane forwarding, and control plane helps users to centralize the intelligence of the network and bring more network automation, operations simplification, and centralized provisioning, monitoring, and troubleshooting. SD-WAN applies these principles of SDN to the WAN.

SD-WAN solution fully integrates routing, security, centralized policy, and orchestration into large-scale networks. It is multitenant, cloud-delivered, highly automated, secure, scalable, and application-aware with rich analytics. The SD-WAN technology addresses the problems and challenges of conventional WAN deployment. The following are some benefits of SD-WAN:

- Centralized network and policy management with operational simplicity, saving time to control and deployment.

- Merge 3GPP network (such as 5G network connection), MPLS and cheap internet line or along with any combination of transports in an active/active fashion, provide flexibility and reduce bandwidth costs.

- A transport-independent overlay that extends to the edge, data center, branch, campus, and public cloud.

- Deployment freedom. Due to the separation of the control plane and data plane, WAN-Controllers can be deployed on premises or in the public cloud. WAN Edge Router can be physical or virtual or container and can be deployed anywhere in the network.

- Robust and comprehensive security with strong encryption of data, end-to-end network segmentation, router and controller certificate identity and a zero-trust security model, control plane protection, application firewall, firewalls, and other network services.

- Seamless connectivity to the public cloud and movement of the WAN Edge Router to the data center, branch, campus, edge, 3GPP network enabled sites, etc.

3.4.1   Architecture

The SD-WAN system contains separate orchestration - Beacon, management, control, and data planes.

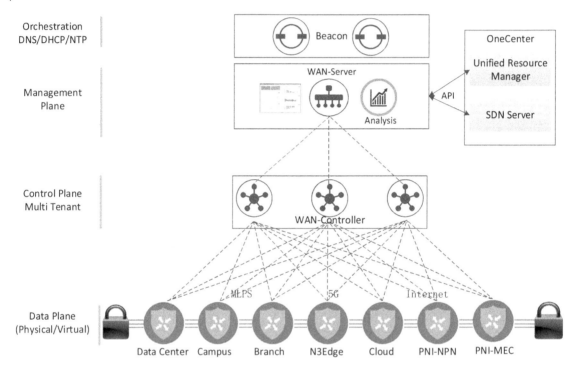

Figure 3-32 Overview of SD-WAN Solution

The Beacon - Performs the automatic onboarding of the WAN Edge routers into the SD-WAN overlay.

The Management Plane - WAN- Server provides an API to the Unified Resource Manager and SDN Server, as well as a response to the Unified Resource Manager.

The Control Plane - WAN-Controller builds and maintains the network topology and controls traffic flows.

The Data Plane - WAN Edge Router is responsible for forwarding packets based on decisions from the control plane.

3.4.2   Components

The main components for the SD-WAN solution consist of the WAN- Server network management system - management plane), the WAN-Controller - control plane, the Beacon - orchestration plane, and the WAN Edge router - data plane.

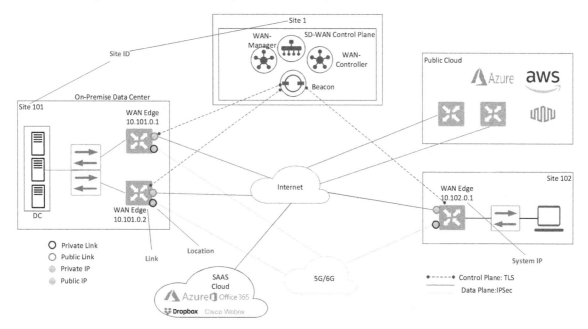

Figure 3-33   Example SD-WAN Topology

WAN-Server is a centralized network management system that provides a GUI interface to easily monitor, configure, and maintain all SD-WAN devices and their connected links in the underlay and overlay network.

WAN-Controller takes the responsibility for control plane of the SD-WAN network. It maintains a secure connection to each WAN Edge router and distributes routes and policy information via the WAN Management Protocol (WMP), acting like a route reflector. It also orchestrates the secure data plane connectivity between the WAN Edge routers by reflecting crypto critical information originating from WAN Edge routers, allowing for a very scalable, IKE-less architecture.

Beacon is a software-based component, which is presented in section [7.3.3 Networking]. For the detailed information, you can refer to it.

WAN Edge Router is either a hardware appliance or software-based router, resides in an on-premises physical Distributed Cloud site or in the public cloud, and provides secure data plane connectivity with the sites over one or more WAN transports. It is responsible for traffic forwarding, security, encryption, quality of service (QoS), routing protocols such as BGP and Open Shortest Path First (OSPF), and others.

The Figure 3-33 demonstrates several concepts of the SD-WAN architecture. This sample topology depicts multiple WAN Edge sites, each directly connected to a 5G or future 6G transport and a public Internet transport. The cloud-based SD-WAN controllers (the two WAN-Controllers, the Beacon and the WAN-Server) are reachable directly through Internet transport. Besides, cloud access to SaaS and IaaS applications will also be present in this solution.

Datagram Transport Layer Security (DTLS) or Transport Layer Security (TLS) can be used for each transport over the connection between WAN Edge routers and WAN-Controllers. The WAN Edge routers also form a permanent DTLS or TLS control connection to the central WAN-Server, but over just one of the transports. The WAN Edge routers securely communicate with other WAN Edge routers using IPsec tunnels over each transport.

Site ID

A site ID is a unique identifier of a site in the SD-WAN overlay network, and it identifies the source location of an advertised prefix. Site ID must be configured on every WAN Edge device, including the WAN-Controllers, and must be the same for all WAN Edge devices that reside at the same site. A site can be a data center, a branch office, a campus, a 3GPP NPN factory location, a PNI-MEC edge, a non-3GPP IoT edge, a public cloud, or something similar. This detailed design of Site ID is shown in Figure 6-3.

System IP

A System IP is a persistent, global system-level IPv4 address that uniquely identifies the device independently of any interface address. It acts much like a router ID, so it doesn't need to be advertised or known by the underlay.

Organization

The Organization is a name that is assigned to the SD-WAN overlay. It must match the organization name configured on all the SD-WAN devices in the overlay. It is used to define the Organization Unit (OU) field to match in the Certificate Authentication process when an SD-WAN device is brought into the overlay network.

IP Addresses

- **Private IP Address**

When the WAN Edge routers behind a NAT device, the private IP address has its value. On WAN Edge routers, the private IP address is the IP address assigned to the interface of the SD-WAN device. In case of no NAT device with the edge router, the private IP address and public IP address can be the same actually.

- **Public IP Address**

The Post-NAT addresses detected by the beacon. This address can be either a public address -publicly routable or a private address. The private and public IP addresses of the SD-WAN device are the same when no NAT exists.

Location

Location is the attachment point where a WAN Edge router connects to the WAN transport network. A Location is uniquely identified and represented by a three-tuple, consisting of system IP address, Link, and encapsulation - Generic Routing Encapsulation (GRE) or IPsec.

Link

The Link attribute applies to WAN Edge routers or WAN-Server and WAN-Controllers and helps to identify an individual location; different locations are assigned different Link labels. The example SD-WAN topology in Figure 3-33 uses a public link called the Internet for the Internet transport Location and a private Link named 5G or future 6G for the other transport location. You cannot use more than two Links on a single WAN Edge router at the same time.

WAN Management Protocol (WMP)

The WMP routing protocol, similar to widely used BGP, manages the SD-WAN overlay network. The protocol runs between WAN-Controllers and between WAN-Controllers and WAN Edge routers where control plane information, such as route prefixes, next-hop routes, crypto keys, and policy information, can be exchanged over a secure DTLS connection. The WAN-Controller acts similarly to a classic BGP Route Reflector; it receives route information from WAN Edge routers, processes and applies any policy to them, and then advertises the routes to other WAN Edge routers in the overlay network.

Virtual Private Networks (VPNs)

Virtual private networks (VPNs) provide segmentation for SD-WAN, like VRFs instances, which is widely used in many scenarios. Each VPN is isolated from one another, and each has its own space and forwarding table. An interface or sub interface is explicitly configured with a single VPN and cannot be part of more than one VPN. Labels are used in WMP route attributes and in the packet encapsulation, which identifies the VPN a packet belongs to.

Each VPN has a VPN number with a four-byte integer. There are several VPNs reserved for special usage.

3.5   OVN-Kubernetes

In addition to providing network services to virtual machines, OVN also provides network virtualization for containers in the "overlay" mode. OVN can create a logical network amongst containers running on distributed multiple hosts. In this mode, OVN programs the traditional Open vSwitch instances running inside multiple hosts. These hosts can be bare-metal machines or virtual machines.

OVN-Kubernetes-Node is started by the OVN and OVS communities, it uses OVN on OVS as the abstraction to manage network traffic flows on the node and also uses Geneve (Generic Network Virtualization Encapsulation) protocol rather than VXLAN to create an overlay network between nodes.

The features that OVN-Kubernetes support include egress firewall, egress service, Hybrid Overlay, OVN multicast, Network Policy, OVS Hardware Offload, OVN central database High-availability, External IP and Load Balancer Ingress and Egress IP, etc.

3.5.1   Architecture

OVN-Kubernetes is powered by OVN and provides an overlay-based networking implementation. In a cluster, each node runs OVS, and the OVN-Kubernetes Adaptor controls the OVN to configure OVS on each chassis to implement the declared network configuration.

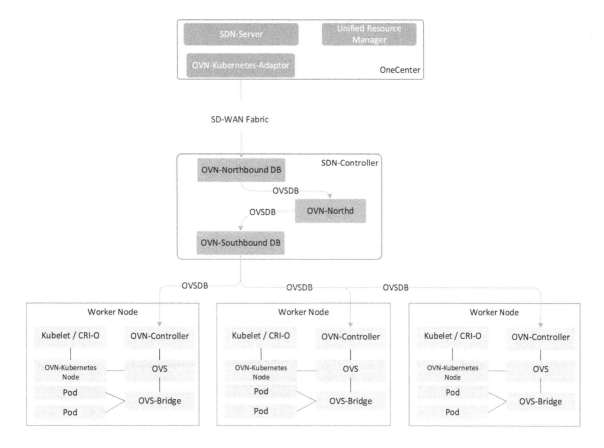

Figure 3-34   OVN-Kubernetes Architecture

3.5.1.1   OVN-Kubernetes Adaptor

In the OneCenter, the SDN Server is the interface between OneCenter and the OVN System, which routes and forwards the OneCenter configuration and user command to OVN-Kubernetes-Adaptor, the OVN-Kubernetes Adaptor converts the configuration and command into OVN format and writes it to OVN Northbound Database through the Open vSwitch Database (OVSDB). All networking information is registered to the Unified Resource Manager.

OVN-Kubernetes Adaptor watches cluster Events-pods, Namespaces, Services, Endpoints and Network Policy. It also responds to translating cluster events into OVN logical network elements stored in OVN-North DB, tracks Kube-API state, and manages pod subnet allocation to nodes.

3.5.1.2 SDN-Controller

This SDN-Controller is a native OVN component which process that converts northbound DB network representation to the lower-level logical flows that are stored in southbound DB.

About the detail feathers of the OVN Northbound Database, OVN Southbound Database and OVN-northd components of original OVN in section [3.3.1 OVN Architecture].

3.5.1.3 Worker Node

Open vSwitch

This is the original Linux open vSwitch, an alternative to Linux native bridges, mainly for pushing the new "edge of the network" to the hypervisor. In open vSwitch, multilayer Open Virtual Switch is used to implement OpenFlow rules.

OVN-Controller

This is the OVN agent that interacts with Open vSwitch and hypervisors, for any information or update that is needed for OVN- Southbound DB. The OVN-Controller reads logical flows from the OVN-Southbound DB, translates them into OpenFlow flows, and sends them to the hypervisor node's OVS daemon.

OVN-Kubernetes Node

This component also termed a CNI plugin (just an executable) from kubelet/CRI-O (Container Runtime Interface - Open Container Initiative), is mainly in charge of digesting IP address management (IPAM) annotation written by OVN-Kubernetes-Adaptor, setting up firewall rules and routes for host Port and service access from node, creating OVS port on bridge, moves it into pod network namespace, sets IP details/QoS and deleting entities when pods die.

3.5.2 Topology Architecture

The topology provides a clear path for three traffic flows, and this is achieved with the feature of a Distributed Gateway Port(DGP), Policy Based Routing (PBR), and 1-to-1 NAT. The three traffic flows include as the following:

- Traffic Between Overlay-Network Pod and Node's IP.

- Traffic Between Overlay-Network Pod and Cluster IP with Host-Network Endpoints.

- Traffic Between Host-Network Pod and Cluster IP with Host-Network Endpoints.

3.5.2.1 OVN's Support for PBR

PBR provides a way to configure reroute policies on the logical router. These policies are captured in a policy-routing table in the router's ingress pipeline. This table takes effect after the IP routing table, so it can override the routing decisions to provide another different next hop. In this method, the traffic of the pod on the node in the topology can be directed to the local service of the node.

3.5.2.2 OVN Support One-to-One NAT

You can configure 1-to-1 NAT for a logical port so that all the packets from the logical port heading out of logical topology will be SNATed to this exclusive IP (external_ip), set aside for it. Since the external_ip is dedicated to the logical_port, the NATing can occur on the chassis where the logical port is bound. The topology leverages this feature on every chassis.

3.5.2.3 Packet Processing with Distributed Gateway Port

First, we need to add a DGP on the DR.

- Add a logical router port (LRP), and then

- Connect this LRP to a logical switch with a localnet port, which can communicate to the underlay network.

For DGP, we also need to bind this DGP to a chassis(node). After that, there are two processing locations for the DGP packages:

- Send to the chassis(node) that the DGP is bound to for processing.

- Process on the local chassis where the logical port is located (the node hosting the Pod).

Hence there are two types of DGPs:

- **Chassis-redirect-DGP (cr-DGP)** - Centralized, the packet will go through the Geneve tunnel to the gateway chassis to which DGP is bound to.

- **DGP** - Distributed.

Traffics that require centralized processing:

- If a packet comes from a logical switch (connected to a logical router), and (the internal IP corresponding to the packet) is not configured with point-to-point NAT mapping, then this packet needs to be redirected to cr-DGP.

- The ARP resolution of the next-hop physical gateway is done through the localnet port on the chassis it is bound to.

Traffics that can be processed natively: If there is a matching one-to-one NAT rule for outbound network traffic (such as the public network), then it will be sent to the DGP of the local chassis (if it exists locally).

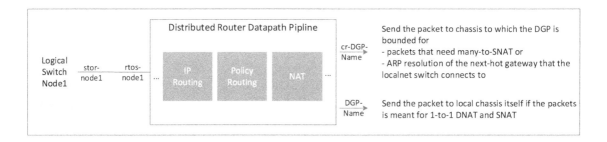

Figure 3-35   Packet Processing with Distributed Gateway Port

3.5.2.4   OVN Logical Topology Based on DGP

The following Figure shows the logical topology with the distributed gateway port created on the distributed router, OVN_Cluster_router. All the pods in a given node are connected to a node specific logical switch. The east-west traffic between pods on a node with all pods on all nodes, without NAT, is provided by the distributed logical router (OVS_Cluster_router in Figure 3-36). The north-south traffic between the pod and the external network is provided by the gateway logical router connected to the external logical switch. The outbound traffic is SNATed on the gateway logical router and then sent out to the underlay physical network. The node-specific external gateway logical router is connected to the distributed logical router by a node-specific join logical switch (shown as ❶ in the following Figure 3-36).

All pods on the node are based on OVN_Cluster_router for east-west traffic. This traffic path is definite. The traffic path from the local pod node pod to the public network needs to pay attention to:

❶pod --> (pod) logical-switch --> OVN_Cluster_router --> (node) logical-switch --> gw_router --> (external) logical-switch--> eth0. The traffic from the pod to the local SVC goes through the local distributed gateway.

❷pod--> (pod) logical-switch --> OVN_Cluster_router --> DGP_ls (localnet) --> br-int --> br-local. Since everything is distributed in the topology, we don't need to handle HA for DGP, nor do we need to run Bidirectional Forwarding Detection (BFD) between all chassis and high availability gateway chassis.

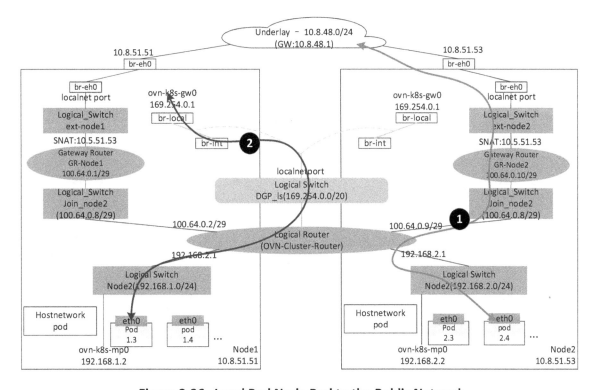

Figure 3-36 Local Pod Node Pod to the Public Network

The Figure 3-37 is a graph of the access paths of network traffic in below all three scenarios:

❶Traffic Between Overlay-Network Pod and Node's IP.

❷Traffic Between Overlay-Network Pod and Cluster IP with Host-Network Endpoints.

❸Traffic Between Host-Network Pod and Cluster IP with Host-Network Endpoints.

Logical Static Routes, Logical Policies, NAT rules, and the packet trace of each traffic flow will be discussed in other book.

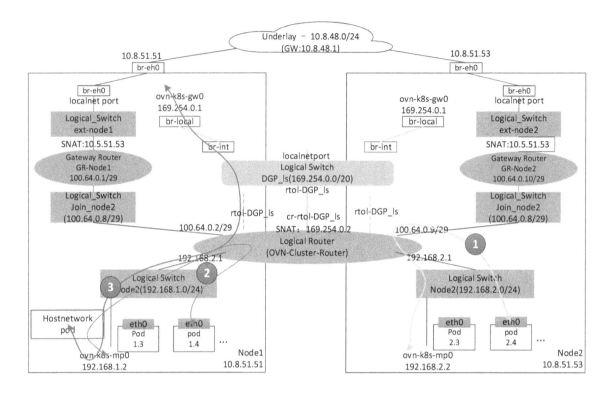

Figure 3-37 Network Traffic Scenarios

3.5.2.5 OVN-K8s-MP0 and OVN-K8s-GW

Ovn-k8s-mp0 is used to provide egress IP reachability. In order to allow hosts to access Kubernetes services, packets from hosts must enter OVN to hit the load balancer and route to the appropriate destination. Typically, when accessing a service backed by an OVN backend pod, a single interface (ovn-k8s-mp0) can be used in order to enter the local node switch, hit the load balancer (LB), and reach the pod endpoint. However, when services are backed by host network pods, things get more complicated. For example, if a host accesses a service where the background endpoint is the host itself, the packets are hair pinned back to the host after load balance.

Chapter 4　The Distributed Cloud Storage System

This chapter take the Ceph as the example of storge backend, it introduces the Ceph architecture, Ceph block device storage, Ceph multi-site object storage, and how those Ceph components can be applied as the backend for the unified software-defined block device storage system of the Distributed Cloud.

By leveraging the OneCenter, the Ceph object storage system, a public cloud object storage system that is S3 compatible, big data massive storage like HDFS or Ozone can all be integrated as a unified and global object storage platform to present the applications and user of Distributed Cloud.

4.1　Ceph Introduction

Ceph is one of the outstanding open-source alternatives to proprietary software-defined storage solutions from traditional vendors, with a vibrant community collaborating on the software.

4.1.1　Ceph Architecture

Ceph is versatile because it makes storage available in multiple ways: as a Portable Operating System Interface (POSIX) compliant file system through CephFS lib, as block storage volumes via the Ceph's RADOS Block Devices (RBD) driver, and for object storage, compatible with AWS S3, thronging the Reliable Autonomic Distributed Object Store (RADOS) gateway API.

In this book, take the Ceph to provide block and object store backend to the Distributed Cloud for bare metal node, virtual machine, and container. Kubernetes has similarly adopted Ceph as a popular way for physical volumes (PV) as a Container Storage Interface (CSI) plugin.

The lower part of Ceph is a RADOS system. RADOS provides functions such as data consistency, high availability, and reliability. The algorithm of the CRUSH map is used to provide data balance (so that files can be allocated to Object Storage Daemons (OSD) dispersedly). On top of this architecture, we will build a pool to isolate files in different spaces. Pool provides on-demand use of three file systems (object storage, block storage, and file storage) mapped out through the LibRADOS interface. Mon holds OSD metadata. Metadata Server (MDS) holds the metadata of the CephFS file system.

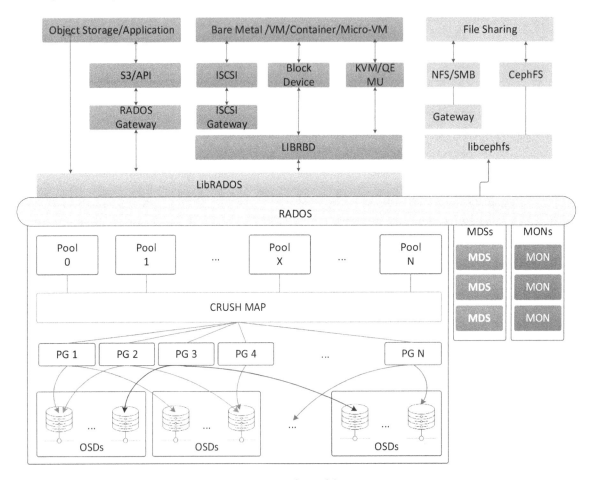

Figure 4-1 Ceph Architecture

Each functional component of the Ceph cluster is described below:

OSD is the Object Storage Device, which is the process responsible for returning specific data in response to client requests. A Ceph cluster generally has many OSDs. Storage devices map a running OSD daemon process with one to one relationship. OSDs utilize the CPU and RAM of the participating cluster member host aggressively. In the hyper-converged edge or small-size site cluster architecture, you should carefully balance the number of OSDs with the number of CPU cores and memory.

Mon is used when a Ceph cluster requires a small cluster composed of multiple Monitors, which synchronize data through Paxos to save OSD metadata.

MDS's full name is Ceph Metadata Server, which is the metadata service that CephFS services depend on.

PG (Place Group)'s full name is Placement Groups, which is a logical concept. A PG contains multiple OSDs. The purpose of introducing the PG layer is to better allocate and locate data.

RADOS is the essence of the Ceph cluster. Users can implement data distribution, failover and other cluster operations.

LibRADOS is a library provided by RADOS. Because RADOS is a protocol that is difficult to access directly, the upper layer RBD, RADOS Gateway (RGW), and CephFS are all accessed through LibRADOS.

CRUSH map is the data distribution algorithm used by Ceph, similar to consistent hashing, which allows data to be allocated to the dispersive and expected place.

RBD's full name is RADOS block device, which is a block device storage service provided by Ceph.

RGW means RADOS gateway, which is an object storage service provided by the Ceph cluster. The interface is compatible with AWS S3.

CephFS's full name is Ceph File System, which is a file system service provided by Ceph.

4.1.2   Ceph in the Distributed Cloud

This section explores how Ceph can be positioned as a storage system that is capable of exposing different types of storage capacities to be consumed by external systems, applications, or clients with diverse requirements. The following pictorial Figure 4-2 illustrates that the Ceph storage system can cater to different sorts of endpoints using standard and renowned protocols.

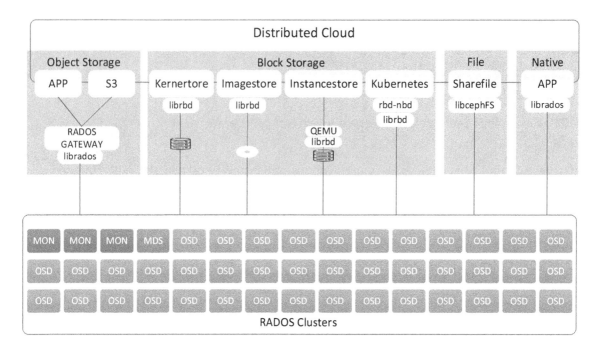

Figure 4-2   Ceph in Distributed Cloud

4.2   Block Device Storage

In the Distributed Cloud, block storage is typically designed for image datastore, instance datastore, kernel datastore, and storage for Kubernetes. In this book, only the Ceph backend will be emphasized and introduced, several other available options can be chosen (such as NFS, Internet Small Computer System Interface (iSCSI), DAS, etc.).

4.2.1   Architecture

The block storage solution design should meet the following requirements:

- Access to global marketplaces that act as public image repositories. Examples include OneCenter Marketplace, Docker Hub, private HTTP repositories and container registries.

- Minimize image transferring and maximize application I/O performance. Sites can use a center-site deployment model over dedicated WAN or public internet links. Moreover, on-premises provisions can scale to a large number of hosts. Storage and image transformation should not be a bottleneck for any of these situations.

- Deployment simplicity. Ease the complexity and technology footprint of the solution by using technologies that already exist in the operating system to accommodate any deployment model, including on physical, virtual resources and containers, as well as increasing the reliability of the backend.

The Distributed Cloud Architecture combines a 3-Tiers architecture for image distribution with an enhanced datastore with replica caching, snapshotting, and backups within each distributed site. The 3-tiers storage architecture (see Figure 4-3) includes:

Tier 1- Marketplace. This Tier consists of the distributed servers and storage implementing the global application image repositories. The marketplace can be a global marketplace and a local marketplace. Typically, in Max type site, a local marketplace is created at the site location, and this local marketplace co-works with the central global marketplace.

Tier 2 - Image Datastores along with the OneZone instance. This tier consists of the zone image data stores and provides the primary image storage location for the cloud zone. This storage area can be provided by the site edge. Its contents are cached and replicated on demand to each site or each local cluster host depending on the OneZone instance's location. This supports the Distributed Cloud cluster deployment on any location as well as scales the on-premises infrastructures such as data centers, branches, campuses, 3GPP NPN sites, 3GPP PNI-MEC sites, and non-3GPP edge sites.

Tier 3 - Cluster/Site Replicas. Operation System or Applications images are cached within a site in the site edge to minimize image transferring costs. The site edge makes use of a specialized distribution system to make the images available to all site hosts and support snapshotting for host failure recovery.

Within each Tier-3 site scope, disk images are transferred between the image and instance datastores by using an enhanced transfer mode (like SSH) with replica caching and snapshotting that greatly improves its scalability, performance, and reliability. The new replica mode caches the images in the site edge, so they are available close to the host and hypervisors to reduce the bandwidth requirements to the Tier -2 Image datastore servers and considerably reduce deployment times. This is especially important in highly Distributed Cloud deployments where copying images from the Tier-2 OneZone instance (reside in OneCenter or site location) to the Tier-3 site hypervisors can be very slow.

In addition to caching and using the local marketplace to speed up the performance, other aspects also can improve the performance:

Image Deployment Performance - Operation System or Application images can use qcow2 format to reduce file transfer and instantiation times with minimal overhead. The qcow2 based type files to back disk images also eases backup solutions, reduces image transfer times, and implements advanced features like snapshotting in an efficient way.

Image Snapshot Performance - To improve the availability of the Distributed Cloud Site blocks, live migration should be supported within the same site. Image snapshots are also kept within the site (Tier 3) to enable fast recovery from the last application checkpoint.

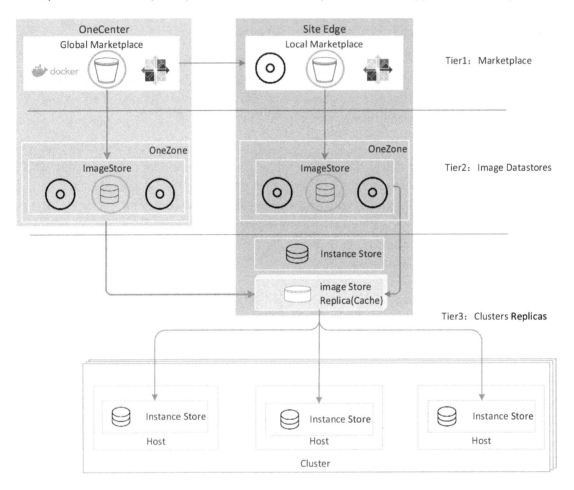

Figure 4-3 The 3-tier Storage System of the Distributed Cloud Architecture

4.2.2   Image Datastore

This section introduces the image datastore backend architecture, catalogs, storage model and the usages etc.

4.2.2.1 introduction

An Image can be a virtual machine disk. Images can have multiple formats (e.g., filesystem or block device) and can store OS installations, data filesystems, images, or kernel files. This book will only introduce about different Image types.

Types and Persistency

There are three main types of Images in the Distributed Cloud, those images represent VM disks, and a VM can use multiple Image types simultaneously:

Operating System (OS) is the main disk, the VM system will boot from this Image. Every VM must include one OS Image at any given time.

CD-ROM ISO (CDROM) is read-only data. Only one Image of this type can be used in a VM.

Data Disk (DATABLOCK) is the generic disk, you can store data in it. These Images can contain existing user data, e.g., a normal document or a database, it can be formatted as an empty drive.

In addition, file Images represent plain files that can be used as:

OS Kernel (KERNEL) is the temporary kernel used in bare metal provision or as a kernel for the Guest OS to start the VM.

RAM Disk (RAMDISK) is loaded by initrd at boot time, for instance in the bare metal provision process.

Generic File (CONTEXT) stores meta data that can be used for cloud-init, a plain file to be included in the context CD-ROM. It May be the source of configdrive for bare metal provision or the VM will have access to this file once it is started.

Image Modes

All types of images can be operated in persistent and non-persistent two modes:

1. Persistent mode: any modifications on this image will be preserved after the instance termination. There can be only one VM using a persistent certain Image at any given time.

2. Non-Persistent: the modifications will not affect the original image. The operation of the VM always takes place at its own workspace, isolated from the original image, so non-persistent images can be used by multiple VMs at the same time.

4.2.2.2 Images Datastore Backend

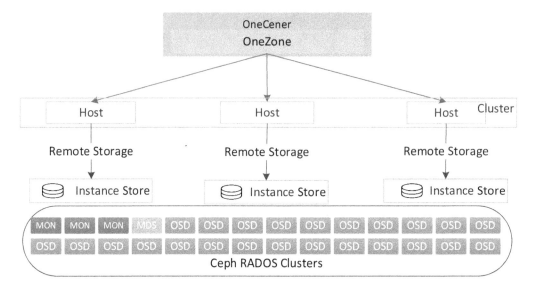

Figure 4-4 Images Datastore Backen Architecture

The images Datastore is the most important datastore, which stores the base operating system images, persistent data volumes, and CD-ROM images.

Marketplaces are shared locations across multiple on-premises, clouds, and edges. They can be global or for private use. Marketplace stores OS Image and Marketplace Applications or Appliances, which include the application definition together with the disk images.

4.2.3   Instance Datastore

An Instance Datastore is the place that contains disks of running Container or Virtual Machines. Disks are moved from/to the Images when the VMs are deployed/terminated. Ceph, Storage Area Network (SAN), or iSCSI can be used for the Instance Datastore back end (only the Ceph back end is presented in this book).

4.2.4   Files & Kernels Datastore

The Files & Kernels Datastore can only store plain files (not disk images) to be used as VM kernels, ramdisks, or any other files that need to be passed to the VM through the contextualization process. This type of Datastore does not expose any special storage mechanism but is a simple and secure way to use files within VM templates.

Keep in mind to make sure that there is enough space in the OneCenter and site hosts for the datastore location to hold the instance files.

4.2.5   Block Storage Backend

In Ceph, a block is a sequence of bytes (commonly 512). Combining many blocks together into a single file can be used as a storage device that the host and applications can read from and write to. Block-based storage interfaces are the most common way to store data with rotating media such as HDDs, SSDs, CDs, and even tape.

The ubiquity of block device storage interfaces makes a virtual block storage an ideal option for interacting with a mass data storage system in the cloud environment.

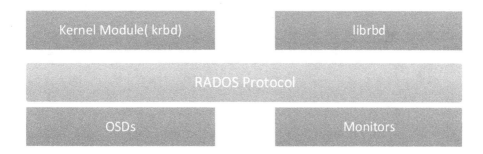

Figure 4-5 Ceph Block Device Storage Components

Ceph block storage are thin-provisioned, resizable, and store data striped over multiple Object Storage Devices (OSD) in a Ceph storage cluster. Ceph block devices storage are also known as Reliable Autonomic Distributed Object Store (RADOS) Block Devices (RBDs). Ceph block devices leverage RADOS capabilities, including Snapshots, Replication, and Data consistency.

Ceph block storage interact with OSDs by using the librbd library or Linux kernel based krbd.

Ceph block devices deliver high performance with infinite scalability to Kernel Virtual Machines (KVMs) based Quick Emulator (QEMU), and the Distributed Cloud relies on the libvirt and QEMU utilities to integrate with Ceph block storage. You can use the same storage cluster to offer the Ceph Object Gateway and Ceph Block Devices simultaneously for the workload.

4.3 Universal Object Storage in Multi-Site Model

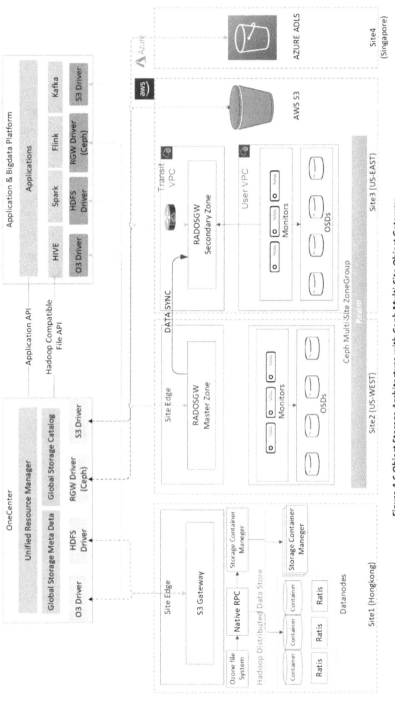

Figure 4-6 Object Storage Architecture with Ceph Multi-Site Object Gateway

In the Distributed Cloud environment, object storage is a comprehensive global unified storage system. It should integrate the Hadoop Distributed File System (HDFS) for big data processing and object storage designed for data applications, based on public cloud S3 compatible distributed object storage also generally includes local S3 compatible distributed object storage systems like Ceph that can be applied to on-premises data centers.

In the Distributed Cloud environment, each Ceph zone colocated with one cloud zone can bring convenience. About the details of site ID and Zone concepts, you can see the section [6.2 Sites Taxonomy].

4.3.1   Architecture

As shown in Figure 4-6, the following describes the several components, related concepts, and how Object Storage Architecture with Ceph Multi-Site Object Gateway works.

Multi-Zone - The Ceph Object Gateway implements a more advanced topology, the "multi-Zone" configuration. In this multi-zone configuration, one Zonegroup consists of multiple zones, with each zone consisting of single or multiple Ceph-radosgw instances. Each zone is backed by its own Ceph Storage Cluster.

The presence of multiple zones in a given zone group provides disaster recovery for that zone group in the event that one of the zones experiences a catastrophic failure. Each active zone can receive write operations. A multi-zone configuration that contains multiple active zones enhances disaster recovery solutions and can also be used as a foundation for content delivery networks(CDN), which Is one of the most important use scenarios in the Distributed Cloud.

Multi-Zonegroup - Ceph Object Gateway supports multiple zone groups, which is similar to AWS regions. Each Zonegroup contains single or multiple zones. If two zones are in the same Zonegroup, and if that Zonegroup is in the same realm as a second Zonegroup, then the objects stored in the two zones share a global object namespace. This global object namespace guarantees the unique object IDs across Zonegroup and zones.

Multiple Realms - The Ceph Object Gateway supports "realms.", Realm is the biggest space of storage configuration. Realms make it possible to set policies that apply to multiple zone groups. Realms have a worldwide unique namespace and can contain either a single zone group or multiple zone groups. If you choose to make use of multiple realms, you can define multiple namespaces and multiple configurations (this means that each realm can have a configuration that is distinct from the configuration of other realms).

At the top of Figure 4-6, there are applications (also be thought of as "clients") and some big data platforms (such as Spark, Flink, Kafka, etc.). The application can both write and read data from the Ceph Cluster by means of the RADOS Gateway (RGW). The big data platforms are only reading data from the Ceph Cluster by means of an instance of RGW. In both cases (read-and-write and read-only), the transmission of data is handled Restfully (REST means representational state transfer).

In the middle of this diagram, we see multiple zones, each of which contains an instance of RADOS Gateway (RGW). These instances of RGW handle the movement of data from the applications to the zone group. The line from the master zone (US- WEST) to the secondary zone (US-EAST) represents an act of data synchronization.

A Ceph realm can extend to the public cloud, such as AWS, using Muti-Site architecture with a Ceph cluster to be built onto the cloud.

Setting up Failover to The Secondary Zone

If the master zone fails, you can fail over to the secondary zone for disaster recovery. By default, Ceph Object Gateway runs in an active-active mode. However, if the cluster is configured to run in an active-passive configuration, the secondary zone is read-only. To allow the secondary zone to receive write operations, you need to remove its read-only status.

Reverting from Failover

If the former master zone recovers, you can revert the failover operation, you should from within the recovered zone, pull the latest realm configuration from the current master zone, make the recovered zone the master and default zone, and so on.

4.3.2   Cloud Object Storage

In Distributed Cloud environment, in order to optimize the costs or for latency for agility, enterprises can use public cloud infrastructures to enhance their design. Utilizing the powerful unlimited public object storage is a beneficial choice. Following, take AWS as an example to present how cloud object storage can be used as an underlying storage backend.

AWS S3 Object Storage

You have several available ways to inter communicate to the AWS S3 system:

1. The first one is to make REST API calls directly from your code. This method works but is cumbersome, it requires you to write the necessary code to calculate a valid signature to authenticate your requests.

2. The second one is using the AWS SDKs to send your requests. This option is without writing code to calculate a signature for request authentication because the SDK clients authenticate your requests by using access keys that you provide. This method is a good choice unless you have some special reasons.

3. The last one is using the AWS CLI to make Amazon S3 API calls.

Other Public Cloud Object Storage

As you know, AWS S3 has become the de facto cloud object storage, so other public object storage has some similarities with AWS S3 little or more, such as Azure Data Lake Storage (ADLS), Google Cloud Storage (GCS), and the popular OpenStack object storage swift. This book omits the detailed API information of the rest of the object storage systems.

4.4 Ceph Disaster Recovery in Distributed Cloud

It is well known that Ceph has some native backup and restore capacity. For example, RBD images can be asynchronously mirrored between two Ceph clusters, and the Multisite bucket-granularity sync policy provides fine-grained control of data movement between buckets in different Ceph zones; the following Figure 4-7 shows how it works.

As shown Figure 4-7, we designed the backup cloud image (image datastore and instance datastore) and other application files from US-EAST (site 2) to US-WEST (site 1) on the left by RBD Mirroring Deamon, while on the right, we plan to sync object files from the Ceph object gateway in US-EAST (site 2) to the remote AWS S3 bucket in site3.

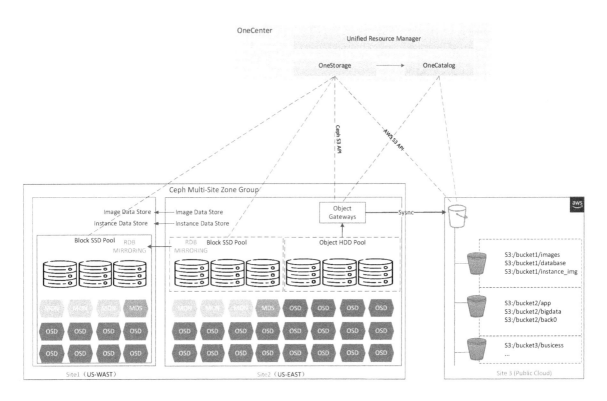

Figure 4-7 Ceph Disaster Recovery

Snapshots

A snapshot is a read-only logical copy of an image at a particular point in time, say a checkpoint. One of the advanced features of Ceph block storage is that snapshots can be created to retain point-in-time state history. Ceph also supports snapshot layering, which allows you to clone images (for instance, VM images) quickly and easily.

RBD Mirroring

As shown in Figure 4-7, RBD images can be asynchronously mirrored between two different Ceph clusters (US-WEST site1 and US-EAST site2). This run in two modes:

Journal-based Mirroring - This mode uses the RBD journaling image feature to ensure point-in-time, crash-consistent replication between Ceph clusters. When writing to the RBD image, it first records to the associated journal before modifying the actual RBD image. The peer remote cluster will read from this associated journal and replay the updates to its local copy of the image. Since each write to the RBD image will result in two writes to the Ceph cluster. Writing latency almost doubles when using Journal-based Mirroring.

Snapshot-based Mirroring - Unlike Journal-based Mirroring, this mode uses periodically scheduled or manually created RBD image mirror-snapshots to replicate crash-consistent RBD images between Ceph clusters.

Mirroring is configured on a per-pool basis within peer Ceph clusters and can be configured on a specific subset of RBD images within the pool. You can also mirror all images within a given pool when with journal-based mirroring mode. According to the application requirement, the Ceph RBD mirroring can be configured for one-or two-way replication:

One-way Replication - When data is only mirrored from a primary cluster to a secondary cluster, the rbd-mirror daemon runs only on the secondary cluster.

Two-way Replication - When data is mirrored from primary images on one cluster to non-primary images on another cluster (and vice-versa), the rbd-mirror daemon runs on both clusters.

RBD Mirroring Level

The RBD Mirroring has two kinds of level, one is the pool Mirroring, and another is the Image Mirroring.

Pool Mirroring configuration should be performed on both peer clusters. These procedures assume that both clusters, for example, "Site-A" and "Site-B", are accessible from a single host for clarity.

Image Mirroring is different from pool mirroring configuration, image configuration only needs to be performed against a single mirroring peer Ceph cluster.

Mirrored RBD images are designated as either primary or non-primary. This is a property of the image, and the pool has no such concept. Images that are designated as non-primary cannot be modified.

RBD Mirroring Operation

On both the local and remote Ceph cluster, create the rbd-mirror daemon processes, respectively. The rbd-mirror daemon synchronizes Ceph images from one cluster to another based on RBD image features (Journal-based Mirroring and Snapshot-based Mirroring).

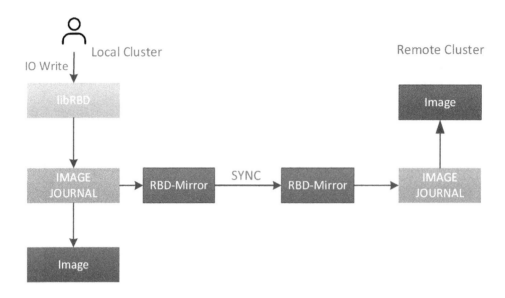

Figure 4-8 Ceph RBP Mirroring Flow

Image mirroring needs to configure the pool at the peer clusters. You can set it to automatically back up all images in a storage pool or only a specific subset of images. Before taking the RBD actions, the user needs to set up the RBD Mirroring. First, guarantee the connectivity is routable using connectivity routable, then configure the same pool at both Ceph cluster sites after adding peering Ceph pool and finally add RBD image settings. Below are the RBD Mirroring processes:

1. IO goes into the RBD's image journal.

2. Once the writing is finished, acknowledge the client.

3. Write what happens to the local RBD image.

4. The local RBD mirror daemon plays journal content to the remote RBD mirror daemon.

5. Replication is being done at the local site.

6. Replication is being done at the remote site

Chapter 5   The Distributed Cloud
Computing Infrastructure

Distributed Cloud aims to manage and control any location or infrastructure and run any application anytime. This chapter discusses the underlying on-premises physical machine provisioning, public cloud resource provisioning, and the enterprise's existing vCenter Cluster infrastructure integration into the OneCenter/OneZone. It presents several critical computing workload technologies (such as bare metal, standard virtual machine, a light virtual machine with firecracker and container managed by Kubernetes) and how the underlying Heterogeneous and inconsistent computing infrastructures can be integrated to abstract as a global unified resources plane for applications and users in the Distributed Cloud.

5.1   Infrastructure Heterogeneous Architecture

The Distributed Cloud target is to build a powerful but easy-to-use, open-source solution to build and manage distributed Enterprise Clouds. Provides a single, feature-rich, and flexible platform that unifies management of all kinds of IT infrastructure and applications, preventing vendor lock-in and reducing complexity, resource consumption, and operational costs.

The Distributed Cloud can treat any heterogeneous infrastructures as its managed resources, including on-premises physical servers in branches/campuses, most popular public clouds,3GPP NPN sites, 3GPP PNI-MEC sites, and non-3GPP IoT edge.

It not only combines bare metal, standard virtual machine, micro-virtual machine, and container technologies with multi-tenancy, automatic provision, and elasticity to offer on-demand applications and services, it also takes other data center cloud platform into a unified cloud platform, such as VMware vSphere offering.

The front and back ends of the computing virtualization system (hypervisor) are decoupled, and the hypervisor software needs to be reasonably tailored and offloaded on the computing nodes. The CPU host side retains the lightweight front-end Hypervisor, KVM completes the virtualization management of CPU and memory, and the Hypervisor back-end on the Infrastructure Processing Units (IPU) side cooperates with QEMU to complete the initialization of the virtual machine and cooperates with Libvirt to complete the life cycle management of the virtual machine. The front-end and back-end communication of the hypervisor should be standardized, and at the same time, the operating system kernel needs to be deeply modified and concise.

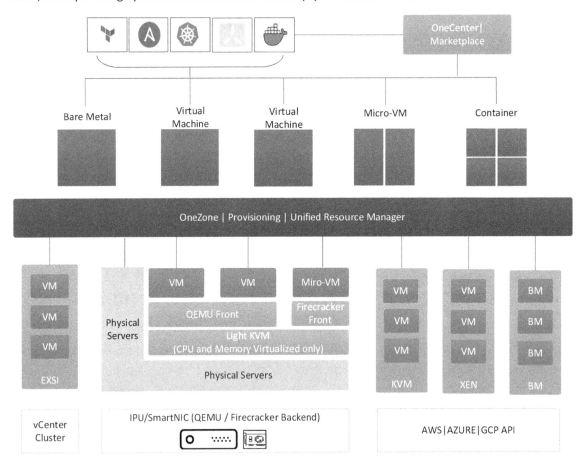

Figure 5-1 Computing Infrastructure Architecture

5.2   ScaleMaker for Bare Metal Provisioning

Although virtualization with hypervisor and containerization with docker have become the main cases in cloud scenarios, bare metal is still necessary in some special conditions. There are several scenarios for bare metal provisioning in a Distributed Cloud:

- High-performance computing clusters.

- Computing tasks that require access to hardware devices that can't be virtualized.

- Big Data platform and Database hosting (big data process and some databases run poorly in a virtual machine or container).

- Dedicated hardware for performance, security, dependability, and other special regulatory requirements.

- Or, rapidly deploying a massive Distributed Cloud infrastructure for virtualization or containerization.

In the actual world, deploying a massive Distributed Cloud infrastructure for The instances can be auto-scaled both within a site scope and across the distributed sites. Figure 2-10 depicts how the two tiers auto-scaling works. The simplest site application consists of one single component, as follows:

- **Application Image** contains the application runtime and the needed support for the operating system (OS). The OS pieces may depend on the compute node used by the site location of the provider.

- **Public Internet IP** address.

- **Capacity Specification** is about CPU, Memory, and Disk.

- **Hardware** requirements are additional requirements to run the application, e.g., a specific processor layout or access to specific hardware like single root I/O virtualization (SR-IOV) or graphics processing units (GPUs).

Hypervisor virtualization or docker containerization technology has some little differences from bare metal, which is directly for user application. For example, hypervisor virtualization or docker containerization cases need one more extra network interface to provide an overlay network for virtual machines or containers.

5.2.1   ScaleMaker - Physical Machine Booting Evolution

In the Distributed Cloud, UEFI HTTP Boot is recommended because it's convenient and flexible. This section also introduces the evolution of system booting. Other traditional and legacy booting methods and technologies (such as MBR, GTP PXE iPXE, etc.) are important to understand the principle of physical machines when booting an operation system. Meanwhile, these traditional options can be used in case of booting legacy hardware.

5.2.1.1 Boot Process Services

PXE (Pre-boot eXecution Environment) is a method of booting computers via a network device instead of a local hard drive. In simpler terms, the network card requests and gets the files it needs to boot the system from an image server over the network rather than from a hard drive inside the computer.

iPXE (formerly gPXE) extends the functionality of PXE and is a superset of previous PXE implementations, supporting more protocols. Most importantly, iPXE supports flexible configuration scripts.

Dynamic Host Configuration Protocol (DHCP) is a standardized networking protocol used on Internet Protocol (IP) networks for dynamically distributing network configuration parameters, such as IP addresses for interfaces and services. In the PXE environment, the BIOS uses DHCP to obtain an IP address for the network interface and to locate the server that stores the network bootstrap program (NBP). DHCP server is required by PXE, iPXE, and UEFI HTTP Boot client.

Network Bootstrap Program (NBP) is the first link in the boot chain process, it is equivalent to GRUND Unified Bootloader (GRUB) or Linux Loader (LILO). Loaders which are traditionally used in local booting. Like the boot program in a hard drive environment, the NBP is responsible for loading the Operating System kernel into memory so that the OS can be bootstrapped over a network. Common NBPs include iPXE, PXELINUX GRUBx64, etc.

Trivial File Transfer Protocol (TFTP) is a simple file transfer protocol that is generally used for automated transfer of configuration or boot files between machines in a local environment. In a PXE environment, when a PXE client requests the DHCP server, the DHCP Server redirects the client to the TFTP server where the NBP file is downloaded.

BMC (Board Management Controller) is another independent system, which is not affected by the normal shutdown of this OS system. This independent system is implemented on the server mainboard through an additional hardware controller, namely the Baseboard Manager Controller (BMC for short).

IPMI (Intelligent Platform Management Interface) is a standardized computer system interface used by system administrators for out-of-band management of computer systems and monitoring of their operation. It is a method to manage systems that may be unresponsive or powered off by using only a network connection to the hardware rather than to an operating system. Because this management system is independent of the system used by the user application, it is also called an Out of Band (OOB) system.

BIOS stands for Basic Input/Output System. The system BIOS is the lowest-level software near the hardware in the machine; it interfaces between the hardware and the Operation System. The

BIOS provides access to the system hardware and enables the load of the higher-level operating systems from which applications are running. You can control your computer by changing some settings through the BIOS.

UEFI stands for "Unified Extensible Firmware Interface". Because BIOS has some limitations, The UEFI is the updating of BIOS and brings some modern features such as supporting bigger disk volume, UEFI supports more hardware devices and standards, such as USB3.0, nonvolatile memory express (NVMe), etc.

Most servers, support both BIOS and UEFI, which means you can operate manually or use ILO or IPMI to set/switch the boot mode. The boot server can be configured in the Bare Metal service in the following ways:

1.   Only one boot mode (UEFI or BIOS) can be configured for the node at any given time.

2.   If the operator wants a node to boot always in UEFI mode or BIOS mode, then they may use capabilities parameters within properties field of a bare metal node. The operator must manually set the appropriate boot mode on the bare metal node.

5.2.1.2 Local Boot with BIOS and MBR

Normally, the system boots from the local disk, thus the diskless booting is the PXE/iPXE boot we need to focus on.

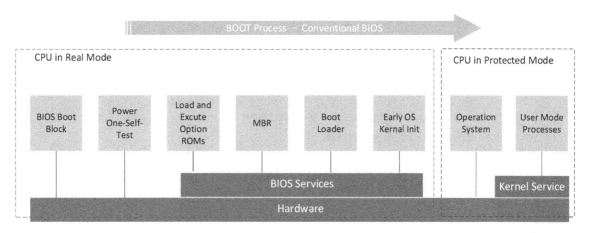

Figure 5-2 Legacy BIOS and MBR Boot Process

A server or device running an operating system needs to go through a series of processes from power-on to the GUI provided by the operating system visible to the users. Below is the Legacy BIOS + MBR Boot Process:

1. After the physical machine is powered on, the CPU loads the BIOS ROM which then initializes and executes a power-on self-test (POST) and initialization.

2. After the power-on self-test (POST) is completed, the BIOS will search for Option ROMs in sequence and execute them. Option ROMs execute with full control over the system and can perform operations without restriction. Moreover, only after the execution of the Option ROM is completed, the CPU is returned to the BIOS, and then the BIOS can continue to execute the next Option ROM or other operations.

3. After the BIOS initialization procedure, allow access to other types of storage (hard disk or RAM). The BIOS stores the boot order of the disks, and then the BIOS looks for the MBR in order. if found, the boot code in the MBR will be copied to RAM. And transfer control to the CPU.

4. The Bootloader is the last stage of the whole boot process. GRUB2 is the most popular bootloader used on almost all Linux distributions. GRUB2 uses a graphical UI menu that allows the user to choose (or default) to load the kernel into RAM.

5. vmlinuz is a bootable, compressed kernel. After the system kernel vmlinuz is loaded into the memory, it starts to provide underlying support. With the support of the kernel, various modules and services are loaded and run.

6. initrd.img is a small image, a virtual RAM disk with a root file system, and some programs in the file system are necessary when Linux boot. this image includes a minimal Linux system.

7. The Linux kernel of server uses this initrd to mount the final real root file system, and then removes this initrd from the memory. In this case, the initrd is actually a transitional thing.

8. The final stage of system startup is actually to load vmlinux and initrd.img, of course, you can continue to load the real system.

5.2.1.3 Local Boot with UEFI and GTP/MBR

GUID Partition Table (GPT) is a newer partitioning standard that has fewer limitations than Master Boot Record (MBR), such as allowing for more partitions per drive and supporting larger volume drives.

 GPT is more robust and provides better data protection and recovery options compared to MBR, but MBR is still necessary for compatibility with older systems.

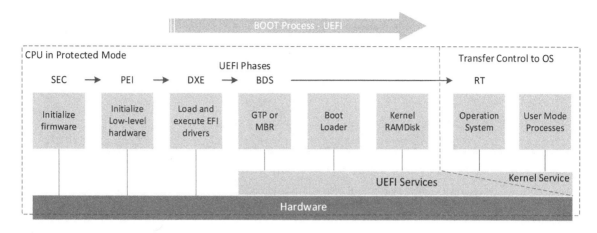

Figure 5-3 Local Boot with UEFI and GTP/MBR

UEFI booting include following several phases:

Security (SEC) Phase - After the system is powered on, the CPU starts to execute the first instruction, and the system enters the SEC phase. The memory at this stage has not been initialized and cannot be used. Therefore, the main work of the SEC stage is to create some temporary memory and switch the CPU to protected mode. The temporary memory can be processor cache or system memory.

Pre-EFI Initialization (PEI) Phase - The main work of the PEI phase is to initialize key devices such as memory, CPU, and chipset. Since this part of the code is not compressed, the code must be as compact as possible. Moreover, in the PEI stage, the boot path of the operating system must be determined, and the memory required by the UEFI driver and firmware must be initialized.

Driver Execution Environment (DXE) Phase -DXE is the most important stage of UEFI, and most of the driver and firmware loading work is done at this stage.

Boot Device Selection (BDS) Phase - The main work of the BDS phase is to initialize the environment variables of the console device, try to load the driver recorded in the environment variable list, and try to start from the boot device recorded in the environment variable list.

Transient System Load (TSL) Phase - Depending on the Boot Device selected in the previous BDS phase, the firmware boots an Operation System loader, the EFI Shell, or a UEFI application.

Run Time (RT) Phase - Here, the UEFI Program is cleared from memory and released to the Operation System. Run time service occupies a small amount of memory to be called by the Operation System as during UEFI BIOS update.

NOTE: *In case of boot from UEFI HTTP Boot model, Boot Device Selection will provide the boot options for HTTP Boot. Once a boot option for HTTP Boot is executed, a particular network interface is selected. HTTP Boot driver will perform all steps on that network interface.*

5.2.1.4 Network Boot with BIOS/UEFI and PXE

As introduced in the above section, after the BIOS is running, it will be booted by the MBR/GPT in the disk. If the disk here is replaced by a network device, then it is what we call PXE (Preboot eXecution Environment) to start. The PXE specification describes a standardized client ↔ server environment where communication uses several standard Internet protocols such as UDP/IP, DHCP, TFTP, and more. In this environment, when the computer starts, it can interact with the server side, allowing the client to dynamically obtain the resources needed for startup from the remote server through the network, so that the computer can be started without relying on the local data storage device (such as a hard disk). Then, load an installation file or an entire operating system.

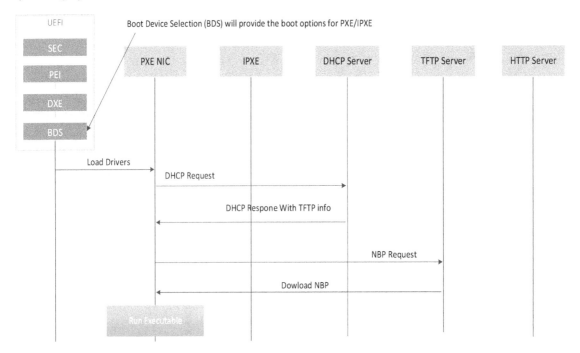

Figure 5-4 Network Boot with BIOS/UEFI and PXE

Here's a simple flow of how standard PXE booting works.

1. When the boot mode is switched to PXE with a computer, the network card makes a DHCP request to the network.

2. The DHCP server gets configured to respond to DHCP requests with not only an address, but also the TFTP server name, and the file name of the PXE executable, a Network Book Program (NBP).

3. When the client (bare metal node) receives this DHCP server response, it connects to the specified TFTP server to download and run the PXE NBP.

4. The PXE NBP connects to the TFTP server again and looks for the default menu configuration file on the server.

5. Finally, the NBP downloads configs, scripts, and/or images it requires to run an Operation System.

NOTE:

1. *In BIOS with PXE case, NBP can be pxelinux.0 and work with pxelinux.cfg.*

2. *In UEFI with PXE case, NBP can be grubx64.efi and work with grub.cfg.*

3. *For BIOS and UEFI with PXE, except the above two different points, Other processes are the same.*

5.2.1.5 Network Boot with BIOS/UEFI and iPXE

iPXE is the leading open source network boot firmware. It provides a full PXE implementation enhanced with additional features.

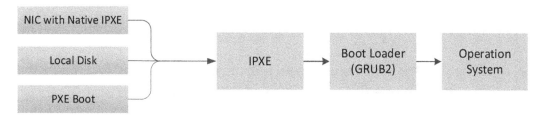

Figure 5-5 Three Cases to Chain the iPXE Booting

Essentially, just like PXE, it allows you to get the files needed to boot from another computer on your network. However, iPXE provides additional protocols that traditional PXE booting doesn't. There are a number of other different methods to set up your computer to start iPXE:

1. The most straightforward method is to flash the iPXE firmware to your network card ROM. The BIOS/EFI can run iPXE directly via the ethernet card in this way.

2. The easiest method is to copy iPXE images to local storage, such as a CD or USB Disk, to boot the computer.

3. PXE boot into iPXE. This is a bit more convoluted than the other options, but it allows you to run a completely diskless boot on the client machine smoothly in a chain loading mode.

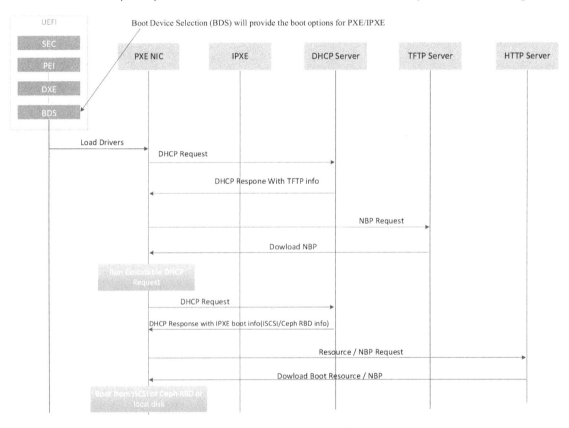

Figure 5-6 Network Boot with BIOS/UEFI and iPXE

In the case of chain loading PXE to iPXE, the steps are slightly different. The DHCP server gets configured to respond differently based on the indication information it receives. The first time, it responds with the filename of the iPXE image. The second time, it responds with the filename that iPXE should load. Following are the detailed steps:

1. The network card makes a DHCP request, which indicates a PXE client to the network.

2. The DHCP server responds with an address, TFTP server name, and the filename of the PXE executable (NBP).

3. The client connects to the specified TFTP server to download and run the PXE executable (NBP).

4. The PXE NBP initiates a new DHCP request, specifies the iPXE option in the request, and indicates this request is from an iPXE client.

5. The DHCP server recognizes that the iPXE option has been specified and provides the iSCSI disk to boot.

6. The iPXE executable (NBP) connects to the specified iSCSI disk and boots from it.

NOTE: *In addition to booting from the iSCSI disk, you also can boot from a variety of other remote storage backends such as NVMe-over Fabric target and Ceph RBD target.*

1. *In BIOS with iPXE case, NBP may be ipxe.pxe, you can download it from http://boot.ipxe.org*

2. *In UEFI with iPXE case, NBP may be ipxe.efi, you can download it from http://boot.ipxe.org*

3. *For BIOS and UEFI with iPXE, except above two different points, other processes are same.*

5.2.1.6 Network Boot with UEFI HTTP Boot

UEFI HTTP Boot is a client-server communication based application. By default, it combines the Dynamic Host Configuration Protocol (DHCP), Domain Name System (DNS), and Hypertext Transfer Protocol (HTTP) to provide the capability for bare metal system deployment and configuration over the internet network. UEFI HTTP Boot replaces Trivial File Transfer Protocol (TFTP) based Preboot Execution Environment (PXE) Boot methods of network deployment with higher performance, simplicity, and convenience.

5.2.1.6.1 Boot from URL

UEFI HTTP Boot defines a related method indicated by other codes in the DHCP options, in which the name and path of the NBP are specified as a URI string in one of several formats specifying the protocol and unique name identifying the NBP for the specified protocol. In this method, the NBP will be downloaded via IPV4 or IPV6 HTTP protocol if the tag indicates UEFI HTTP Boot.

Compared to PXE or iPXE Boot, HTTP Boot can handle much larger files than TFTP and spread out the network scope limitation to the internet environment. You can easily download multi-megabyte files, such as an Operation System kernel and a root file system, and you can download it from servers that are out of your local area network from remote.

5.2.1.6.2 Message Exchange in HTTP Boot

Generally, the UEFI HTTP Boot Client should be able to enter a heterogeneous network, acquire a network address from a DHCP server, and then download an NBP to set itself up.

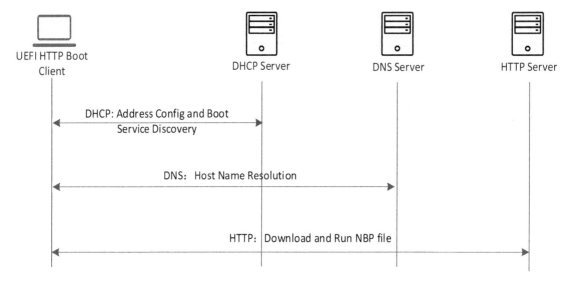

Figure 5-7 UEFI HTTP Boot Flow

The concept of the HTTP Boot message exchange sequence is as follows. The UEFI HTTP Boot Client initiates the DHCPv4 D.O.R.A. (Discover, Offer, Request, Acknowledge) process by broadcasting a DHCPDISCOVER message containing the extension that identifies the request as coming from a client that implements the HTTP Boot functionality. Assuming that a DHCP server or a Proxy DHCP server implementing this extension is available, after several intermediate steps, besides the standard configuration such as address information, subnet, router information, DNS-server address, boot resources location will be provided to the client in the format of a URI. The URI can be the address of N.B.P., which is used for client target hardware configuration. Then, the client executes the downloaded N.B.P. image from memory. This image can then consume other UEFI interfaces for further system setup, such as the operation system installation.

Message Exchange Using DHCP Client Extensions

1. **Client Broadcast**

The HTTP Boot client broadcasts a DHCP Discover message to the standard DHCP port (67).

2. **DHCP Server Response**

The DHCP server responds by sending a DHCPOFFER message on the standard DHCP reply port (68).

The UEFI HTTP Boot Client may possibly receive multiple DHCPOFFER packets from different sources of DHCP Services, possibly from DHCP Services that recognize the HTTP extensions or from Standard DHCP Services.

A service recognizing HTTP extensions must respond with an offer that has the Vendor Class Identifier Option 60 parameter set to "HTTPClient", in response to the Vendor Class Identifier requested in option 55 in the DHCP Discover message.

Some parameters are mandatory for each message that the standard DHCP has, for example, an IP address for the client and any other parameters that the administrator might have configured on the DHCP or Proxy DHCP Service. The DHCP service or Proxy DHCP, which recognizes the HTTPBoot extension, will provide DHCPOFFER with HTTP Client extensions. The client IP address field will fill with 0.0.0.0 in the case of Proxy DHCP service. If this is from a DHCP service, then the returned client IP address field is the normal correct one.

3. **DHCP Request**

The HTTP Boot Client selects an IP address offered by a DHCP server, and then it completes the standard DHCP protocol by sending a DHCP Request packet for the address to the DHCP Server and waiting for acknowledgment from the DHCP server.

4. **DHCP ACK**

The DHCP server acknowledges the IP address by sending a DHCP ACK packet to the HTTP Boot client.

Message Exchange not Using DHCP Client Extensions

In a Lite site or Mini site, there may not exist a DHCP Server within the site locally. The Boot URI Information will not be provided by the DHCP Offers. We need another way to provide this information. The implementation suggestion is provisioning this information by the Original equipment manufacturer (OEM) or input by the end user through Setup Options when booting. Henceforth, make sure the UEFI Boot Client already knows the Boot URI before contacting the DHCP server.

Message in DNS Query/Reply

The DNS Query/Reply is a standard process. Multiple IP addresses might be retrieved from the DNS process. It's the HTTP Boot Client driver's responsibility to select the proper IP address automatically or show the user interface for the customer to decide the proper IP address to select.

Message in HTTP Download

In the UEFI HTTP Boot environment, an HTTP GET message is used to get an image from the Web server where the boot related file is stored.

5.2.2   ScaleMaker - On-premises Bare Metal Provisioning

Traditionally, Physical servers are managed manually, including operation systems installation by inserting a CD-ROM media disk and installing software utilizing a USB stick, but in a cloud environment, especially the Distributed Cloud, this process should be automated and on-line approach.

Bare metal refers to hardware without any software installed on the host. Bare-metal provisioning means installing an operating system directly into the computer's host hardware.

A target physical machine may contain a CPU host and an IPU device. It only refers to the CPU host hardware when we say bare metal is hardware without any software installed on it, and IPU hardware typically has special pre-installed software, including an operation system.

Bare metal node is a new type of computing service that combines the elasticity features of virtual machines and the performance and characteristics of physical machines. Its user experience is consistent with that of ordinary CPU hosts. It also fully supports nested virtualization technology and retains the resources of ordinary cloud servers. Elastic and retain the experience of a physical machine with the help of nested virtualization technology. There is almost no loss in performance, no different from a physical machine.

Bare Metal uses hardware devices (such as smart NIC, Data Process Unit (DPU), IPU, or GPU device) virtualization technology to achieve performance, multi-tenant, absolute isolation in security, and lock the scope of security risks.

5.2.2.1 Bare Metal Capacity

Following are some features and several design targets of the bare metal node and system:

1. **Bare Metal** with Firmware Isolation supports the BIOS/UEFI and BMC standard server disable in-band update and management, only permitting out-of-band operation. The SmaritNIC or IPU device enables restrict mode and only allows out-of-band to make it can not be managed and updated.

2. **Storage** provides hot plug NVMe cloud disk and the NVMe cloud disk can be booted from as operation system disk.

3. **Networking** supports standard GVPC network and elastic network card with hot plug feathers and VF capacity.

4. **Computing** manages and schedules the full life cycle of bare metal instances. And support monitoring collection and Virtual Network Computing (VNC) Console to Debug.

5. **Operation and Maintenance** support the automated operation and maintenance of smartNIC/IPU devices, including installation, and out-of-band serial port login management.

5.2.2.2 Bare Metal Service Integration Architecture

Figure 5-8 below demonstrates the general architecture of bare metal provisioning. It shows the basic components that form the Bare Metal Controller, the relation of the Bare Metal controller with other cloud services in the OneCenter, and the logical flow of a boot instance request resulting in the provisioning of a physical target. The Bare Metal controller instance can reside in the site edge location, IPU device, or be located in the OneCenter location according to the different provisioning scenarios.

A user's request to boot a target is passed to the Scale Maker via the user API and the Unified Resource Manager. The Scale Maker understands and forwards this request to the Bare Metal

Controller, where the request passes from the Bare Metal API to the Bare Metal Director(BM-Director), to a driver to successfully provision a physical target for the user.

Bare metal is a node adding an IPU to the physical server so that users can use the entire physical machine like a virtual machine.

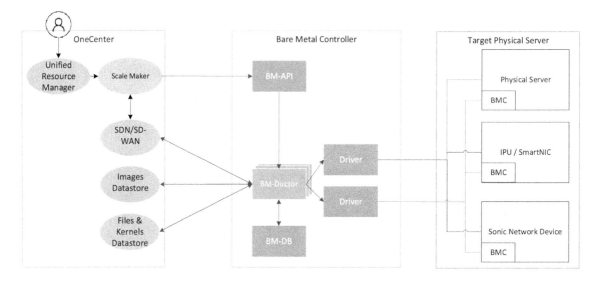

Figure 5-8 Logical Architecture of Scale Maker Integration with Bare Metal Service

Compared to a physical machine (or physical server), the bare metal node has the following characteristics:

- The performance of CPU and memory is exactly the same as the physical machine.
- vCPU scheduling latency is exactly the same as a physical machine.
- Interrupt response times are exactly the same as physical machines.
- Storage software path is slightly longer.
- Performance may slightly slow down in some virtual network scenarios.

The Bare Metal service may, depending upon configuration, interact with several other Distributed Cloud services. This includes:

- The Distributed Cloud Image service (marketplace and image store) from which to retrieve images and image meta-data through HTTP/HTTPs.
- The Distributed Cloud Networking service (Beacon) for DHCP, NTP, and DNS and network configuration.

- The Distributed Cloud Compute service (OneZone Instance) works with the Bare Metal service and acts as a user-facing API for instance management, while the Bare Metal service provides the admin/operator API for hardware management.

- The Distributed Cloud Object Storage (Ceph Object Store with S3 API) can be used to provide temporary storage for the configdrive, user images, image metadata, deployment logs, inspection data, etc.

5.2.2.3   Bare Metal Controller

As the main controller of the bare metal node life-cycle, the Bare Metal Controller includes the following components:

Bare Metal API (BM-API) is a RESTful API that processes application requests by sending them to the BM-Director.

Bare Metal Director (**BM-Director**) is responsible for adding/editing/deleting nodes; powering on/off target nodes with IPMI or other vendor-specific protocol; provisioning/deploying/cleaning bare metal nodes.BM-Director uses drivers to execute operations on target hardware.

Bare Metal Agent (BM-Agent) is a service that is run in temporary ramdisks to play director and inspector roles with remote access, in-band hardware control, and target hardware introspection.

A Database to store target hardware information and states. Each Bare Metal Controller instance can have its own separate database because this controller probability can be deployed in a geo-distributed model. In the Distributed Cloud architecture, all Bare Metal Controller instance databases should keep synchronization with the Unified Resource Manager.

Deployment Architecture

The Bare Metal RESTful API service is used to enroll hardware that the Bare Metal Controller will manage. Bare Metal targets the physical server's special attributes, such as MAC address, IP address, boot image information, and IPMI credentials, which should be automatically using a certain tool or manually registered by the cloud administrator. There can be multiple instances of the API service at the same time.

There can be multiple instances of the director service to support various classes of drivers and also to manage failover. Each director can run many drivers to operate heterogeneous hardware. This is depicted in Figure 5-8.

5.2.3 ScaleMaker - Cloud Bare Metal Provisioning

In the Distributed Cloud, the public cloud is one of the most important infrastructure providers. The public cloud offers unlimited resource sources. It allows companies to build hybrid and multi-cloud architecture environments. About the more benefits of public cloud for the Distributed Cloud architecture, you can read [Chapter 8 Hybrid Multi-Cloud in The Distributed Cloud].

This section briefly describes the public provider and how to provision a public cloud site with AWS as an example.

5.2.3.1 Amazon AWS Provider

A cloud provider represents a cloud where resources such as hosts (bare metal or virtual machine), networks (VPN and Elastic IP (EIP), etc.), or storage are allocated to implement a provision. Usually, a provider includes a zone or region in the target cloud and an Identity and Access Management (IAM) account that will be used to operate (create, update, or delete) the resources needed.

An AWS provider contains the credentials to interact with Amazon and also the region to deploy your Provisions. The Distributed Cloud can come with pre-defined AWS providers in AWS regions.

In order to define an AWS provider, you need the following information:

Credentials are used to interact with the remote AWS provider. You need to provide an access key and a secret key. About how to create and get the access key and secret key from AWS, you can refer to https://docs.aws.amazon.com for detailed information.

Region is the location in the world where the resources are going to be allocated. All the available regions are listed on https://docs.aws.amazon.com, too.

Instance Types and Amazon Machine Image (AMI) specify the capacity of the resources that are going to be deployed and the operating system that is going to be installed on them.

5.2.3.2 Create an AWS Provider

To add a new provider, you can create a YAML template file. This template at least contains the Credentials, Region, and Instance types, and AMI's related information. After defining the provider YAML template file, the Distributed Cloud provides a command to create the provider.

The above method can be done by command line. Of course, the GUI approach also should be supported by the tenant console of the Distributed Cloud.

5.2.3.3 Customize an Existing Provider

The provider information is stored in the Distributed Cloud unified resource manager database and can be updated just like any other resource. In this case, you can use the CLI to achieve this. It will open an editor so you can edit all the information there. You can also use the tenant GUI console to update all the information.

5.2.3.4 Mini Site Provision from AWS

As described in section 6.2, the public cloud site can be deployed as four types of sites: Max site, Pro site, Mini site, and Lite Site. This section focuses on a Mini site with an AWS Hyperconverged Infrastructure (HCI) Cluster.

Mini Site features a hyper convergent storage configuration based on the Ceph cluster. Compared to the Lite site, the Mini site with an HCI cluster provides a highly available solution. The Mini site is based on bare-metal servers and can support the LXC and KVM hypervisors.

5.2.3.5 AWS Mini Site Implementation

Site Nodes

The AWS Cloud Mini site consists of three different types of cloud servers:

Full Nodes, run Ceph OSD, and Monitor daemons as well as the selected hypervisor. For getting a fault-tolerant cluster, a number of 3 nodes of this type site is suggested.

OSD Nodes, run Ceph OSD daemon and the selected hypervisor.

Hypervisor-only Nodes, run the selected hypervisor and the Ceph client utilities.

Ceph Specific AWS Resources

The following resources are allocated to build the Ceph cluster:

- AWS Amazon Elastic Block Store (EBS) Volume, each Ceph node running the OSD daemons includes an EBS backed block device to store the cluster data.

- AWS Ceph Subnet, each instance includes a dedicated interface to isolate Ceph cluster communication.

Networking Design

A cloud site includes two different networks:

Public Networking is implemented using elastic IPs (EIP) from AWS and the global IPAM from OneCenter of the Distributed Cloud. When the virtual network is created in OneCenter, the EIP is requested from AWS. Then, inside the CPU host, IP forwarding rules are applied so the VM can communicate over the EIP assigned by AWS.

Private Networking is implemented using MP-BGP-EVPN with VXLAN. For more information about MP-BGP-EVPN and VXLAN, please see section [Chapter 3 The Distributed Cloud Enterprise Networking].

As shown in Figure 5-9, extending the Distributed Cloud to the public cloud can use two approaches: one is onRamp using an SD-WAN edge router located in the AWS transit Virtual Private Cloud (VPC), and the other one is connecting to AWS Internet Gateway (IGW) using EIP offered by AWS directly. About the WAN Edge Router method, please refer to section [8.2 Hybrid Multi-Cloud Design] for more detail. This section focuses on the IGW method.

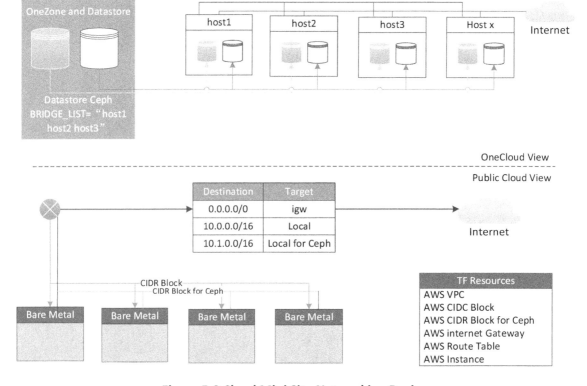

Figure 5-9 Cloud Mini Site Networking Design

These network elements are created with the following resources in AWS:

AWS VPC contains an isolated virtual private network for all the deployed resources.

AWS Subnet allows communication between AWS Instances that are running in the provisioned hosts.

AWS Internet Gateway (IGW) lets AWS Instance have public connectivity over the Internet to OneCenter and other sites.

AWS Security Group custom security rules can be defined by the user to allow only specific traffic to the AWS Instance.

5.2.3.6 AWS Mini Site Definition

To create a Mini site in AWS, the following information should be provided and configured:

Table 5-1 AWS Mini Site Configuration Infromation Example

Configuration Items	Example Value	Descriptions
num_ceph_full_hosts	3	Number of instances for Ceph full nodes:OSD+MON
num_ceph_osd_hosts	0	Number of instances for Ceph OSD (only for OSD)
num_ceph_client_hosts	1	Number of instances for hypervisor (Ceph client)
ceph_disk_size	500	Disk size of CEPH disk volume for the OSD, in GB
aws_instance_type	c5.metal	AWS instance type, use bare-metal instances
aws_root_size	200	AWS instance root volume size, in GB
aws_ami_img	Default	AWS AMI image used for host deployments
num_public_ips	1	Number of EIP to get from AWS for virtual machine
dns	8.8.8.8	DNS name servers for public network

5.2.3.7 The Distributed Cloud Site Resources

In the Distributed Cloud there are following resources can be created:

1. **Site** - containing all other resources.

2. **Hosts** - for each instance in AWS.

3. **Datastores** - image and instance datastores backed by Ceph.

4. **Virtual Network** - for public networking.

5. **Virtual Network Template** - for private networking.

5.3   Infrastructure Virtualization

From the top view of the Distributed Cloud, the bare metal provisioning from on-premises, edge, and the public cloud can be looked at as cloud underlay infrastructure provision. At the resource layer, the administrator may virtualize the underlay bare metal nodes for application tasks and also can allocate the underlay bare metal node to run an application or service such as bigdata platform directly. This section introduces following virtualization technology in the Distributed Cloud:

KVM/QEMU

KVM/QEMU is the mainstream virtualization solution for Linux on x86 architecture hardware, which supports virtualization extensions (Intel VT or AMD-V) technology. KVM itself resides in the Linux Kernel space to provide base CPU and Memory core virtualization and several processor-specific modules. KVM cooperates with QEMU, which contains the user-space machine hardware emulator and virtual machines management tool libvirt to complete a full virtualization stack to run a virtual machine. With KVM, you can run multiple Virtual Machines with unmodified Linux or Windows images. Each Virtual Machine has private virtualized hardware - network card, disk, graphics adapter, etc. by default. In the Distributed Cloud, providing standard virtualized hardware is not enough, and a KVM based virtual machine must have the following capacity:

PCI Passthrough - The hypervisor can discover Peripheral Component Interconnect (PCI) devices in the hosts and directly assign them to Virtual Machines in the KVM hypervisor.

NVIDIA Virtual Graphics Processing Unit (vGPU) - The user need assure SR-IOV and IOMMU settings in the BIOS configuration are enabled.

SR-IOV and RDMA (Remote Direct Memory Access) - These feathers may be necessary in the case of Telco Edge (CSP CORD, 3GPP NPN, 3GPP PNI-MEC) and Distributed Storage System.

LXC

LXC (LinuX Containers), an operating system layer virtualization technology, is a user space interface for the Linux kernel container function. It packages the application software system into a software container, which contains the code of the application software itself, as well as the operating system core and libraries required by the code. The available hardware resources of different software containers are allocated through a unified name space and shared API, creating an independent program running environment for applications so that Linux users can easily create and manage various application containers.

LXC utilizes the functions of cgroups and namespaces to provide an independent operating system environment for application software. LXC does not require the Hypervisor software layer. The software container itself is extremely lightweight, which improves the speed of creating virtual machines.

Such a container environment is just an additional process tree along with other hypervisor processes. Inside the environment, it looks like a standard Linux installation that sees only its own private resources that share the whole host operation system kernel.

Firecracker

Firecracker is an open-source virtualization technology that is purpose-built for creating and managing secure, multi-tenant container and function-based services. And Firecracker enables users to deploy workloads in lightweight virtual machines, called microVMs, which provide enhanced security and workload isolation over traditional VMs, while enabling the speed and resource efficiency of containers. Firecracker was developed at Amazon Web Services (AWS) to improve the customer experience of services such as serverless services.

A firecracker is a virtual machine monitor (VMM) that uses the Linux KVM to create and manage micro-VMs. It has a minimalist design. It excludes unnecessary devices and guest functionality to reduce the memory footprint and attack surface area of each micro-VM. This improves security, decreases the startup time, and increases hardware utilization. Firecracker runs in user space and is based on the Linux KVM to create microVMs. Starting up microVMs is very fast, and with low memory overhead, these can let you pack thousands of microVMs onto a single physical machine. This means that every function, container, or container group can be encapsulated with a virtual machine barrier, enabling workloads from different customers to run on the same physical machine without any tradeoffs to security or efficiency. Firecracker's other option is QEMU, an established VMM with a general purpose and broad feature set that allows it to host a variety of guest operating systems.

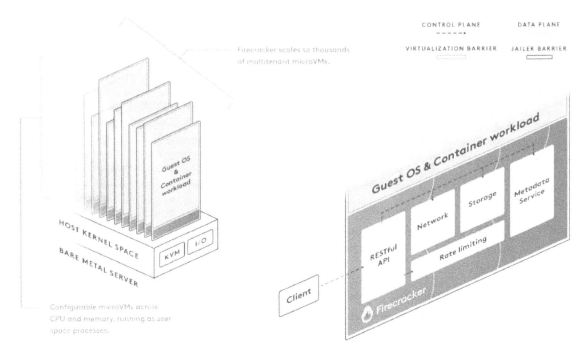

Figure 5-10 How Firecracker Works (source: https://firecracker-microvm.github.io)

5.4 Infrastructure Containerization

Application container technologies have a long history with several main streaming related solutions, and this section introduces two docker container ecosystem solutions. The first one is a simple but powerful approach for running containerized applications and workflows by directly using the Docker official images available from the Docker Hub and running them on lightweight Firecracker micro-VMs that provide an extra level of efficiency and security or running your containers on a cloud environment based on LXC system containers if you need full bare-metal performance and isolation is not a requirement, the second other most important solution is using Kubernetes Clusters Manager to control Kubernetes clusters with Docker. At the same time, a container managing tool, Docker Machine, will be briefly described in section [5.4.2 Manipulate Global Containers with Docker Machine].

We say the first solution is cloud-native containerization, and the second one is a heterogeneous Kubernetes cluster manager. The Figure 5-11 shows the architecture of those two solutions.

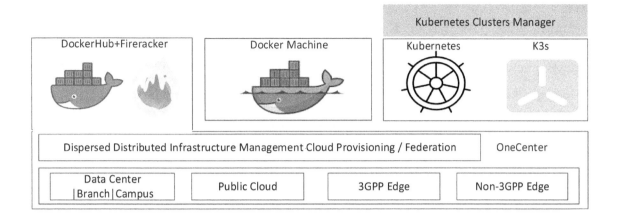

Figure 5-11 Available Solutions for Container Orchestration

5.4.1   Running Containers on MicroVMs

This approach combines all the benefits of containers with the security, orchestration, and multi-tenant features but without adding extra functions of management, thus reducing the complexity and costs compared with Kubernetes. The Distributed Cloud is designed to support the LXC system and let you can also run your containers on the Distributed Cloud based on LXC system containers in case you do not need full bare-metal performance and isolation.

Orchestrating Containers

In the current cloud era, cloud-native and shifting from a "monolithic" approach to a microservice approach is becoming the trend. Deploying a single container can be an easy task, but things get a bit more complex when deploying multi-container applications in a distributed environment, given that, in these cases, a Docker Engine alone fulfills the requirements. This is where container orchestrators like Kubernetes play an important role in scheduling containers to run on different hosts in a cluster environment, migrating containers to a new host when the original host becomes bad, restarting containers when they fail, managing overlay networks to allow containers to communicate on different hosts, orchestrating storage to provide persistent volumes for stateful applications, and so on.

Running Containers on MicroVMs

Firecracker can be incorporated into OneCenter as a new supported virtualization technology. This microVM technology, developed by AWS and widely used as part of its Fargate and Lambda services, has been specially designed for creating and managing secure, multi-tenant container and function-based services. By taking this step, OneCenter can manage to bridge the gap between two technological worlds, leaving behind the old dilemma of whether to use containers - lighter, but with weaker security - or Virtual Machines - with strong security but high overhead.

By adopting the increasingly popular approach of running microservices based on containerized applications, and thanks to its seamless integration with Docker Hub, OneCenter may become a powerful alternative to deploy and orchestrate containers as secure and fast Firecracker microVMs.

Making the Best of Both Worlds

The Distributed Cloud can bring new features to the container orchestration ecosystem by providing an innovative solution for companies who need to build and manage a secure, self-service, multi-tenant cloud for serverless computing. Users of a Distributed Cloud can easily run isolated containers without the need to provision and manage hosts or additional control layers, thus allowing them to focus on designing and building their applications instead of managing the underlying container infrastructure.

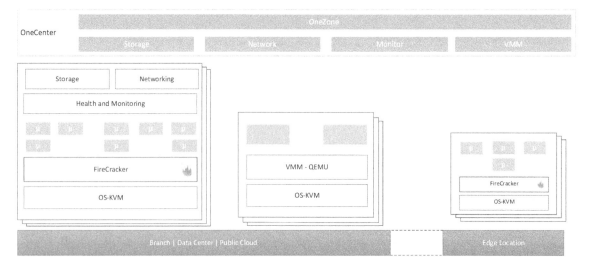

Figure 5-12 Integration of Firecracker as a Virtualization Technology Officially

The Distributed Cloud's pioneering solution towards container orchestration is based on the innovative integration of two main technologies:

Firecracker is the VMM that provisions, manages, and orchestrates micro Virtual Machines.

Docker Hub is the public marketplace for application containers from which users can obtain and seamlessly deploy Docker images as micro VMs.

Firecracker is an open-source virtualization technology developed by AWS that is based on KVM to launch lightweight Virtual Machines - termed micro-VMs - for enhanced security, workload isolation, and resource efficiency. Firecracker technology opens up a new world of possibilities as the foundation for serverless solutions that need to quickly start critical applications with containers while keeping them in secure isolation. With the integration of Firecracker as a supported virtualization technology, the Distributed Cloud can provide an innovative solution to the dilemma of whether to use containers - lighter but with weak security - or Virtual Machines - with strong security but high overhead.

The Distributed Cloud's integration of Docker Hub as a new native marketplace provides organizations with immediate access to Docker Hub images. Through this integration, Docker images can be easily imported into a Distributed Cloud, following a process similar to that of The Distributed Cloud's Global Marketplace. The Distributed Cloud context packages are installed during the import process so that once an image is imported, it becomes fully functional.

5.4.2 Manipulate Global Containers with Docker Machine

Docker Machine lets you create Docker hosts on an edge site, public cloud providers, or inside an on-premise data center. It can automatically create hosts, install Docker on them, and then configure the Docker client to talk to them. Here a "machine" refers to the combination of a Docker host and a configured client. With a single Docker client, you can deploy Docker containers anywhere and in any type of infrastructure provider worldwide.

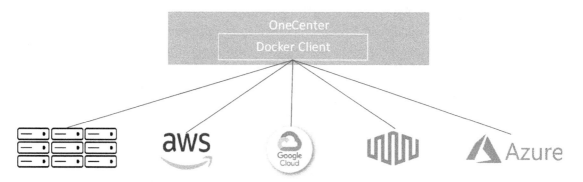

Figure 5-13 Docker Machine in The Distributed Cloud

The integration with the Distributed Cloud is extraordinarily simple and easy to use for the users as the Figure 5-13.

5.4.3   Dispersed Heterogeneous Kubernetes Clusters

The earlier section [5.4.1 Running Containers on MicroVMs] discussed the native method for container workload in the Distributed Cloud. However, no single size fits all, and there are use cases that still require the running of a Kubernetes cluster, including those cases in which your target application has been defined as a Helm Chart, so you may need to use Kubernetes on the cloud or on-premise.

Docker and Kubernetes are becoming the de facto leading standards for packaging, deploying, and managing applications with increased levels of agility and efficiency. Docker uses OS-level virtualization to deliver software in packages called containers, whereas Kubernetes is a widely used tool to orchestrate the container on the Kubernetes cluster.

A Kubernetes cluster usually runs within a Distributed Cloud site. In order to control and manage the dispersed geo-distributed Kubernetes clusters in worldwide locations, a Kubernetes Clusters Manager is needed and will be presented in the following section:

5.4.3.1 Introduction

Kubernetes Clusters Manager is a Kubernetes management tool to deploy and run clusters anywhere and on any cloud infrastructure provider.

Kubernetes Clusters Manager adds significant value on top of Kubernetes, first by centralizing authentication and role-based access control (RBAC) for all the clusters, giving global admins the ability to control cluster access from one location.

It then enables detailed monitoring and alerting for clusters and their resources, ships logs to external providers and integrates directly with Helm via the application catalog. If you have an external Continuous Integration/Continuous Delivery (CI/CD) system, you can plug it into Kubernetes Clusters Manager.

Kubernetes Clusters Manager is a complete container management platform for Kubernetes, giving you the tools to successfully run Kubernetes anywhere.

5.4.3.2 Deployment Strategy

According to business scale, organizations can deploy a Kubernetes Clusters Manager instance in two recommended deployment strategies: one is Hub & Spoke Strategy, and another is regional. This book omits regional strategy and only presents the Hub & Spoke Strategy.

As in Figure 5-14, in this deployment scenario, there is a single Kubernetes Clusters Manager instance managing different Kubernetes clusters over all Distributed Cloud sites across the globe. The Kubernetes Clusters Manager instance is recommended to be run on a high-availability Kubernetes cluster.

This kind of deployment has some advantages. For example, you can view all regions and environments from a single control plane interface, and Kubernetes clusters do not require Kubernetes Clusters Manager to operate and can tolerate losing connectivity to the Kubernetes Clusters Manager instance.

As to the disadvantages, it is obvious that you must be subject to network latencies, and the global provisioning and monitoring of new services are unavailable until the disaster is recovered, but each Kubernetes cluster can continue to be managed individually.

In the regional deployment model, a control plane is deployed together with or in close proximity to the cluster compute nodes. Its details are omitted from this book.

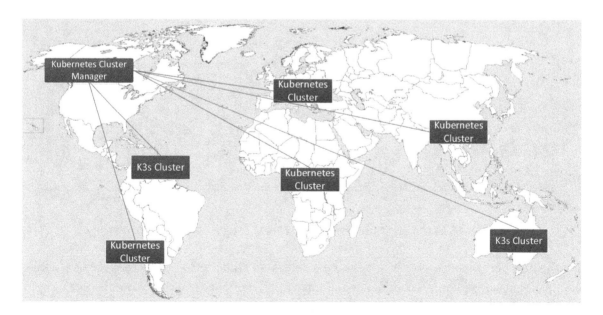

Figure 5-14 Deployment Strategy of Kubernetes Clusters Manager

5.4.3.3 Kubernetes Clusters Manager Components Architecture

The majority of Kubernetes Clusters Manager software runs on the Kubernetes Clusters Manager Server. Kubernetes Clusters Manager Server includes all the software components used to manage the entire Kubernetes Clusters Manager deployment.

Figure 5-15 below illustrates the high-level architecture of Kubernetes Clusters Manager. This figure depicts a Kubernetes Clusters Manager Server installation that manages three downstream Kubernetes clusters: middle one (Tokyo) created in the on-premises data center, right one (New York) created by Amazon Elastic Kubernetes Service (EKS) in the public cloud, and left one (Singapore) which is created with k3s cluster.

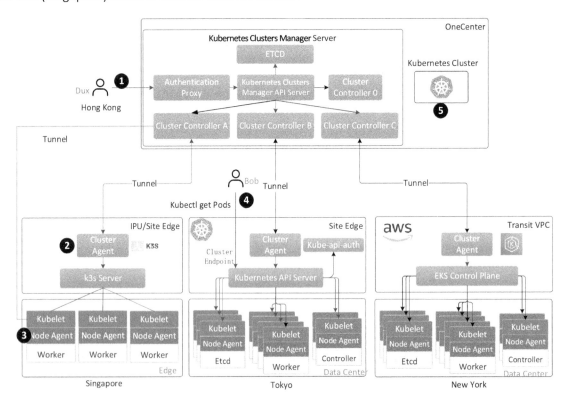

Figure 5-15 Managing Kubernetes Clusters through Authentication Proxy

For the best performance and security, using a dedicated Kubernetes cluster for the Kubernetes Clusters Manager server is recommended. Running user workloads on this cluster is not encouraged. After deploying Kubernetes Clusters Manager, you can create or import Kubernetes clusters for running your workloads.

You can install Kubernetes Clusters Manager on a single node or a high-availability Kubernetes cluster (this is recommended for production). The Kubernetes Clusters Manager backup operator can be used to migrate Kubernetes Clusters Manager from the single Docker container install to an installation on a high-availability Kubernetes cluster.

The Kubernetes Clusters Manager server, regardless of the installation type, should always run on nodes that are separate from the tenant downstream user clusters that it controls and manages. If Kubernetes Clusters Manager is installed on a high-availability Kubernetes cluster, it should run on a separate cluster from the cluster(s) it manages.

❶The Authentication Proxy

In Figure 5-15, a user named Dux wants to see all pods running on a downstream user cluster called User Cluster 1. From inside Kubernetes Clusters Manager, he can run a kubectl command to see the pods. Dux is authenticated through Kubernetes Clusters Manager 's authentication proxy. The authentication proxy forwards all Kubernetes API calls to downstream clusters. It integrates with authentication services like local authentication, FreeIPA, Active Directory, and GitHub. On every Kubernetes API call, the authentication proxy authenticates the caller and sets the proper Kubernetes impersonation headers before forwarding the call to Kubernetes masters.

❷Kubernetes Cluster Controllers and Cluster Agents

Each downstream Kubernetes cluster has a cluster agent, which can reside in IPU or site edge and opens a tunnel to the corresponding Kubernetes Cluster Controller within the Kubernetes Clusters Manager server.

Typically, the Kubernetes Cluster Controller resides in the central controller, OneCenter, and there is one Cluster Controller pair and one Cluster Agent for each downstream Kubernetes cluster. Each Kubernetes Cluster Controller:

- Watches for resource changes in the downstream Kubernetes cluster.

- Report the current state of the downstream cluster to the desired state.

- Configures access control policies to clusters and projects.

- Provisions clusters by calling the required Docker machine drivers (for more information about Docker machines, refer to section [5.4.2 Manipulate Global Containers with Docker Machine]) and Kubernetes engines, such as AKE and Google Kubernetes Engine (GKE).

By default, to enable Kubernetes Clusters Manager to communicate with a downstream cluster, the Kubernetes Cluster Controller connects to the Cluster Agent. If the Cluster Agent is not available, the Kubernetes Cluster Controller can connect to a node agent (described in later this section) instead.

The Cluster Agent is a component that runs in a downstream Kubernetes cluster. For example, With Mini or Lite of the Distributed Cloud site, the Cluster Agent usually resides in the IPU device, while with Max or Pro site, the Cluster Agent usually resides in the site edge node. It mainly performs the following actions:

- Connects to the Kubernetes API of Kubernetes Clusters Manager-launched clusters.

- Manages workloads, pod creation, and deployment within each cluster.

- Applies the roles and bindings defined in each Kubernetes cluster's global policies.

- Communicates between the Kubernetes cluster and Clusters Manager server (through a tunnel to the Kubernetes Cluster Controller) about events, status, worker node information, and health status.

❸Node Agents

As its name implies, the Node Agent runs in each Kubernetes worker node. If the Cluster Agent meets trouble, one of the Node Agents creates a tunnel to the Kubernetes Cluster Controller to communicate with the Kubernetes Clusters Manager.

The Node Agent is deployed using a DaemonSet resource to make sure it runs on every node in a Kubernetes Clusters Manager-launched Kubernetes cluster. It is used to interact with the nodes when performing Kubernetes cluster operations, such as upgrading the Kubernetes version and creating or restoring ETCD snapshots.

❹Authorized Kubernetes Cluster Endpoint

An authorized cluster endpoint allows users to access the Kubernetes API server of a downstream cluster without having to route their requests through the Kubernetes Clusters Manager authentication proxy. Note that the authorized cluster endpoint only works well on Kubernetes Clusters Manager -launched Kubernetes clusters. It is difficult to become available for imported Kubernetes clusters or for clusters in a hosted Kubernetes provider, such as GKE.

There are two main reasons why a user might need the authorized cluster endpoint:

- To connect a downstream user cluster while Kubernetes Clusters Manager fails.

- To reduce latency in the case that the Kubernetes Clusters Manager server and downstream cluster are separated by a long distance.

Like the authorized cluster endpoint, the kube-API-auth authentication service is also only available for Kubernetes Clusters Manager-launched Kubernetes clusters.

As shown in Figure 5-15, the Kubernetes Clusters Manager server is located in Hong Kong, and User Cluster B is located in Tokyo. A user, Dux, also lives in Tokyo. Dux can manipulate resources in User Cluster B by using the Kubernetes Clusters Manager UI, but her requests will have to be sent from Tokyo to the Kubernetes Clusters Manager server in Hong Kong, then be proxied back to Tokyo, where the downstream user cluster is. The geographical distance may cause significant latency; which Bob can reduce by using the authorized cluster endpoint.

With this endpoint enabled for the downstream Kubernetes cluster, Kubernetes Clusters Manager generates an extra Kubernetes context in the kubeconfig file in order to connect directly to the cluster.

❺Local Kubernetes Cluster

In addition to the geo-distributed Kubernetes managed by the Kubernetes Cluster Manager, a single or multiple local Kubernetes Clusters will be created within the Distributed Cloud OneCenter location to serve OneCenter components.

5.4.3.4   Approaches for Provisioning Kubernetes Clusters

The approaches and tools that Kubernetes Clusters Manager uses to provision downstream user clusters depend on the type of cluster that is being provisioned.

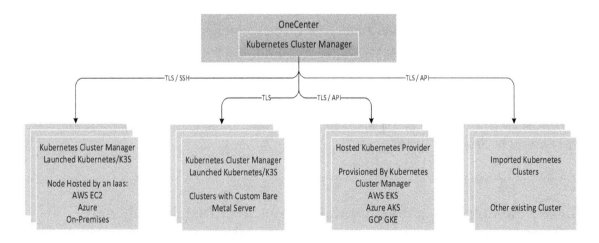

Figure 5-16 Approaches for Provisioning Kubernetes Clusters

3. Kubernetes Clusters Manager Launched Kubernetes/K3s for Nodes Hosted in an Infrastructure Provider

Kubernetes Clusters Manager can dynamically provision nodes in an Infrastructure provider such as Amazon EC2, Azure, OpenStack, or VMWare, then install Kubernetes clusters on them.

Kubernetes Clusters Manager can provision this type of cluster using a Docker machine. For detailed information on Docker-Machine, please refer to section [5.4.2 Manipulate Global Containers with Docker Machine].

4. Kubernetes Clusters Manager Launched Kubernetes/K3s for Custom Nodes

When setting up this type of Kubernetes cluster, Kubernetes Clusters Manager installs Kubernetes on existing nodes, which creates a custom cluster. This type of deployment can typically be applied in an on-premises infrastructure.

5. Hosted Kubernetes Providers

When setting up this type of cluster, Kubernetes cluster is installed by Kubernetes cluster providers such as Google Kubernetes Engine, Amazon Elastic Container Service for Kubernetes, or Azure Kubernetes Service.

6. Imported Kubernetes/K3s Clusters

In this type of cluster, Kubernetes Clusters Manager connects to a Kubernetes/K3s cluster that has already been set up. Therefore, Kubernetes Clusters Manager does not provision Kubernetes but only sets up the Kubernetes Clusters Manager agents to communicate with the existing Kubernetes cluster.

NOTE: *The Kubernetes cluster also refers to both the standard Kubernetes and the lightweight Kubernetes (K3S) in this section.*

5.4.3.5 Managing Lightweight Kubernetes over Distributed Edge

K3s is an official Cloud Native Computing Foundation (CNCF) project that provides a lightweight yet powerful certified Kubernetes distribution designed for production workloads across less power devices, remote edge, or edge end point. Managed by Kubernetes Clusters Manager (shown in Figure 5-17), it is easy and simple to install, configure and operate the K3s instance.

K3s is a simple yet full-function solution to run Kubernetes at the edge, especially when it is managed and controlled under Kubernetes Clusters Manager. With a simple deployment way, you can quickly launch thousands of clusters at the edge site, and users can manage the high volume of clusters with Kubernetes Clusters Manager Continuous Delivery, which gives users a controller that allows them to efficiently manage lightweight Kubernetes at the edge site.

K3 architecture is different from Kubernetes. Let's take a look at the architecture briefly. K3s cluster contains two kinds of processes: the server and the agent. In one process, you can run both the server and agent, and you can run them separately.

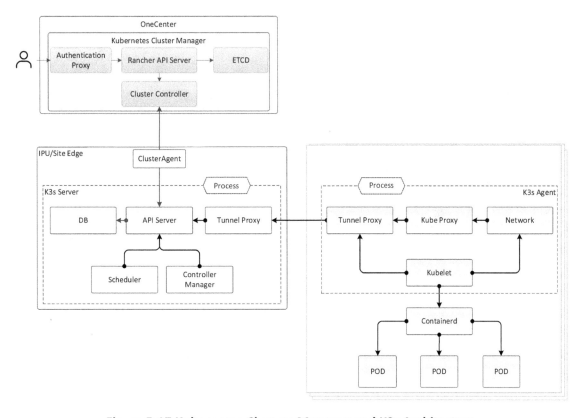

Figure 5-17 Kubernetes Clusters Manager and K3s Architecture

The K3s server process runs several components that contain:

- The main control plane components such as Kubernetes API, controller, and scheduler.
- Lightweight databases that are the default storage backend.

- Reverse tunnel proxy, which eliminates the need for bidirectional communication between server and agent, which means you don't have to punch holes in firewalls for servers to communicate with agents.

The K3s agent is responsible for running the kubelet and kube-proxy. Also including:

- Networking as an embedded process.

- Containerd as the container runtime.

- Internal load balancer that load-balances connections between all API servers in HA configurations.

- Network policy controller to enforce network policies.

5.5   Infrastructure Reuse - Integrating with vCenter

The Distributed Cloud is intended for companies willing to create a cloud environment on top of their VMware infrastructure without having to abandon their past investment in VMware and retool the entire stack. In these environments, OneCenter can seamlessly integrates with the existing vCenter cluster to leverage advanced features - such as vMotion, HA, or DRS scheduling - provided by the VMware vSphere product family. The Distributed Cloud provides a multi-tenant, cloud-like provisioning layer on top of vCenter, including features like VDC, Sites federation, or hybrid cloud computing connecting in-house vCenter infrastructure with public clouds. Resources like Virtual Machine, Virtual Machine templates, data stores, and networks can be easily imported from vCenter infrastructures to OneCenter.

5.5.1   High Level Reference Architecture

You can manage a distributed collection of vCenter instances across multiple sites and data centers with a single OneCenter instance. Seamlessly integrates with existing vCenter infrastructures to leverage advanced features provided by the VMware vSphere product family. In this way, it enables infrastructure provisioning, elasticity, and multi-tenancy features on top of vCenter and is very easy to install, upgrade, and maintain with a convenient OneUI.

The simplest way is taken: one vCenter cluster (with all its ESXi hosts) will be represented as one Distributed Cloud host in the OneCenter view. In this method, the host should be grouped in vCenter clusters. This book will omit how to import individual ESX Hosts from vCenter vSphere cluster to the Distributed Cloud.

The VMware vCenter drivers of Distributed Cloud enable OneCenter to access single or multiple vCenter servers, which then manage one or more ESXi clusters. Each ESXi cluster is shown in OneCenter as a logical aggregated hypervisor. Note that OneCenter scheduling decisions are made at the ESXi cluster level. vCenter then uses the DRS component to select an ESXi host and Datastore to deploy the Virtual Machine.

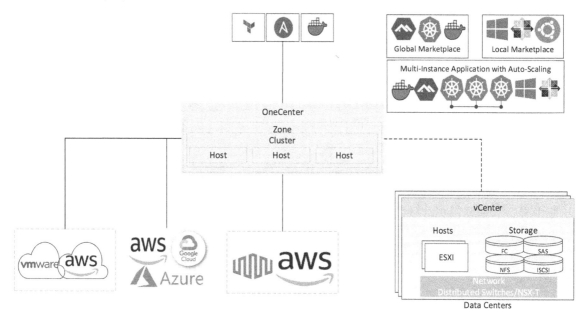

Figure 5-18 Architecture of Integrating vCenter with ESXI Infrastructure

5.5.2   Multi-Site Deployments

Leveraging the vCenter RESTful API, OneCenter interacts with the vCenter instances to communicate remotely. A single OneZone instance can remotely orchestrate several vCenter instances located in different separate sites. To achieve good performance and reliable management, a low latency path is necessary from the OneZone to the separate remote vCenter instances. (see Figure 5-19).

There are some reasons why a zone federation configuration is necessary based on the vCenter infrastructures. For example, administration domains need to be isolated, the data center contains a huge scale of servers, workload, and services, or the interconnection between data centers does not allow a single controlling entity. Each OneZone instance of the federation is called a Zone, one of them configured as master and the others as secondaries. A Zone federation is a tightly coupled integration, with all the instances sharing the same user accounts, groups, and permission configurations by default (see Figure 5-20).

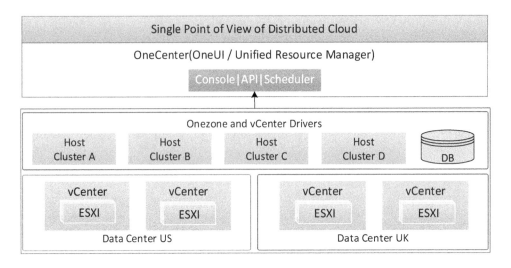

Figure 5-19 Single OneZone Instance Multi-Datacenter Deployment

The federation allows end-users to consume resources allocated by the federation administrators regardless of their geographic location. The integration is seamless, and the zone switch is smoothy, meaning that a user logged into the GUI of a zone will not have to log out and enter the address of another zone. OneUI allows users to change the active zone at any time, and it will automatically redirect the requests to the expected OneZone instance.

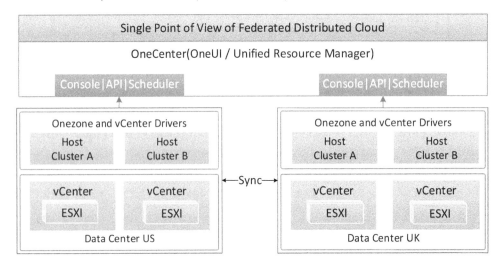

Figure 5-20 Multi-datacenter Deployment Based on Two OneZone Instances

Chapter 6   The Distributed Cloud Site Architecture

This book proposes a new concept, Distributed Cloud Site. A Distributed Cloud Site is a cloud workload location. Those locations are dispersed geo-distributed worldwide (including public cloud, data center, branch, campus, SoHo,3GPP NPN edge site,3GPP PNI-MEC edge site, non-3GPP edge site, or even colocation). The Distributed Cloud consists of OneCenter, a marketplace, and sites. OneCenter is the unique instance that plays a central controller role in taking responsibility for networking, storage, and computing of all sites' infrastructure control and management. The sites are operated by OneZone instances in a multi-layer model.

This Chapter provides some critical terminology and concepts associated with the Distributed Cloud site and clarifies those easily confused concepts. Besides mainly depicting the site taxonomy, the most important thing is this Chapter offers an elaborate site architecture design of computing, networking, and global storage systems in the Distributed Cloud.

This Chapter gives the design of Max and Lite-type sites. Pro and Mini sites be omitted because most contents of the Max site design have covered that of the Pro and Mini site. Besides, the Cloud site is skipped in this Chapter. About the design of a cloud site, please refer to section [8.2 Hybrid Multi-Cloud Design].

6.1   Key Terminology and Concepts

For easy understanding and neutrality, this reference architecture of Distributed Cloud is based on some open-source software that brings some concepts and terms that may be similar or confused with those of the Distributed Cloud. Now, let us clarify and differentiate them.

SD-WAN Site and Distributed Cloud Site

SD-WAN Site means an end and exit point of WAN / Internet, while the Distributed Cloud Site refer to the geo-distributed physical location.

In Figure 3-25 in section [3.2.6.3 External WAN Edge Router – Single Zone with Multiple Data Centers], a zone contains multiple data centers, and each data center has one Distributed Cloud site hosting one VXLAN fabric. These multiple data centers (sites) share a single WAN Edge Router exit point. In this case, one SD-WAN Site with Site ID is mapped to multiple Distributed Cloud Sites. In all other cases, shown as ❶ in Figure 6-2, the SD-WAN Site with its Site ID and Distributed Cloud Site with its Site ID have a one-on-one relationship. typically, when the Distributed Cloud sites are Max type, shown as ❶ in Figure 6-2, and Figure 3-24 in section [3.2.6.2 External WAN Edge Router - Single Zonegroup with Multiple Zones], the sites can connect to the external/WAN through a separate WAN Edge Router although those Distributed Cloud sites (zones) belong to a single Zonegroup.

The Site concept and Site ID design architecture of SD-WAN have been described in section [3.4 Software-Defined WAN - SD-WAN] and section [6.2 Sites Taxonomy].

Ceph Site, Zone, Cluster and Zonegroup

In the Ceph Multi-site architecture, each Ceph Zonegroup contains one or more Ceph Zone(s), which are backed by its own Ceph Storage Clusters that are in geographically separate Site(s). In most cases, the Ceph Cluster, Ceph Zone and Ceph Site have the one-to-one relationship.

VXLAN Data Center, Site and Fabric

In Distributed Cloud, it is assumed that each data center with one VXLAN Fabric. Because a zone can contain single or multiple data center, that means a zone can contain one or several VXLAN fabrics. The EVPN Multi-Site architecture allows you to interconnect data center Fabric(s) built on VXLAN EVPN technology.

Distributed Cloud Infrastructure: Site, Zonegroup, Zone, Cluster, Host and Data Center

Like the AWS cloud region and available zone, the infrastructure of the Distributed Cloud has the concept of Zonegroup. Typically, each Zonegroup is consists of single or multiple Zone(s). Note that one Zone doesn't mean only one Data Center. That is each Zone can contain a single or multiple Data Center(s), depending on the scale of the Zone (depicted in Figure 6-2). The interconnection between the Zone can be a low latency resilient fiber link, third-party direct connection, WAN connection, or even a public internet link (this is different from the interconnection between of availability zone in AWS region, which requires high speed fiber connection). The Distributed Cloud Cluster, Public Cloud Site and Site ID are present in the next section [6.2 Site Taxonomy].

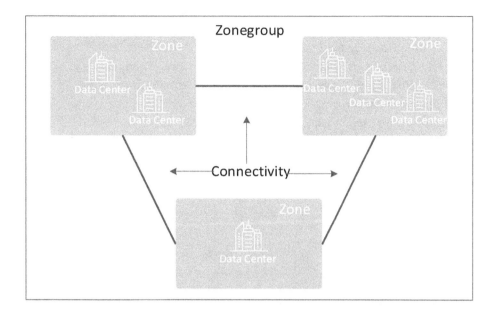

Figure 6-1 The Distributed Cloud Zonegroup Deployment

Distributed Cloud Infrastructure: Physical Machine/Server, Bare Metal, Node and Host

In most cases of the Distributed Cloud, the Physical Machine and Physical Server usually have the same means and are exchangeable. Bare Metal is a node without any hypervisor and containerization virtualization software. A Node contains a CPU host and (or) IPU host, and the Node can be bare Metal or hypervisor. A Host can be a cloud / CPU host that runs a standard operation system with the cloud workload or an IPU host that runs a particular operation system for the acceleration and burden offloading. Usually, the CPU host and IPU host cooperate to form a flexible, powerful, and versatile cloud infrastructure for the Distributed Cloud.

6.2   Sites Taxonomy

In the Distributed Cloud, at the top-level view and from the distribution attribute, it is divided into OneCenter and Sites. In OneCenter, there are one Unified Resource Manager and at least one OneZone instance. OneCenter manages multiple zones by respective OneZone instance, and the sites can be Lite, Mini, Pro, and Max site according to the scale and role of the location.

Later of this section will describe several typical site architecture designs. In the Distributed Cloud, except for the on-premises site, the sites located in the public cloud are often used.

NOTE: *Any kind of site belongs to a particular OneZone instance. In the case of Pro, Mini, or Lite type, it is managed by the OneZone instance residing in the OneCenter location remotely, while if a site is Max site, it should be managed by a local OneZone instance located within the site, in this case, one Max site can be federated with others. About how to federate the different zones within a Zonegroup, you can refer to later of this section and section [5.5.2 Multi-Site Deployments & 6.2 Sites Taxonomy].*

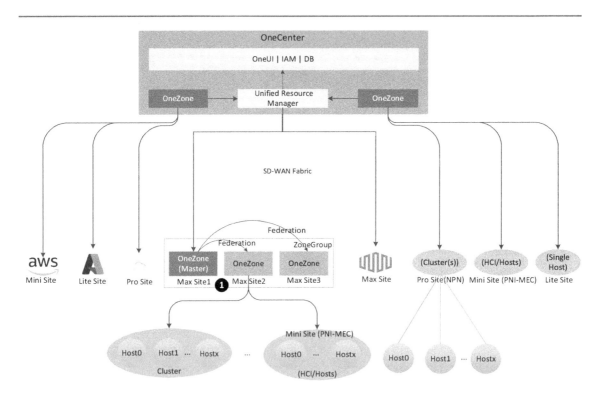

Figure 6-2 Site Taxonomy

The Distributed Cloud Site Category: Basing on the Scale or Size

From above Figure 6-2, we can see that Distributed Cloud sites can be cataloged into the following several types:

1. Lite Site

A Lite type of site with only one single host, this type of site can be a 3GPP and non-3GPP edge computing site. Typically, this type of site may bring a smartNIC or IPU device for a

WAN connection. The Lite site CPU host operates operation system provisioning, host network offloading, host storage offloading, etc. The user case of this type of site can be a LoRa WAN gateway, LoRa WAN network server,3GPP MEC host (SNPN or PNI-MEC), and so on. Section 6.5 (Lite Site) describes some more on Lite Site. Note that this type of site can not provide host-level high availability capacities.

2. Mini Site

A Mini type of site is typically made up of two to four nodes for minimal high availability. The type of site typically presents as an HCI system with minimal converged computing, storage, and networking infrastructure.

3. Pro Site

A Pro site can contain single or multiple clusters. A campus hub, enterprise headquarter, branch, a 3GPP SNPN edge location or a single data center can host a Pro site. The Pro site workload hosts in the clusters are controlled by the OneZone instance located in the separate remote OneCenter location.

4. Max Site

If a site is designed for an available zone, it should be a Max-type site. Like the Proc site, the Max site contains single or multiple clusters. As to architecture aspects, the main difference between the Max site and Pro site is the location of the OneZone instance: in the Max site, the OneZone instance is collocated with workload clusters at the site location, while in the Pro site, the workload clusters at the site location are managed by the separate remote OneZone instance in the OneCenter location.

Distributed Cloud Site Category: Basing on the Deployment Location

1. Public Cloud Site

Public Cloud Site is a logical term that refers to the Distributed Cloud sites previous presented residing in the public cloud provider, based on the network connection approach and the infrastructure scaling needed from the cloud. The site on the public cloud can also be a Lite, Mini, Pro, or Max Site, according to the site size and role. For example, the organization can design a Mini site or Lite site in AWS with IGW connection among OneCenter and other sites, while the direct connect and SD-WAN edge router can be applied for the interconnection across the Max site, Pro site, OneCenter, and remote other public cloud sites.

When a site is offered from the public cloud provider, you can deploy any size of site in it. Note that the network architecture may greatly vary from the certain site type to be built.

Examples of public cloud providers with bare metal offerings include classic public cloud providers like famous AWS, Google Cloud Engine, and Azure Cloud, as well as smaller infrastructure providers like Equinix, Linode, and vultr and on son.

For the Distributed Cloud, this type of site is able to offer a common site architecture across different public cloud providers. They can typically offer a latency for services above 20 ms.

2. Data Center Site

This type of site refers to on-premises datacenter-like providers such as an enterprise data center, branch, campus, or even a colocation location with a bare-metal server offering. They can also provide the bare metal offering with similar service latency above 20 ms like the above public cloud case.

3. Edge Site

This type of site has greater proximity to the end-user (compared with a public cloud) and enables a lower latency for the edge application, in the order of 1-5 ms. The typical case for this type of site can be 3GPP NPN and the public cloud substation location.

A typical example is the 3GPP NPN edge described in section [9.3.2   Non-Public Network (NPN)], which provides specific infrastructure deployments that embed the Distributed Cloud computing, networking, and storage services right within the data centers at the edge of the growing 5G network of carrier operator. it can provide renders the closest computation to the end-users and can deliver latencies.

4. Access Site

This type of site is able to house computing resources. the scenario can be the non-3GPP IoT edge, such as Wi-Fi 6, LoRa WAN, and so on, it also renders the closest computation to the end-user and can deliver latencies in the order of about 2ms.

Global ID and Index Design

The node index is responsible for presenting the physical machine sequence, using the node flag to indicate the server purpose, such as physical network devices like SONIC enabled switch, network gateway node, site edge node, Lite type site node, or the cloud workload node, etc. The Host index indicates the host type, such as the cloud workload host or IPU host with ARM for acceleration/burden-offloading.

The global flag indicates the zone features and some common purposes. From Figure 6-3, we can calculate the rest Distributed Cloud Infrastructure Identity (including Site ID, Cluster ID, and Zone ID) and deduce the site type from Host ID by pre-definition of the flag of or index of each field.

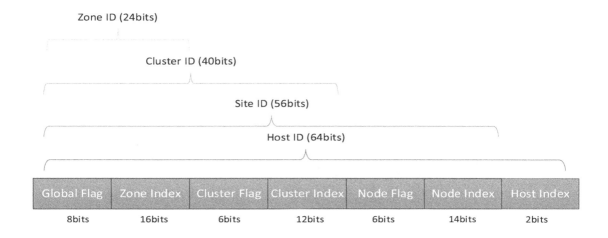

Figure 6-3 Global ID and Index Desgin

Distributed Cloud Zone Federation

If administration domains need to be isolated, or the interconnection between data centers does not allow a single controlling entity, Zone can be configured in a federation. Each OneZone instance of the federation is called a Zone, one of them configured as master and the others as secondary. A Zone federation is a tightly coupled integration, with all the instances sharing the same user accounts, groups, and permission configurations.

The integration is seamless, meaning that a user logged into the GUI of a Zone will not have to log out and enter the address of another Zone. OneCenter portal allows users to change the active Zone at any time, and it will automatically redirect the requests to the right OneZone.

6.3   Site Edge

The physically independent site edge node(s) exists in the Max, Pro, or Mini type of site in the on-premises case. In the Lite site, the site edge is implemented in the IPU host. Only a single node can be deployed in the site edge location by default. In some special conditions, the site edge can also be scalable and consist of more than one physical server depending on the resource's requirement, for example, when a data gateway is deployed in the site edge since the data gateway may consume many more resources. In any case, all control plane functions, and software must be deployed in a master node representing the identity of the site location.

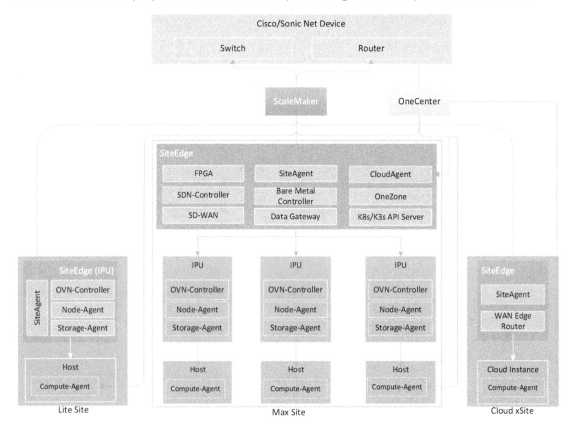

Figure 6-4 Monitoring the Multiple Sites Resources

In the Lite site case, although it isn't configured with a physical site edge node, the IPU host implements the site edge role as that is implemented in the Max, Pro, or Mini sites. In the public cloud site case, the transit VPC with WAN-Edge Router plays the site edge role.

In the site edge, the SiteAgent plays a site proxy role, talking with components ScaleMaker and OneCenter, and the SD-WAN is responsible for the WAN secure connection from the site to other sites, WAN, internet, ScaleMaker, and OneCenter. SDN-Controllers are in charge of the underlay and overlay network inside the site. The Bare Metal Controller and OneZone instance play the same roles as in the OneCenter for the local site's physical servers and virtual machines. The Kubernetes and K3s-related components play a proxy role for the Kubernetes cluster or K3s Cluster to communicate with the Kubernetes Cluster Manager in the OneCenter.

The Node-Agent collects the physical level status and metrics of the node (including the IPU host and cloud host) to report to the ScaleMaker, while the Compute-Agent does that at the hypervisor level. The storage agent relays the command from the storage controller to operate the storage device through the NVMe-oF Target, NVMe-oF Initiator RDMA, etc. The OVN-Controller is the OVN agent that resides in each node and interacts with Open vSwitch and hypervisors for any information or update needed for the OVN- Southbound Data Base.

6.4   Max Site

This Max-type site will be fully described in the section because the Max-type site contains comprehensive components and functions of a Distributed Cloud site, which covers all aspects of a site. Meanwhile, it has a special characteristic in that it deploys the OneZone instance at the site edge, this instance is collocated along the workload cluster within the site location.

6.4.1   Site Model - Networking

The SD-WAN, EVPN VXLAN, and OVN can be integrated into a comprehensive solution to implement the complete enterprise networking environment for the Distributed Cloud.

The OVN is good at E/W traffic between the computing node, typically through the Geneve tunnel. EVPN VXLAN benefits the Multitenant and Layer 2 and Layer extension features to offer global network solutions for end-to-end communication and user mobility. The SD-WAN fully integrates routing, security, centralized policy, and orchestration into large-scale networks. It is also multitenant, cloud-delivered, highly automated, secure, scalable, and application-aware with rich analytics.

Within the Max type site, you can deploy multiple SDN-Controllers that can be responsible for the physical network device, such as the SONIC switch and OVN overlay network fabrics (for example, in Figure 6-5, the SDN-Controller 0 is serving for spine and leaf nodes for the underlay EVPN VXLAN fabric, the SDN-Controller 1 is in charge of overlay OVN network control).

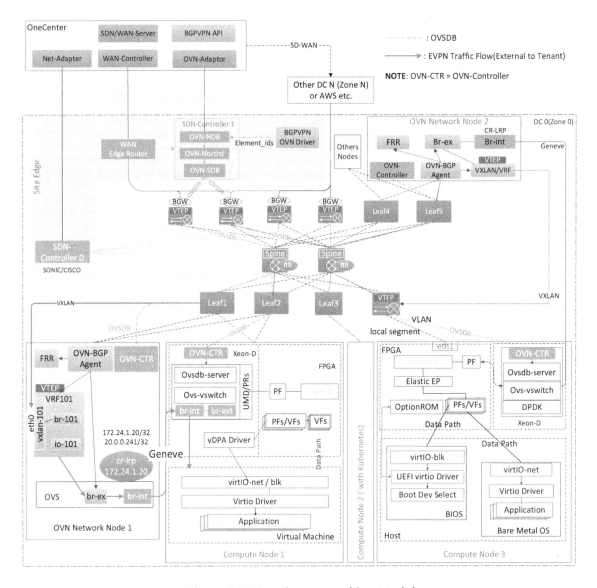

Figure 6-5 Max Site Networking Model

6.4.1.1 Networking Offloading

With the rapid development of cloud computing technology and the enrichment of enterprise services, the bandwidth and low latency requirements of virtualized networks continue to increase, and offloading virtualized networks to hardware has become essential and mandatory in the Distributed Cloud.

6.4.1.1.1 Hardware Offload for Network Interfaces

Mainstream virtual network interfaces mostly use two I/O virtualization technologies, virtio and Single Root I/O Virtualization (SR-IOV). SR-IOV is an I/O virtualization solution based on network hardware. It realizes the sharing and exclusive resource of physical network cards by dividing physical resources and virtualizes a single PCIe device into multiple virtual PCIe devices directly to the container of the physical machine, in the application of the machine or the virtual machine managed by the hypervisor, the kernel protocol stack is bypassed thus to obtain extremely high performance. However, the pure SR-IOV solution does not support live migration, and the virtual machine needs to be specifically adapted to the network card driver manufacturer. Virtio is an I/O paravirtualization technology that adopts a front-end and backend separation architecture. A general virtio driver is installed in the application, container, or virtual machine OS to interact with the virtio backend. With the continuous rise of performance requirements, the virtio backend has experienced the evolution of virtio-net, vhost-net to vhost-user, and virtio full offload, but there are always software processing network I/O bottlenecks, or the virtual machine live migration function can not be supported. Virtio technology is more flexible than SR-IOV due to the interaction between the control plane and QEMU. Uses Virtio driver in the VM, making the VMs hardware independent and enabling support of a broad array of guest operating systems and live VM migration. From the perspective of ensuring the flexibility of computing resources and reducing the complexity of business migration to the cloud, virtio technology is more in line with the requirements of the cloud computing environment.

As the virtual switching network sinks to the IPU hardware for processing, the implementation of the virtio backend also sinks from the user mode vhost-user mode to the IPU hardware. virtio Data Path Acceleration (vDPA) is an open-source implementation framework for the hardware offloaded virtio backend. Its data plane is directly connected to the virtual machine like SR-IOV. The control plane interacts with QEMU through the vhost-user protocol to implement the live migration function of the virtual machine. This solution takes both high performance and flexibility into account and has become a standard solution for network interface hardware offloading. From the perspective of implementation, vDPA has a DPDK-based user mode framework and a Linux kernel-based kernel mode framework. The Max type site networking architecture design is shown in Figure 6-5.

6.4.1.1.2 Hardware Offload for Virtual Switched Networks

OVN and OVS are the implements of the network in the Distributed Cloud known as SDN; the virtual switch (vSwitch) is an important part of the overlay network. Among the current implementations of various vSwitches, OVS is the most widely used virtual switching software in the industry. The OVS architecture is divided into the control plane and the data plane. The original OVS data plane data processing path needs to go through the kernel protocol stack, so emerge a technical solution for DPDK data forwarding plane user mode acceleration. OVS-DPDK processing can bypass the kernel protocol stack and relying on the way of binding CPU core polling to complete the forwarding processing action based on the flow table match-action, the performance has been greatly improved. However, as the bandwidth is up, more CPU resources need to be reserved to ensure forwarding performance. Therefore, it has become a trend and necessity to offload vSwitch, even the both OVN-Controller and OVS to the IPU host.

The control plane software of the virtual switch is deployed on the CPU core of the IPU card, and the forwarding data plane is offloaded to the hardware acceleration engine on the IPU. The DPDK standard rte_flow method is used to interact between the control plane and the traffic forwarding plane to achieve full offloading of the virtual switch and release the CPU resource overhead of network forwarding on the cloud host side. Unloading the virtual switch is a necessary pre-condition for unloading the virtio backend. After the data packets received by the IPU complete vSwitch forwarding processing on the IPU card, they are passed to the virtual machine or the standard virtio-net front end inside the bare metal through the virtio-net backend implemented by the vDPA framework. Data is transferred without CPU intervention, achieving higher network forwarding performance.

6.4.1.1.3 SDN-Controller

In this network model, the SDN-Server still resides in the OneCenter, whereas the SDN Controller is located in the site edge to serve the whole internal site scope (including the cluster hosts and site edge node itself). In this network architecture, all OVS and OVN-controller are offloaded into the IPU device, and the CPU host does not process the OVS related workload.

6.4.1.2 VXLAN Networking with EVPN

In Distributed Cloud, there are several critical networking requirements, for example end-to-end multitenant, Interconnect for multiple sites, Internet and WAN Connectivity among OneCenter and sites, etc. Distributed Cloud leverages VXLAN, OVN and along with eBGP technologies to implement the internal-site and inter-site networking.

6.4.1.3 OVN Networking with EVPN

The main purpose of adding OVN BGP Agent and EVPN Driver is to be able to provide multitenancy aspects by using BGP in conjunction with EVPN and VXLAN. It allows tenants to have connectivity between Virtual Machine hosts running in different edges, data centers, or clouds, without worry about overlapping subnet Classless Inter-Domain Routing (CIDR) among tenants.

6.4.1.3.1 EVPN with OVN BGP Agent

In order to add support for EVPN, the OVN-BGP Agent functionality must be extended with a different "mode" for EVPN. For the BGP mode, the VMs on provider networks or with Floating IPs were exposed directly on the OVN chassis where the VM was allocated. Therefore, there was a need for running the agent in all the chassis. However, the EVPN mode targets to expose the VMs on tenant networks (on their respective EVPN/VXLAN). Given that in OVN networking, the N/S traffic to the tenant VMs without Floating IPs needs to go through the networking chassis (the ones hosting the Router Gateway Ports, i.e., the cr-LRP OVN ports). Therefore, there is no need to deploy the BGP Agent in all of the nodes. Only the nodes that are able to host router gateway ports (cr-LRPs), i.e., the ones with the enable-chassis-gw tagged. Consequently, the VM IPs will be advertised through BGP/EVPN in one of those nodes. From those, it will follow the normal path to the compute node where the VM is running - the Geneve tunnel.

6.4.1.3.2 BGP Agent with EVPN mode

In the BGP mode, the agent exposed the IP addresses by adding the VM host IP to a dummy interface associated with a VRF instance. The VRF device, where the dummy interface is linked to, is connected to nothing and was only used for exposing routes through BGP. By contrast, with the EVPN mode, the VRF is used for the traffic associated with that tenant and for the EVPN. Note that the VRFs are associated with Router Gateway Ports, not cloud tenants. This means that if a tenant has several virtual routers connected to the provider network, it will have a different VRF associated with each one of them.

To configure the EVPN, the agent creates the following related elements:

> **VRF device**, using the VNI number for the table number associated to it, as well as for the name suffix: vrf-101 for vni 101.

> **VXLAN device**, using the VNI number as the VXLAN ID, in the name suffix: vxlan-101.

> **Bridge device**, where the VXLAN device will be connected, and belonging to the previously created VRF; also using the VNI number as name suffix: br-101.

> **Dummy device**, virtual machine IPs will be created in this device to be exposed through BGP and be associated to the previously created VRF with the VNI number as name suffix: lo-101.

In this way, the BGP Agent is able to expose/withdraw virtual machine IPs through BGP EVPN by adding/deleting them from the dummy device. However, the BGP Agent also needs to ensure the Free Range Routing (FRR) configuration is correct to be able to expose those IPs to remote peers.

At last, the BGP Agent needs to ensure the traffic arriving at the node can be redirected from the VRF to the OVN overlay and vice versa. To do that, the agent also performs the actions:

- Add a VRF device to the OVS provider bridge (use 'br-ex' in this case, but it can be an arbitrary name).

- Add routes into the VRF associated routing table (101 in this example) for both the cr-LRP IP (router gateway port IP) and the subnet CIDR so that the traffic is redirected to the OVS provider bridge (use 'br-ex' in this case, but it can be arbitrary name).

- Ensure not exist route on the VRF table for the VM IPs pointing to the dummy device.

- Add an OVS flow into the OVS provider bridge to redirect the traffic back to the proper VRF instance, based on the subnet CIDR and the router gateway port MAC address.

6.4.1.3.3 EVPN Routing

Figure 6-5 shows how the traffic flow goes to/from the VM when exposed through BGP EVPN, and this traffic is the N/S traffic flow through the VRF to the VM, including information regarding the OVS flows on the provider bridge (br-ex), and the routes on the VRF routing table.

The EVPN driver response for the networking configuration ensures that VMs on tenant networks can be reached through BGP EVPN (N/S traffic). To achieve this, it needs to ensure:

- VM IPs can be advertised in a node where the traffic can be injected into OVN overlay, in this case, the node where the router gateway port is scheduled.

- Once the traffic arrives at the specific node, the traffic is redirected to the OVN overlay.

The OVN BGP Agent depends on kernel networking capabilities (IP rules and IP routes) to redirect traffic in/out of the Distributed Cloud OVN Overlay. Therefore, DPDK and SR-IOV, bypassing the kernel space, are not supported. About How to make the OVN BGP Agent ready for Hardware Offloading (HWOL) and OVS-DPDK will be introduced in other book.

As shown in OVN Network Node 1 and Compute Node 1 of Figure 6-5 in red solid line, The IPs of both the router gateway port (cr-lrp, 172.24.1.20) and the VM itself (20.0.0.241/32) get added to the same dummy device (lo-101) associated to the VRF (vrf-101) which was used for defining the BGPVPN (VNI 101). Co-located with the other devices created on the VRF (vxlan-101 and br-101), and with the FRR reconfiguration, ensure the IPs get exposed in the right EVPN. In this way, the traffic to reach the node with the cr-LRP will be redirected to the OVN Overlay. To achieve this, the VRF is added to the br-ex OVS provider bridge, and two routes are added to redirect the traffic going to the network (20.0.0.0/24) through the CR-LRP port to the br-ex Open vSwitch bridge. That will inject the traffic properly into the OVN overlay, which will redirect it through the Geneve tunnel (by the br-int OVS flows) to the compute node 1 in Figure 6-5 hosting the virtual machine.

The reply traffic from the virtual machine will come back through the same Geneve tunnel. However, an extra OVS flow needs to be added to br-ex to ensure the traffic is redirected back to the VRF (vrf-101) if the traffic is coming from the exposed network (20.0.0.0/24).

The rule matches the traffic coming from the cr-lrp port from br-int, with the MAC address of the cr-LRP port, i.e., the router gateway port and from the exposed network. If it matches, it changes the MAC to the one on br-ex device and redirects the traffic to the VRF device.

6.4.1.3.4 Event and Trigger

As for the BGP mode, the agent watches the OVN Southbound Database and triggers actions depending on the events detected. The BGP agent in EVPN mode watches the same type of events but with some caveats, such as not reacting to Floating IP (FIP) events.

6.4.1.3.5 BGPVPN API Integration

So far, we have learned how the BGP Agent works internally, the events it reacts to, and shown the network traffic flow process. Now, let's step into the API side: how users can expose their tenant networks and how the needed information is translated and injected into the OVN Southbound Database so that the BGP agent can detect and process it accordingly. For exposing tenant networks through BGP EVPN without overlapping CIDRs from other tenants, the BGPVPN API has:

- An admin API to define the BGPVPN properties, such as the VNI or the BGP AS to be used, and to associate it to a given tenant.
- A tenant API to allow users to associate the BGPVPN to a router or to a network.

This offers an API that allows users to expose their tenant networks and admins to provide the needed EVPN/VNI information. Then, we need to enhance OVN Driver support so that the provided information is stored on the OVN Southbound Database and consumed by the driver (when the watcher detects it).

As regards to the integration architecture, the BGPVPN includes three main components:

BGPVPN API is the component that enables the association of Route Type (RT)/VNIs to tenant networks/routers. It creates a couple of extra databases on the SDN-Server to keep the information. This is the component that the user can leverage, restricting some of the APIs.

BGPVPN OVN Driver is the component in charge of triggering the extra actions to notify the backend driver about the changes needed. In this case, it is a driver that just integrates with the OVN Northbound Database to ensure the information gets propagated to the corresponding OVN resource in the OVN Southbound Database (by adding the information into the external_ids field).

OVN BGP Agent runs on the network or compute nodes and is in charge of configuring the networking layer according to requirements (e.g., RPC handling, ovs-flows, etc.). In this case, the OVN BGP Agent continues to consume information from the OVN Southbound Database (reading the extra information at external_ids) and adds the needed kernel routing and FRR configuration, as well as OVS flows to steer the traffic to/from OVN overlay network.

The only need is for a BGPVPN OVN Driver that reacts to the BGPVPN API calls and adds/removes the BGPEVPN information into/from the OVN Databases so that the OVN BGP agent can consume it. The OVN Adapter (OVN Adapter is described in Figure 7-6 in section [7.3.3 Networking]) already copies the external_ids information of the ports from the Logical_Switch_Port table at the OVN Southbound DB into the Port_Binding table at the OVN Southbound DB, which is what OVN BGP agent consumes. Thus, the new OVN service plugin driver for BGPVPN only needs to annotate the relevant ports at the Logical_Switch_Port table with the required EVPN information (BGP AS number and VNI number) on the external_ids field. That gets translated into the OVN Southern bond DB at the Port_Binding external_ids field. The OVN BGP Agent reacts to it by configuring the extra OVS flows at the provider bridge, creating the needed devices (VXLAN, Bridges, VRFs, Routes), and reconfiguring FRR.

About the API actions, when the tenant associates the BGPVPN to a network, there are the following two scenarios:

1. In the specific network case, the BGPVPN OVN Driver annotates that information into External_ids field of the Network router interface port on the Logical_Switch_Port table. The patch port is associated with the LRP port.

2. In the router where the network is connected case, the BGPVPN OVN driver annotates that information into External_ids field of the Router Gateway Port on the Logical_Switch_Port table. The patch port is associated with the cr-LRP or LRP port.

6.4.2 Site Model - Computing

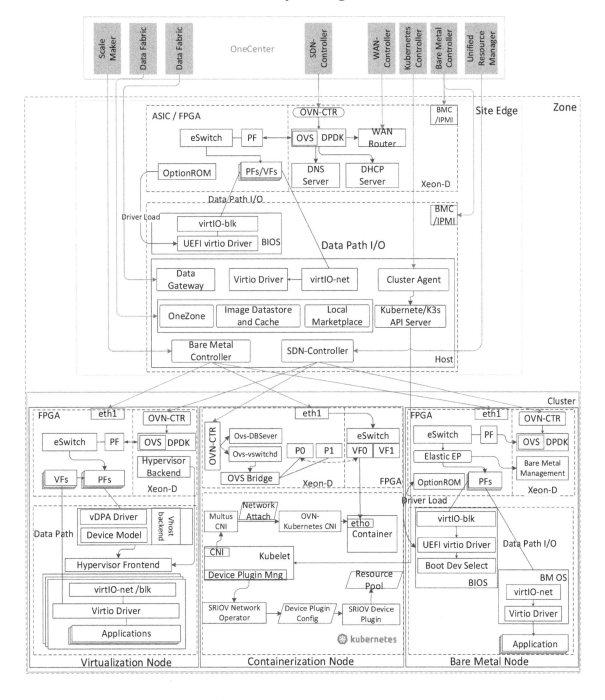

Figure 6-6 Max Site Computing Model

A Max site consists of a OneCenter and OneZone, which contain site edge, and single or multiple clusters offer comprehensive computing capacities. As shown in the Figure 6-6, for illustration convenience, it is assumed that the cluster hosts several types of workloads: bare metal, hypervisor virtualization, and containerization. You can deploy only one kind of workload on a specially dedicated cluster. Actually, that is the best optimal for operation convenience.

6.4.2.1 Site Edge

In Max site case, may exist one or more physical machine farms of cluster worker nodes, the nodes of the physical server farm also with IPU card device which need be provisioned through PXE/iPXE or UEFI HTTP Boot, in this case, the bare metal controller instance should be located within the site network scope to provide mandatory services such as DHCP and DNS Server to serve the physical server provisioning process.

As shown in Figure 6-6, bare metal controllers, SDN-Controllers, OneZone instance, Kubernetes agents/controllers, OVN-Controller, and WAN Edge Routers are deployed in the site edge playing a control plane role in serving the cluster workload of networking, storage, and computing.

6.4.2.2 Physical Server Deployment

In a Max or Pro-type site, the site edge can be a bare metal node that can be provisioned by the bare metal controller instance in the OneCenter through the BMC/IPMI interface located in the site edge. After provision and the system is set up in the site edge, another bare metal controller instance will be set up in the site edge, and then the site physical server can be provisioned by the site resident bare metal controller instance.

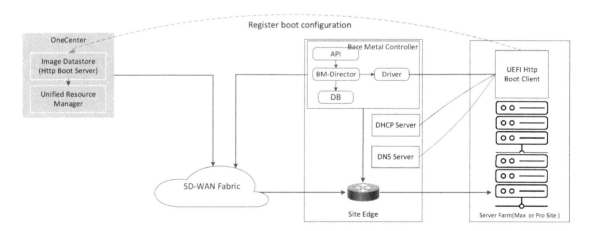

Figure 6-7 HTTP Boot Network Topology Concept - Max and Pro Site Environment

A typical network configuration that supports UEFI HTTP Boot may involve a single or multiple UEFI client and several server systems. Figure 6-7 shows a typical HTTP Boot network topology for a Max and Pro Site environment.

UEFI HTTP Boot Client first initiates the communication between the client and different kinds of server systems.

DHCP Server with HTTPBoot Extension Service Discovery. Besides the standard host configuration information such as address, subnet segment, gateway address, name-server address, etc., the DHCP server with the extensions can also provide the discovery of URI locations for boot resources (images) on the HTTP server.

HTTP Server can be located either inside the site edge of the corporate environment or OneCenter or on an Internet location, etc. The boot resource itself is deployed on the HTTP server. For example, "http://onedux.com/boot/Distributed Cloud-boot.efi" is used as the boot resource. Such an application is also called NBP. NBPs are used to set up the target client system, which may include inspecting the target, loading configuration, installation of an operating system, or running a service OS for maintenance and recovery tasks and more.

DNS Server is optional and provides standard domain name resolution service.

6.4.2.3 Bare Metal Deployment Process

The following is a possible process to install an operation system on a physical machine.

Port Planning

The server and IPU each have a Baseboard Management Controller (BMC) out-of-band management interface, which is an electrical port connected to a twisted pair line and connected to a Gigabit network switch and assigned a management IP.

Optical Port P0 of the IPU - the system interface is a shared interface, connected to a fiber optic cable, a switch over 100G or 200G capacity, and can be assigned 1 or 2 IP addresses.

Optical Port P1 of the IPU - used for storage systems, connected to a fiber optic cable, a 100G /200G or above capacity switch, and can be assigned 1 IP address.

IPU Serial Port - for network card out-of-band management, externally connected twisted pair to the serial port server. No network IP address is assigned to it.

Information Registration

The metadata information of the physical server must be registered with the Unified Resources Manager; the work order system can pull that information from the Unified Resources Manager. The metadata information includes:

- System IP, MAC, Gateway, and Mask used for networking.

- Management IP, Gateway, and Mask used for BMC interface.

- Data IP, Gateway, MAC, and Mask used for storage interface.

- SmartNIC Management IP, MAC, Gateway, and Mask used for SOC management interface.

- SmartNIC Control IP used for SOC debug interface.

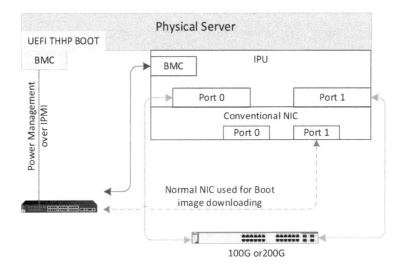

Figure 6-8 Bare Metal Port Planning

System Deployment

System deployment includes SOC System Installation and host system deployment, and the Host system deployment includes Compute, Networking, and Storage Installation.

Ending Work

Finally, Set UEFI boot mode, Disable PXE, and Disable local disk boot to close up.

6.4.2.4 Bare Metal Node

The Field Programmable Gate Arrays (FPGA) present different devices to the CPU host and the IPU host. The CPU host and the IPU host accelerate the hardware according to the seen devices. The IPU host runs basic software such as OVN-Controller, OVSDB-Server, OVS-vSwitchd, DPDK, and SDPK (Storage Performance Development Kit).

In terms of storage, through the SDPK software running in the IPU host, the virtio-blk device is provided to the CPU host, supporting multi-queue, multi-disk features, and a variety of remote storage backends (such as NVMe-over Fabric target, Ceph RBD target and iSCSI target).

You can use virtio-blk to start UEFI boot and UEFI HTTP boot, or you can use virtio-net to start PXE for booting. BIOS detects the Option ROM in FPGA, loads the specific program(virtio-blk driver) provided by the FPGA Option ROM, configures the network , pulls the image from the image repository (can be PXE server, HTTP server, remote storage backend) to executes PXE, UEFI or UEFI HTTP book booting, since FPGA presents standard virtio-blk device and virtio-net device to CPU host, CPU host side can use Linux kernel or the virtio driver in the DPDK/SDPK of user space without additional modification, so as to meet the needs of tenants to deploy any operating system on Bare Metal.

FPGA plays the role of connecting the CPU host and IPU host for storage. The read and write requests of the host are sent to FPGA, and then FPGA forwards these read and write requests to SDPK. After SDPK completes reading and writing to the backend storage, it returns the results in the same way.

In order to meet the dynamic expansion needs of Bare Metal users, the Elastic Endpoint (Elastic EP) technology in FPGA is used to dynamically increase or decrease the number of Physical Functions (PF) that the CPU host can use. When users need more data disks, they can increase the number of PF, otherwise delete PFs, and this can be achieved by using the management software of the IPU host and configuring the IP of Elastic EP.

NOTE: The CPU host refers to the main host with a general standard operation system that runs the cloud workload on a standard server, while the IPU host refers to the ARM or Xeon D CPU host that runs a network and storage acceleration system to the control software in the IPU/SmartNIC device.

6.4.2.5 Hypervisor Virtualization Node

FPGA presents to the CPU host the VF that supports the SR-IOV function, and the operator allocates the corresponding number of VF according to the actual needs (the number of virtual machines, etc.), The bare metal CPU host can see PF, while the hypervisor virtualization CPU host can see both VF and PF.

FPGA receives data on the function that the CPU host can see and sends it to the PF that the IPU host can see. The IPU host can see the standard virtio PF and support virtio driver that is in Linux kernel mode or user space's DPDK/SDPK.

The IPU host also sees the standard virtio PF, which supports the virtio driver in the Linux kernel space or DPDK/SDPK in the user space. SDPK gets the reads and writes requests from PF; the requests come from the CPU host, and then SDPK processes these requests. SDPK supports the use of Ceph, NVMe-oF, and iSCSI to process remote storage requests. SDPK brings performance, flexibility, and scalability, and it can also use SDPK to develop a custom third-party block device storage backend, SPDK backend for cloud remote booting.

According to the configuration of SDPK, when the virtual machine starts, it starts through the Operation System image matched by the host VF, and the Datapath is the same as the one mentioned above, so it will be omitted here.

As shown in Figure 6-6, both the OVS Datapath and control plane (OVN-Controller) can be offloaded to the IPU device. In this architecture, all OVS and OVN-controller are embedded in IPU, and the CPU host does not process any OVS related workload.

Virtio-net/blk FPGA support host VM live migration, converged virtio-net/blk vDPA driver combination be used for acceleration.

Computing System Offloading

The computing system here mainly refers to the hypervisor system of the KVM-QEMU architecture. The virtual layer provides a virtual machine environment for virtual network elements (VNF, virtual network function) or application virtual machines through the Hypervisor. Computing system offloading mainly offloads the Hypervisor to the IPU. The traditional Hypervisor needs to reserve CPU computing resources. By dividing the Hypervisor into a front-end and back-end architecture, the front-end runs on the CPU host side but only retains some necessary memory functions and logical CPU context synchronization functions on the CPU host side, and the back-end is offloaded to the IPU host. The remaining computing resources are reduced to close to "zero", and the impact of VM jitter caused by VM-Exit on system performance can be reduced greatly. As shown in the Hypervisor Virtualization Cloud Node section in Figure 6-6, the specific implementation method is as follows:

1. The front-end host mainly plays the essential functions of virtual machine management, interacts with the KVM module in the kernel, implements the vCPU and memory allocation functions of the virtual machine, and interacts with the backend device model to determine the virtual machine IO and memory mapping table.

2. The backend mainly plays the device model and life cycle management functions. The device model is based on QEMU's QOM mechanism to complete the initialization of the virtual device. At the same time, when the virtual machine is started or shut down, it interacts with the front end to complete the resource allocation and release of memory and vCPU, meanwhile interacting with Libvirt to complete the life cycle management function of the virtual machine

In order to achieve the full utilization of host CPU resources, the CPU host OS needs to reduce resource usage as much as possible. Since most IOs are directly connected to virtual machines by IPU, the CPU host OS basically does not need to manage IO hardware devices. At the same time, CPU host OS only needs to support the running of virtual machine vCPU threads and management service agents is enough, so you can consider not using the complex initialization system and package management tools based on the system and directly adopt a more concise initialization system to achieve close to "zero" CPU resource consumption of the CPU host.

6.4.2.6 Containerization Node

In this section, we will describe the work being done to integrate virtio/vDPA into Kubernetes as the primary interface for pods. The Hardware (HW) offloading solution includes the packet processing (for example, moving from OVS running in the kernel to an IPU hardware card) and the packet steering, where the virtio/vDPA comes into play.

6.4.2.6.1 Running Containerized Workloads with Virtio/vDPA

Virtio/vDPA and the Pod's Primary Interface

In the Distributed Cloud, Kubernetes is used as the default container orchestration platform, and here, we will also present the Kubernetes-based container network. We will start by describing how the bare metal node for the Lite site is configured in practice.

Worker Node and HW Offload

Figure 6-6 shows the target configuration on the node. Note that all the OVN and OVS components must be installed in the system before the IPU provisioning happens.

OVN-Controller and OVS

Both the OVN-Controller and OVS are introduced in section [3.3 Software-Defined Network - SDN]. In this architecture, OVS hardware offloading is enabled in order to offload the packet processing to the IPU.

HW Offload to IPU

Switchdev driver plays an important role when Linux Switch uses it as an abstraction layer. This abstraction layer provides open, standard Linux interfaces, thus ensuring that any Linux application can run on top of it compatible.

Once the Switchdev driver is loaded into the Linux kernel, each of the hardware switch's physical ports and virtual functions (VFs) are registered as a net_device within the Operation System kernel. With switchdev mode, a port representor (PR) is created for each of the VFs and added to the Open vSwitch bridge. In this case, Open vSwitch processes the packet, but this activity is CPU intensive, affecting system performance and preventing full utilization of the available bandwidth resources.

IPU Offloading

When the first packet is received by IPU (packet miss), it is still handled by the OVS module (slow path), but any subsequent packet will be matched by the offloaded flow installed directly in the IPU (fast path). This mechanism is implemented by OVS and Traffic Control Flower (TC flower). As a result, we can achieve significantly higher performance and avoid burdening the associated CPU load.

6.4.2.6.2 vDPA Workflow in Kubernetes

Now let's dive into the vDPA with Kubernetes workflow, introducing the overall architecture and components that take part in the implementation.

SR-IOV Network Operator

The Single Root I/O Virtualization (SR-IOV) Network Operator is a software extension to Kubernetes and follows the Kubernetes operator pattern. It's responsible for coordinating all the different components, as shown in the following Figure 6-9. You can think that Kubelet is the primary node agent of Kubernetes that runs one instance on each node of the cluster.

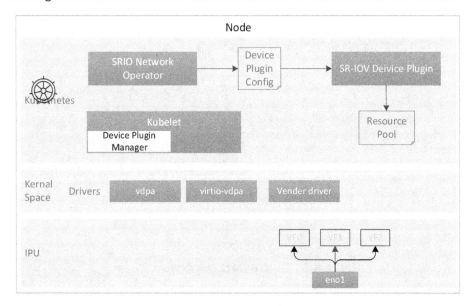

Figure 6-9 SR-IOV Network Operator

The cluster administrator applies the operator triggered by a policy and is mainly responsible for the IPU configuration:

1. The end-user creates a policy and submits it to the operator.

2. The IPU is configured in switchdev mode with HW offload enabled on the PF, Virtual VFs and port representors.

3. IPU is partitioned into SR-IOV VFs.

4. The vDPA drivers are installed in the Linux kernel (such as vdpa, virtio-vdpa).

5. The specific vendor drivers are installed in the Linux kernel and bound to the VFs.

6. The vDPA devices are created and bound to the virtio-vdpa driver.

7. A configuration manifest is generated for the SR-IOV-network-device-plugin to operate.

SR-IOV Network Device Plugin

The SR-IOV network device plugin is a Kubernetes device plugin that is responsible for discovering and advertising networking resources in the form of SR-IOV VFs. The following Figure 6-10 shows the connection between the SR-IOV device plugin and the SR-IOV operator:

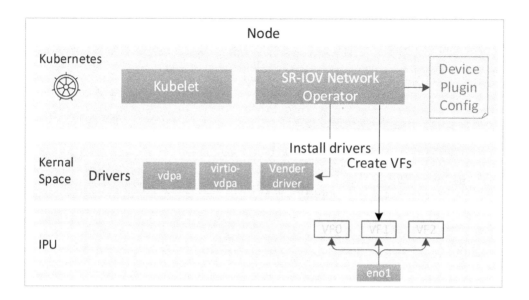

Figure 6-10 SR-IOV Network Device Plugin

The following is the flow of the SR-IOV device plugin performs in the context of virtio/vDPA:

1. Discover vDPA devices and create resource pools as per the configuration manifest coming from the operator. The configuration indicates how to arrange the SR-IOV resources into pools.

2. Register the vDPA devices to the device plugin manager of Kubelet in order to these resources can be allocated to pods.

3. The creation pod action will trigger Allocating vDPA devices. The pod manifest must have a reference to the resource pool for the injection of the requested network interface.

Kubernetes Pod with CNI and OVN-Kubernetes

CNI (Container Network Interface) includes a specification and libraries for writing plugins to configure network interfaces in containers, along with a number of supported plugins.

Multus CNI is a CNI plugin specially for Kubernetes that enables attaching multiple network interfaces to Kubernetes pods. By default, in Kubernetes, each pod only has one network interface besides the local loopback interface. With Multus CNI, you can create a multi-homed pod that has multiple network interfaces.

OVN-Kubernetes Container Network Interface (OVN-Kubernetes CNI) plugin is a network provider for the default cluster network. The Distributed Cloud uses a virtualized network for pod and service networks. OVN-Kubernetes is based on OVN and provides an overlay networking implementation. A cluster that uses the OVN-Kubernetes overlay network provider also runs OVS on each node. OVN configures OVS on each node to perform the declared network configuration.

The following describe the operation flow of "Containerization Node" in the above Figure 6-6.

1. The SR-IOV Operator configures the network interface controller (NIC), loads the drivers and generates a configuration manifest for the device plugin.

2. The SR-IOV Device Plugin creates the resource pools and allocates vDPA devices to pods when requested from Kubelet

3. The user creates a network attachment, a custom resource that brings together the resource pool and the designated CNI plugin for the pod network configuration.

4. The user creates the pod manifest and selects the resource pool for the network interface.

5. When the pod is created, Multus CNI takes in input the network attachment and delegates the OVN-Kubernetes-CNI for performing the pod network configuration.

6. OVN-Kubernetes moves the virtio/vDPA device into the container namespace (eth0 in the container of Containerization Node in Figure 6-6) and adds the corresponding port representor to the OVS bridge.

6.4.3   Site Model - Storage

The global cloud block device storage and unified object storage across the whole Distributed Cloud scope have been discussed in chapter [Chapter 4 The Distributed Cloud Storage System]. This section describes the integration of storage for QEMU/KVM (virtual machine), Docker/Kubernetes, bare metal, and the integrated object gateway for the OneStorage and Hadoop system. in addition, some technology and architecture of the storage acceleration and offloading site also be introduced.

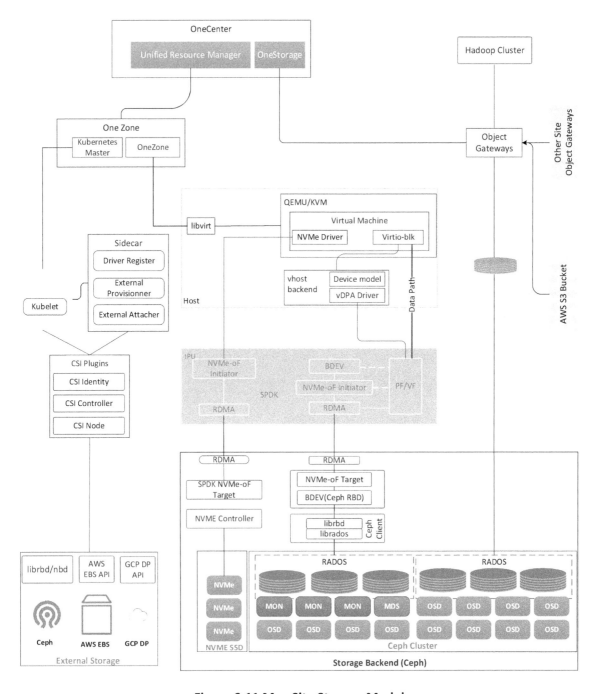

Figure 6-11 Max Site Storage Model

6.4.3.1 Virtual Machine Storage

Libvirt with Ceph RBD

The libvirt library creates a virtual machine abstraction layer between hypervisor interfaces and the software applications that use them. Using libvirt library, developers and system administrators can focus on a common management framework, common API, and common shell interface (i.e., virsh) to QEMU/KVM or LXC, etc.

Ceph block devices support QEMU/KVM. You can use Ceph block devices with software that interfaces with libvirt. The above Figure 6-11 illustrates how libvirt and QEMU use Ceph block devices storage via librbd. The libvirt provides Ceph block devices storage to the Distributed Cloud. The OneCenter uses libvirt to interact with QEMU/KVM, and QEMU/KVM interacts with Ceph block devices via RDMA, NVMe-oF and librbd.

Block Devices Storage and KVM in Cloud

You can attach Ceph Block Device images to the Distributed Cloud KVM instances through libvirt, which configures the QEMU interface to librbd. Ceph stripes block volumes across multiple OSDs within the cluster, which means that large volumes can achieve better performance than local drives on a standalone server.

6.4.3.2 Kubernetes/Docker Storage

For some stateful services and applications, Kubernetes needs a mechanism and technology to ensure that the storage used by the container is durable. This section introduces the integration of CSI plug-in architecture and technology with Kubernetes clusters.

Ceph Block Devices and Kubernetes/Docker

Besides providing Block Device images for QEMU/KVM in the cloud through Ceph-CSI (Container Storage Interface), Ceph can do the same thing for Kubernetes with Docker. Ceph dynamically provisions RBD images to back Kubernetes volumes and maps these RBD images as block devices (another way, you also can mount a file system contained within the image) on worker nodes running pods that reference an RBD-backed volume. Ceph stripes block device images as objects across the cluster, which means that more Ceph Block Device images have better performance than a standalone server.

Kubernetes External Component

The Kubernetes team is completely in charge of implementing and maintaining this component. These extend Kubernetes actions outside of Kubernetes. The vendors need not care about the detailed information and its implementation. They contain three sub-components:

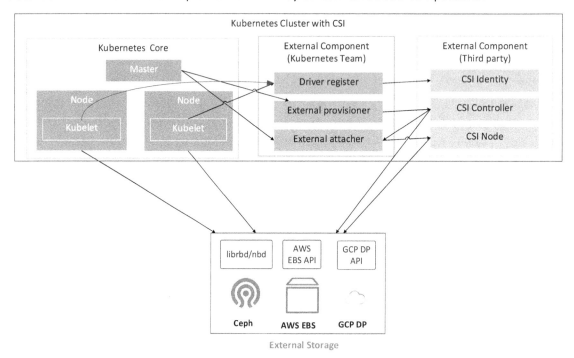

Figure 6-12 Kubernetes Storage Components

Driver Registrar is in charge of registering the CSI driver with kubelet and adding the driver's custom NodeId to a label on the Kubernetes Node API Object.

External Provisioner is responsible for watching Kubernetes PersistentVolumeClaim objects and triggering CSI CreateVolume and DeleteVolume operations against a driver endpoint.

External Attacher is responsible for watching Kubernetes VolumeAttachment objects and triggering CSI ControllerPublish and ControllerUnpublish operations against a driver endpoint.

Storage Vendor External Component

This is a vendor specific implementation. Each vendor should implement their respective APIs into gRPC service functions. E.g., Implementation of AWS EBS, Ceph, etc. this component contains below three sub-components:

CSI Identity is mainly for identifying the plugin service, making sure it's healthy, and returning basic information about the plugin itself.

CSI Controller is responsible for controlling and operating the volumes, such as creating, deleting, attaching, detaching, or snapshotting, etc.

CSI Node is responsible for controlling volume's operation in the Kubernetes node.

6.4.3.3   Storage System Offloading

In the Distributed Cloud, the IPU can provide storage acceleration functions for containers, virtual machines, or bare metals, archive storage protocol offloading through a combination of software and hardware, and flexibly meet the requirements of high storage Input/Output Operations Per Second (IOPS) performance and low host CPU usage.

RDMA

High-speed storage media such as NVMe provide microsecond-level access latency. Typical applications such as Telco Edge networks (the Distributed Cloud architecture only focuses on 3GPP NPN and 3GPP PNI-MEC scenarios) and edge artificial intelligence (AI) rely on low-latency networks to complete operations such as state synchronization, which make higher.

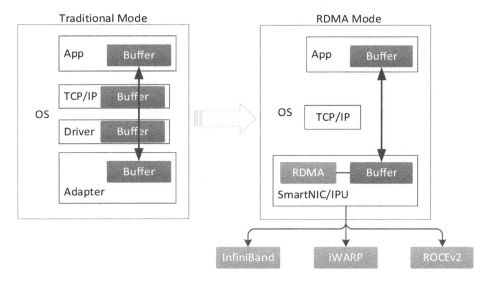

Figure 6-13 RDMA Protocol vs TCP/IP Stack Data Paths

requirements for network latency. Traditional millisecond-level TCP network demand has been unable to be met. RDMA technology uses kernel bypass and zero-copy technology to enable direct data reading and writing between network devices and applications, eliminating the context switching and data copy overhead of the traditional TCP/IP protocol stack so that it can provide end-to-end microsecond-level and low-latency network communication with low CPU load, it is shown as the Figure 6-13.

Compared with the bus IO of traditional DMA, RDMA performs the direct transmission of Buffer between the application software of two endpoints through the network; compared with traditional network transmission, RDMA does not require the intervention of the operating system and protocol stack. RDMA can easily achieve ultra-low latency and ultra-high throughput transmission between endpoints, and almost does not require CPU, OS, and other resources to intervene, and does not need to consume too many other resources for network data processing and migration.

Offloading RDMA protocols (such as ROCEv2) to hardware, including encapsulation, decapsulation, congestion control algorithms, etc., and supporting unilateral operations can further reduce CPU overhead on the passive side. The host installs the RDMA protocol driver and connects to the RDMA primitive, which can greatly reduce the delay and improve the throughput of the business.

Storage Interface Offloading

In the Distributed Cloud, the IPU is the base of the Distributed Cloud platform and can provide the standard storage interface virtio-blk for virtual machines and bare metal instances. Utilize the front-end and back-end vring sharing mechanism of the virtio interface to provide storage data interaction for the standard virtio-blk driver installed in the Guest OS. The native virtio-blk interface can already provide dynamic capacity expansion and hot-swapping of devices.

NVMe has become the industry standard for storage. With the advent of NVMe-native devices in cloud environments such as data centers, virtualization-based NVMe interfaces can provide higher bandwidth performance and lower storage protocol latency than virtio-blk. The virtualization interface based on the NVMe standard protocol has become another standard, and storage devices based on the NVMe protocol can support richer functions and control interfaces.

Use the IPU to offload the storage interface. The approach is to implement the backend of the storage interface on the IPU and provide the device interface of virtio-blk or NVMe to the CPU host. Load the standard virtio-blk or NVMe driver in the CPU host to perform the read and write of block storage. No additional vendor-specific drivers are required.

Storage Network Protocol Stack Offloading

The IPU performs corresponding processing on the received storage network data packets based on the storage network protocol stack, such as Ceph and iSCSI. Offloading the storage network protocol stack (or storage client) to the IPU can reduce the CPU load on the CPU host side, and avoid storage network security risks caused by exposing the storage network protocol stack to the client OS in the bare metal model, shown as Figure 6-11.

Storage nodes work together with storage clients running on computing nodes to provide block storage-level services. The back-end storage platform generally supports different storage media, such as HDD, Serial Advanced Technology Attachment (SATA), Serial Attached SCSI (SAS), SATA SSD and NVMe SSD, etc., so as to build storage services for different applications. The storage client can be installed in the CPU core of the IPU to process the storage network protocol stack of iSCSI or Ceph and cooperate with the SPDK user mode acceleration framework to improve the storage and forwarding performance.

Furthermore, with the development of storage media and the emergence of high-performance storage requirements, the storage interface is evolving to NVMe. Using the NVMe over Fabric (NVMe-oF) protocol can further leverage the advantages of NVMe's high performance, low latency, and low protocol burden. Build a high-speed network based NVMe shared storage system interconnection structure. NVMe-oF can use different high-speed network transmission protocols to implement NVMe functions. That is, it can support various types of Fabric networks, including Fiber Channel (FC), RDMA, TCP, etc., considering the high performance and compatibility of network transmission protocols, the Distributed Cloud uses RDMA (RoCEv2).

The offloading acceleration of the NVMe-oF protocol stack is implemented on the IPU, which can provide a native NVMe back-end storage interface on the computing node, connect to the storage end through a high-performance RDMA network protocol (such as RoCEv2), and use the IPU hardware on the storage node. NVMe Target manages NVMe SSDs, and the entire storage network transmits end-to-end bypass host CPUs without any protocol conversion cost, providing CPU hosts with high-performance, elastic remote storage that is close to the performance of local NVMe.

6.5   Lite Site

The Lite site is composed of CPU host and smartNIC / IPU device at the edge location to close the users. Lite site has limited space, small scale, low power, and uses wireless connection technologies such as 5G network, Lora WAN, WIFI or Bluetooth. At this site scale. the IPU host of

Lite site implements some site edge roles (SiteAgent, Node Agent and so on) that plays an edge gateway role in the Max, Pro, or Mini sites.

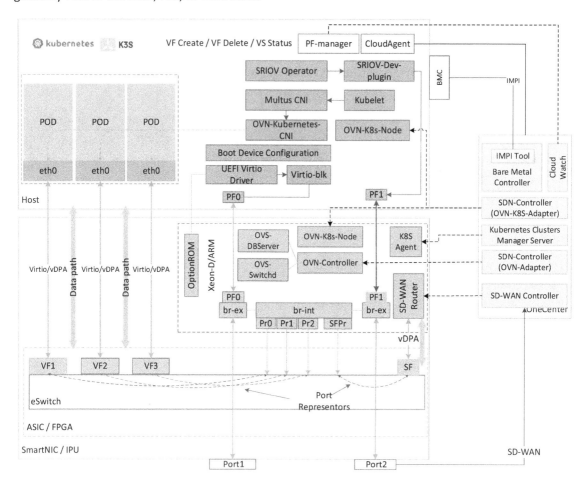

Figure 6-14 Lite Type Site Architecture

Networking

SD-WAN and SDN Controller (in the OneCenter location) directly connect to OVN-Controller and SD-WAN Edge Router (both located in the IPU host of target Lite site). The Kubernetes network in the Lite site use CNI and OVN-Kubernetes. That means the SDN-Controller with OVN-Kubernetes-Adapter communicate with OVN-Kubernetes-Node located in both the IPU host and Cloud host. About the deployment of Kubernetes Pod with CNI and OVN-Kubernetes in the Distributed Cloud, you can refer to section [6.4.2.6.1 Running Containerized Workloads with Virtio/vDPA].

Like the normal computing node in the previous discussed Max type site, the OVN-Controller and Open vSwitch (OVS) software is offloaded into the IPU host of Lite site node.

Storage

In the Lite site case, Generally, data will not be stored on a large scale, nor will a highly available distributed storage system be deployed. This type of node is mainly responsible for data collection, data caching, and real-time push and transmission of data to the remote central node or data center in the form of streaming data.

Computing

1. Workload Infrastructure

In the Lite site, bare metal is not presented to users and applications directly. Docker with Kubernetes or docker with lightweight Kubernetes (K3s) is mainly used as the workload of the Lite site. For the Kubernetes, Docker, and K3s, refer to section [5.4 Infrastructure Containerization].

2. Bare Metal Provisioning

Unlike the Max or Pro Site environment, a standard DHCP server can be enhanced to support the HTTPBoot extension. In the Lite site network, generally, only an optional standard DHCP server may be available for host configuration information assignment. Figure 6-15 shows the concept network topology for a typical edge host or site edge of a Max or Pro site environment.

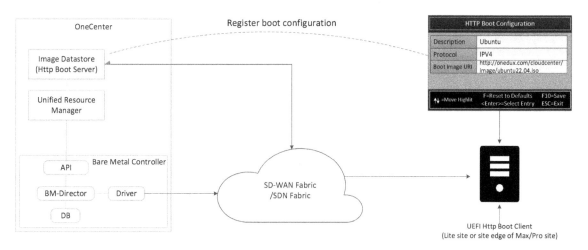

Figure 6-15 HTTP Boot Network Topology Concepts - Lite Site Environments

UEFI HTTP Boot Client first initiates the communication between the client and different servers if configured. In the Lite site environment configuration, however, the client will expect the boot resource information to be available from a source other than the standard DHCP server, and that source does not typically have HTTPBoot extensions. Instead of a DHCP server offering, the boot URI can be created by a UEFI application or extracted from text entered by an end user manually.

DHCP Server is optional and, if available in the network, provides the standard service to assign host configuration information to the UEFI Client. That information can be address, subnet, gateway, name-server address, etc. In case the standard DHCP server is not available, the same host configuration information should be provided by a UEFI application or extracted from text entered by a user prior to the client initiating the communication.

DNS Server is optional too and provides standard domain name resolution service.

Chapter 7　The Distributed Cloud Central Controller - OneCenter

The main innovation and feature of the distributed cloud in this book is that the cloud platform uses an enterprise-controlled central manager, OneCenter, to neutrally and undifferentiatedly orchestrate and control heterogeneous cloud infrastructure spread around the world.

In the Distributed Cloud, OneCenter manages and orchestrates all cloud infrastructure and resources, providing a central point of view for all kinds of users. The OneCenter is responsible for all cloud operations, including security, availability, updates, and governance of the distributed infrastructure. In this chapter, the critical components, and their functions of the OneCenter architecture will be introduced.

7.1　Components Architecture

As an advanced cloud ecosystem, the Distributed Cloud has some Outstanding features compared to conventional cloud platforms, and the Distributed Cloud has a new concept of layered overlay and underlay. At the top view, the Distributed Cloud consists of an infrastructure layer, an abstraction layer (unified resource manager), a resource layer, a workload/consuming layer, and common faculties and other cloud tools out of rest API shown in below Figure 7-1.

Except for the Scale Maker, the database, message queue, and IAM of the Distributed Cloud not be described especially in this section.

Identity and Access Management (IAM) is about Identity authorization, authentication, and user access. IAM allows you to centrally manage permissions that control which cloud resources users can access. These cloud resources include any infrastructure such as Physical Server, IaaS, PaaS, and SaaS, and also include the data in the unified Data Fabric, the file in the OneStorage, and the images in the marketplace.

The Organization needs to unify the Identity and Access of on-promise and third-party cloud providers.

About the design details of IAM and how to integrate the IAM into the on-premises and third-party cloud providers, will be described in other book.

The database is used for OneCenter to persist the state of the cloud. This is a key component that should be monitored and tuned for the best performance by cloud administrators following the best practices of the database product.

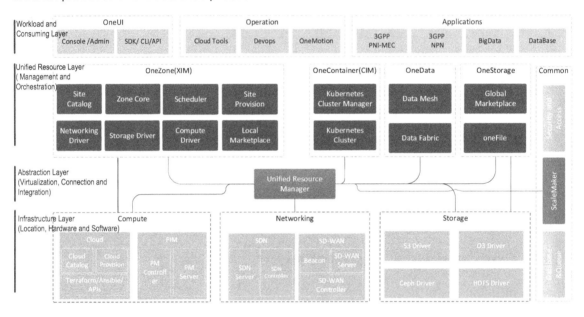

Figure 7-1 OneCenter Components Architecture

7.2   ScaleMaker

The Scale Maker scales, operates and monitors the site, node, and application automatically with DevOps function based on security capacities.

Edge, On-premises, Multi-Cloud, and Hybrid Management (Infrastructure) - Data center, branch, campus, 3GPP NPN, 3GPP PNI-MEC, public cloud, and various non-3GPP edge are implemented by abstraction of network load interface and multi-platform adaptation technology. Help users achieve unified access management, unified operation, and maintenance management experience.

Simple Operation with DevOps - Through the unified operating platform, break down the barriers between development, operation, and maintenance teams, and improve the efficiency of application compilation, launch, and deployment. The logs of application instances can be collected in a unified manner, which can be quickly queried and searched to help quickly locate the problems.

Application Capacity Burst with One Click Scaling - Applications of any size can be managed. Whether it is 10 or 1000 or more instances, elastic scaling can be easily achieved. One-click scaling of application instances, so as to easily cope with the explosive growth of business needs.

Tenant Isolation and Save Cost -Collaborate with the unified account system (IAM) to perform tenant resource isolation, authority allocation, and resource pool management.

Service Fault Tolerance and Never Down - ScaleMaker can automatically migrate and deploy applications for the CPU host running on the failed server while keeping the internal network IP unchanged, ensuring that the business will not be interrupted, and the operation will be highly reliable. This also means you don't have to suffer sleepless nights when one or two servers go down. Container instance service health check, service accidental failure, automatic pull-up, so that service failure self-healing.

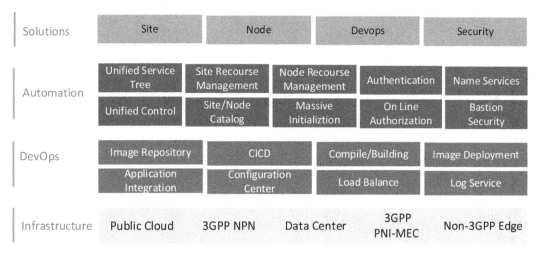

Figure 7-2 Scale Maker Components

7.2.1   Scale the Site

When building up a site, first, we need to set up a site edge. ScaleMaker use site resource management component to helps the Distributed Cloud administrators manage site edge servers throughout their lifecycle, from provisioning and configuration to orchestration and monitoring. Provisioning support gives organizations easy control of setting up new site edge servers and using configuration management (Puppet, Ansible, Chef, or Salt can be used). Users can easily automate repetitive tasks. ScaleMaker scales well to multiple locations (edge, data centers, public cloud, etc.) and multiple organizations, allowing you to grow without losing your single source of infrastructure truth.

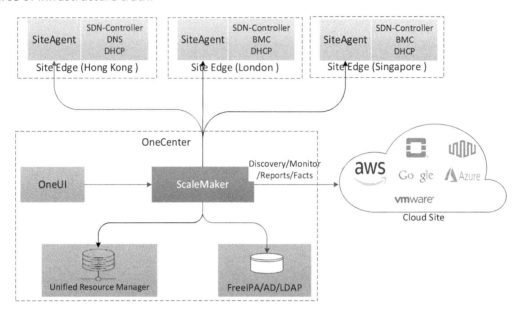

Figure 7-3 The Architecture of Scale Maker for Site

The Site Agent manages remote services and is generally installed with all ScaleMaker installations to manage the TFTP server, DHCP server, DNS server, Puppet, Terraform, Ansible, or Salt. A Site Agent is located on or near the machine that performs a specific function and helps ScaleMaker orchestrate the process of commissioning a new host. Placing the SiteAgent on or near the actual service at the site edge node/cluster will also help reduce latency in the large, distributed infrastructure of organizations. The following list is a high-level overview of Scale Maker for the sites:

- Discover, provision, and upgrade the organization's entire site edge bare metal infrastructure.
- Install operating systems via PXE, iPXE, and UEFI HTTP Boot, local media, or from templates or images to the site edge node.
- Control and gather reports from site edge configuration management software.

For more information about site deployment, you can refer to section [2.3.2 Site Deployment].

7.2.1.1 Site Catalog

The Site Catalog is a component that maintains a list of site resource providers that are certified to work with OneCenter. This catalog is globally centralized and managed by the OneCenter component. The catalog includes bare metal offerings from cloud or on-premises providers, which can be provisioned into the site by the Site Provision tool. The provider can include cloud location from AWS, Azure, Google Cloud or Equinix, etc., and on-premises location from the data center, campus, branch, 3GPP NPN site, 3GPP PNI-MEC site, and non-3GPP edge site, etc.

The Site Catalog data model captures the information needed to decide which provider offers the characteristics better suited for the site application in terms of capacity, latency, traits, regulation, bandwidth, etc. It is available through both the web interface and a command line interface.

Besides, another set of tools is available to filter the catalog using criteria useful for site application deployment. The following are some possible tools:

Latency Calculator Filter - Given a geographic location and a latency threshold, this filter will select those site locations that ensure a latency below the given threshold. The filter will work using heuristics that approximate the value according to periodic tests run by the Distributed Cloud among the locations available in the site catalog.

Cost Calculator Filter - Given a price target per hour and a capacity in terms of available network, disk, memory, and CPU, this filter selects those locations and instance types that will meet the price objective when deployed.

NOTE: *In an enterprise private vCenter cluster or private OpenStack cloud site, the cost may not be a concern in case the infrastructure is on-premises.*

Specific Characteristics Filter - Given some special attributes from a predefined set (which is available in the Catalog metadata, for example, NVMe disks in the instances), this filter selects those site locations and instance types that meet this criterion.

Certificate a New Provider - In order to certify a new location provider, OneCenter can provide a "Site Provider Certification Guide", this guide describes the process of registering and certifying a new provider in the SiteCatalog. At the same time, a "Site Provider Driver Development Guide" can describe the architecture of the SiteProvision drivers needed to interact with the Site Provider API programmatically.

Site Resource Provider Types - There are different types of Site Resource Providers by proximity to their end users, Public Cloud Providers, 3GPP NPN Infrastructure Providers, 3GPP PNI-MEC Infrastructure Providers, on-premises Data Centers (including Headquarters, Branch, Campus, and SOHO, etc.) Providers, non-3GPP IoT edge Providers, can offer resources to the unified resource manager in OneCenter. For detailed information, please refer to [7.4 Abstraction Layer - Unified Resource Manager].

7.2.1.2 Site Provision and Deployment

The Site Infrastructure Provision and Deployment - Site Provision is the component extended for the site to meet the User Experience (UX), usability, flexibility, and improved reliability required in a highly geo-distributed site environment. Site Provision allows organizations to manage the full life cycle of the complete independent site locations, starting with their provision and maintenance until the un-provision. This component is integrated into OneCenter to easily control the site locations from OneUI.

Each site location is defined as a group of physical servers allocated from the remote bare-metal cloud provider or on-premise physical site (data center, branch, campus, 3GPP NPN site, or 3GPP MEC site located in Mobile Network Operator (MNO) data centers) infrastructures. They are fully configured with the user-selected hypervisor and enabled in the edge stack for the end users. In the case of public cloud providers, except for the physical servers, each provision comes with a dedicated virtual machine, virtual networks, PaaS, etc. Every single site location is an independent and complete computing environment.

7.2.2   Scale the Node

When operating the infrastructures of the Distributed Cloud, the site-level aspects always be first considered and then step into the node level inside the site.

ScaleMaker helps the Distributed Cloud administrators manage site servers throughout their lifecycle, from provisioning and configuration to orchestration and monitoring. Provisioning support gives organizations easy control of setting up new site servers and using configuration management (Puppet, Ansible, Chef, or Salt can be used). Users can easily automate repetitive tasks. With ScaleMaker, you can quickly deploy applications and proactively manage change, both on-premises with VMs and bare-metal or in the cloud.

A Node Agent is located in an IPU or CPU host and performs a specific function. The following list is a high-level overview of Scale Maker for the node:

- Discover, provision, and upgrade the organization's entire bare metal infrastructure.

- Create and manage instances in a virtualization environment and across on-promises including edge and public clouds.

- Install operating systems via PXE, iPXE, and UEFI HTTP Boot, local media, or from templates or images.

- Control and gather reports from your configuration management software.

For more information about how the ScaleMaker works with the target node, you can refer to section [5.2 ScaleMaker for Bare Metal Provisioning].

7.2.3   Cloud DevOps

The Distributed Cloud scenarios and features provide nimble and reliable continuous integration (CI) and continuous delivery (CD) of services and simplify the life cycle management of applications such as deployment, monitoring, and operation, thereby greatly improving the efficiency and stability of the Distributed Cloud operation.

7.2.3.1 Configuration Management

Configuration management can provide common operation and maintenance services such as online server tree structure management, automated script execution, automatic distribution of batch files, and unified authority management.

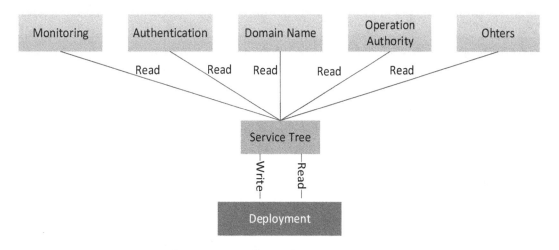

Figure 7-4 Configuration Management

The main functions of configuration management are:

Maintenance of Management Nodes - In order to facilitate the maintenance of the instance-level life cycle, the service tree provides six levels of system, department, product line, system, application, and group to support flexible customization of hierarchical relationships.

Maintain the Relationship - This refers to maintaining the relationship between application and host, application, and instances. Based on the service tree, the relationship between applications and hosts, applications and instances is displayed, and the distribution of hosts where applications are deployed and the running status of application instances are intuitively displayed.

Resource Pool Management - The resource pool includes cloud hosts, etc., and manages all the resources that the deployment depends on.

Access Control - Based on the unified access application process of service tree nodes, it provides authorization Access and identity verification services for various service tree-based subsystems. The authority module manages who has what authority to a certain service tree node (including the machine/instance it belongs to) in each subsystem and the token management of the API call of each subsystem.

7.2.3.2 Continuous Delivery

On the ScaleMaker system, the life cycle management and control of the application can be completed in a unified manner, including compilation and construction, package deployment, start, stop, automatic expansion/contraction, and application offline, etc., to implement the full process management of the application.

The architecture in Figure 7-5 mainly includes the following modules:

1. Service management, providing product tree management based on service tree, providing authority interface and services for upper-level services.

2. Configuration management, providing configuration file derivation, group configuration files take effect, and environment parameter configuration functions.

3. Compilation and construction, providing multiple programming languages and multi-environment building platforms, supporting automatic, and manual compilation, building and packaging.

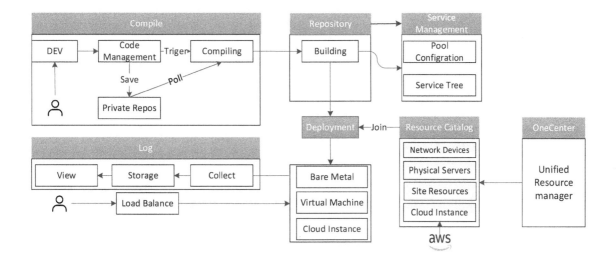

Figure 7-5 Continuous Delivery Architecture

7.2.3.3 Smart Monitoring

According to the upstream and downstream relationship of the service tree, smart monitoring provides full-link monitoring services, which can effectively shorten the abnormal life cycle of operation and maintenance. Through rich monitoring methods and fast computing capabilities, it can accurately detect abnormalities, locate faults, and provide decision support for fault recovery. Smart monitoring also supports rich abnormality detection methods and alarm dependencies and can automatically generate node alarm contact groups according to roles. Send the alarm to the specific person in charge in a targeted manner, so as to achieve the greatest degree of minimizing loss.

7.3 Infrastructure Layer - Location, Hardware and Software

This section presents the geo-distributed heterogeneous underlying infrastructures and how these infrastructures can be provided to the upper layer. The Distributed Cloud users can automatically allocate resources when needed, deploying, and controlling site nodes based on the current demand at those specific geographical locations. This approach significantly simplifies the process of provisioning and managing site resources without the organization that's using this solution having to provide or own those underlying infrastructure resources.

7.3.1   Compute

The underlying public cloud and on-premises physical machine infrastructures provisioning management (also termed PIM) will be introduced. Actually, the legacy vCenter cluster of organizations can also be reused by the Distributed Cloud. It is not captured in Figure 7-1.

7.3.1.1 Cloud Infrastructures

In Distributed Cloud, the preexisting private cloud (such as OpenStack cloud or VMware cloud) and public cloud (the cloud region and substation edge) always is adopted as underlying IaaS and PaaS infrastructures in edge site or extend distributed multiple cloud zones from on-premises data center to the public cloud regions scenarios. Section [10.2 Cloud Edge] and section [Chapter 8 Hybrid Multi-Cloud in Distributed Cloud] present some more detailed information on them.

7.3.1.2 On-premises Physical Infrastructures Management (PIM)

This section mainly provisions the physical server of on-premises infrastructure, and these provisioning targets include physical servers and network devices of the data center, branch, campus,3GPP edge, and non-3GPP edge, etc. About the physical infrastructure deployment, you can refer to section [5.2 ScaleMaker for Bare Metal Provisioning].

7.3.2   Storage

In the Distributed Cloud, the various heterogeneous storage backends are managed by OneCenter in a unified method. As to the Cloud object storage, the heterogenous storage backends can be AWS S3, Azure ADLS, SWS S3 compatible object storage, Ceph, Ozone, HDFS, etc. (Figure 7-1 shows several different drivers) and section [4.3 Universal Object Storage with Ceph Multi-Site Gateway] introduced the global Cloud Object Storage.

7.3.3   Networking

As to the block device storage for the system, although only one storage backend of Ceph is applied in this book, the Distributed Cloud architecture can also provide a storage abstraction layer (offered by the Abstraction Layer shown as Figure 7-1) that enables it to use other storage backends (such as SAN, NFS, iSCSI, etc.). About the block device storage backend related information, you can read section [4.2.5 Block Storage Backend].

The important thing is that there are too many network aspects that need a master for the Distributed Cloud architecture and design. This book focuses on architecture and design, and some other additional network-related technologies and solutions will be presented in the other book, the deeper inspection the related context you read it.

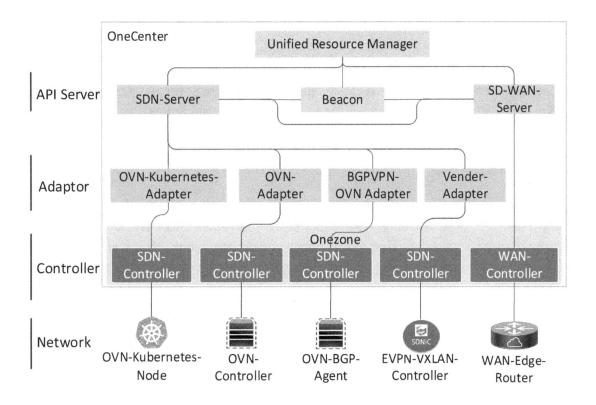

Figure 7-6 Networking Architecture in OneCenter

Beacon is a software-based component that performs the initial authentication of WAN Edge devices and orchestrates WAN-Controller, WAN-Server, and WAN Edge Router connectivity.

At the same time, the Beacon is also responsible for the initial authentication and orchestration of SDN-Controller and ONV-Kubernetes, OVN-Controller, OVN-BGP-Agent, VXLAN-EVPN-Controller connectivity. In addition, Beacon also provides global NTP, DNS, and global IPAM services across the Distributed Cloud. The networking is divided into the following four layers:

1. API Layer

This Server and API layer hosts both SDN-Server and SD-WAN-Server. This service process runs on the OneCenter location and provides RESTful API as the entrance to SDN and SD-WAN. The Servers receive user HTTP requests and route the request to the adapter layer based on user request parameters. For detailed information on the SD-WAN, you can refer to section [3.4 Software-Defined WAN - SD-WAN].

2. Adaptor Layer

The adapter layer mainly serves for the SDN adapter such as OVN-Kubernetes-adapter, OVN-adapter, BGPVPN-adapter, and net Vender-adapter such as for the SONIC or CISCO net devices as switch or router. The API layer dispatches the application and tenant requests to this adaptor layer. Then, the adaptor layer makes routing decisions according to the request parameters.

3. Controller Layer

The controller layer mainly includes the SDN-Controller and SD-WAN-Controller, the SDN-Controller driven by the OVN-Kubernetes-adapter, OVN-adapter, and BGPVPN-OVN-adapter runs the OVN network, the SDN-Controller drove by the Sonic-adapter run the VXLAN and EVPN network, about the detail information of these two controllers, you can refer to [Chapter 3 The Distributed Cloud Enterprise Networking].

4. Network Layer

The network layer is responsible for the SDN and SD-WAN operation targets:

- OVN-Kubernetes-Node in charge of digesting IPAM annotation written by OVN-Kubernetes-Adaptor, setting up routes for host Port and service access from the node, creating OVS port on bridge, moves it into pod network namespace.

- OVN-Controller is the agent in the OVN environment, running on each OVN chasis and connects to ovs–vswitchd as an OpenFlow controller, for control over network traffic.

- OVN-BGP-Agent runs on the network or compute nodes and is in charge of configuring the networking layer according to requirements.

- VXLAN-EVPN-Controller supports the EVPN and VXLAN network on the physical switch or router (typically for the SONIC or Cisco network physical devices).

- WAN-Edge-Router is responsible for forwarding packets based on decisions from the SD-WAN control plane.

At the network layer in Figure 7-6, this section mainly describes the control plane of the network at the workload node and how the internal node and inter node communication between nodes is omitted.

Some network-specific use cases require the deployment of VNF or container network functions (CNF) on the site. In this case, it is extremely important to optimize the performance of the application instances. Typically, the optimization requires fine-grained, NUMA-aware placement of the instances and the use of specialized network toolkits like the data plane development kit (DPDK), SR-IOV, vDPA, and OVS offload, etc. The Distributed Cloud can support these high-performing site application instances.

7.4　Abstraction Layer - Unified Resource Manager

Vary from the conventional cloud, the Distributed Cloud needs to trace and manage many more kinds of and more complex resources, such as AWS, Azure, and legacy VMware infrastructures. That is, the public cloud is one of numerous Distributed Cloud Resource providers.

7.4.1　Unified Resources Model

Unified Resource Manager has its design goals to improve resource utilization, instance performance, and availability; support rich scheduling strategies, high throughput, and low latency; easy to expand, debug, and explain.

The Unified Resource Manager is the global scheduler of the Distributed Cloud for orchestrating the sites, clusters, nodes infrastructures and computing, networking, and storage resources, and it plays the global computing, global data routing, and global traffic schedule. Unified Resource Manager decouples the heterogenous underlay infrastructures and unified overlay resources, playing an abstraction and normalization roles for the Distributed Cloud.

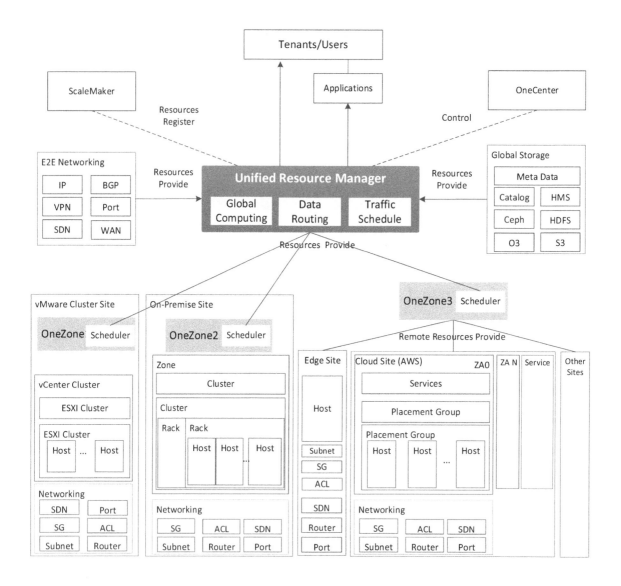

Figure 7-7 The Distributed Cloud Unified Resources Model

7.4.1.1   Resource Concepts and Terminology

Resource provider is the entity that provides resources, such as Worker (Compute) Node, Storage Pool, IP Pool, network elements and storage, etc.

Resource Class is the type of resource, such as traditional vCPU, Memory, Disk, SR-IOV_NET_VF, vGPU, NUMA_Memory, IP_Address, etc. Also include public IPs, VPN links, BGP, WAN, global Storage meta data and category information that are particular for the Distributed Cloud.

Resource inventory is the resource inventory owned by the resource provider, for example, vCPU, Disk, RAM, and other inventories owned by the Worker (Compute) Node.

Resource Provider Aggregates is a function similar to Host Aggregate. When obtaining Allocation Candidates, it supports obtaining from a specific aggregate through the member of the request query parameter. Resource provider aggregates are ideal with different types of host aggregates (e.g. high performance host aggregates, large storage capacity host aggregates, low-latency edge aggregates, etc.).

Resource Traits feature tag function, used to identify the characteristic properties of Resource Provider, each Resource Provider has its own default traits, and also supports custom traits for the specified Resource Provider. Resource Traits is a very flexible design, similar to the role of "tags". Users can build a "tag cloud" and decide to put a "tag" on a Resource Provider. It is an auxiliary tool for resource classification requirements. Resource Traits are very useful in some Workflows. For example, identifying available Disks with NVMe characteristics helps the Unified Resource Manager to flexibly match launching instance requests.

Resource allocation status including the mapping relationship between Resource Class, Resource Provider and Consumer. Record the number of consumers using this type of resource.

Consumers are essentially a string of UUIDs.

7.4.1.2 Standardization of Heterogeneous Resources

Resource Model

In the classic cloud environment, for example, private OpenStack and vMware cloud or other public clouds such as AWS and Azure, the schedule object of cloud resource typically includes the vCPU, RAM, PCI, Non-uniform memory access (NUMA) Topology, and Disk, while in the Distributed Cloud, the resources that must be taken into account are many more than traditional cloud environment as previous discussed.

Modeling with Provider Trees

Unified Resource Manager supports modeling a hierarchical relationship between different resource providers. A parent provider can have multiple child providers, but a child provider can belong to only one parent provider. Therefore, the whole model can be thought of as a "tree" structure, and the resource provider on top of the "tree" is called a "root provider". For example, In the Distributed Cloud environment, we can take the site as the root provider for the computing.

Provider Probe and Discovery

For the on-premises provider, the site proxy connects to the Scale Maker to register the site information to become a candidate site. After the site and Scale Maker set up the link, the site proxy reports the status, metrics, capacity, network status, and network quality to the Scale Maker. For the cloud provider, the Scale Maker continuously probes and detects the possible new provider and new location (region, available zone, substation) of the existing provider.

Provider Monitor

After the provider probing and Discovery, those candidate infrastructures are registered into the unified Resources Manager. As mentioned in section [7.2 ScaleMaker], the Scale Maker is responsible for monitoring the registered and linked resources located in the providers.

Resource Information Registration and Release

The metadata information of the physical server must at least be registered with the Unified Resources Manager; the work order system can pull that information from the Unified Resources Manager.

The following scenarios register or release the underlying heterogeneous resources to the Unified Resources Manager:

1. When provisioning the bare metal node from the on-premises infrastructure (such as edge, data center, campus, branch, etc.) and public cloud from the Scale Maker.

2. When provisioning the bare metal node from the public cloud (including the regional zone resources or the substation) triggered by the Scheduler in case of cloud busting.

3. When the provider resources are not available any more or in case of regulation prohibition, etc., the respective resources will be un-registered or released.

Standardization of Heterogeneous Resources

Unified Resources Manager provides a unified resource API to applications and tenants to standardize the Heterogeneous Resources at this abstraction layer in the Distributed Cloud.

7.4.2   Unified Resource Schedule

In a Distributed Cloud environment, the schedule policy and algorithm are different from traditional cloud such as public cloud and private cloud. The Distributed Cloud manages the dispersed resources across multiple distributed sites worldwide. The sites are heterogeneous and can be a non-3GPP edge, branch, 3GPP edge, data center, and public cloud location.

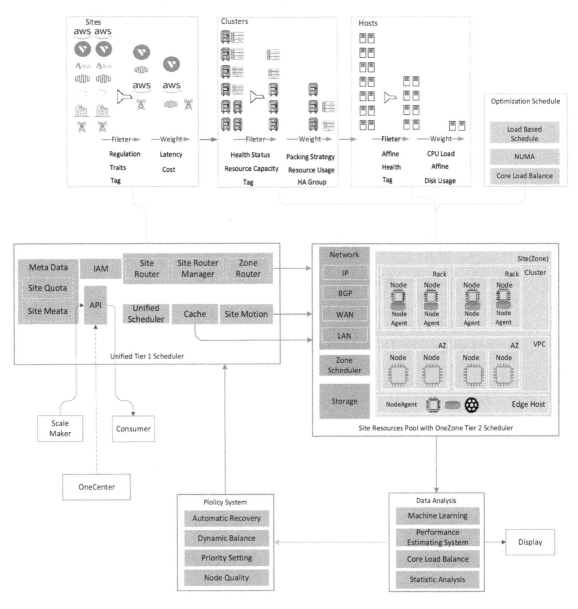

Figure 7-8 The Distributed Cloud Unified Resources Scheduler

The Distributed Cloud expand the schedule targets, schedule scope and schedule tiers. The schedule target combines 2-Tiers architectures for schedule and resource management, the Tier 1 (Unified Scheduler) for global site resources and the Tier 2 (Zone Scheduler) for zone and site internal resources.

In the Distributed Cloud, the network is also the critical schedule object, and the Unified Resource Manager cooperates with the SDN module for site internal and the SD-WAN module for WAN and inter-sites to achieve networking optimal connection management and schedule.

7.4.2.1 Tier 1 Unified Scheduler

The Tier 1 unified scheduler is the top view scheduler that takes the site as the scheduler as the schedule object. That is, this level scheduler decides which one or which group sites are the optimal one/collection to deploy/run the servers or applications.

Site-Router

1. When creating a resource, first apply for a quota from the site quota, then schedule the site and get the site ID.

2. First query from the caching when querying the resource list.

3. When an action may trigger migration, it is directly forwarded to Site-Migrate, such as changing configuration, resetting the system, booting, and other operations.

4. When managing and operating resources, it is necessary to locate the site ID of the resource first and then route the request.

Site - Scheduler

1. It is responsible for scheduling the Site ID when creating resources and needs to consider user attributes (such as VIP or Standard), Host Type, FD, and Zone.

2. The service needs to pre-configure the models supported by each site.

3. If the resource type created by the user does not match the user's attributes, it is necessary to configure a special whitelist for the user or configure the mapping relationship between the special model and the site.

4. When the user attribute changes, the IAM will send a notification message, and the site scheduler will modify the user attribute after receiving the message, thereby affecting the subsequent Site scheduling of user resource creation.

Caching

1. Through the Site-sync, centrally synchronize the data of all Databases under the site to the cache service to support list query and paging functions.

Meta Data

1. When creating a resource, you need to reserve a quota in the site-quota first. When the creation is successful, submit the reserved configuration. If it fails, roll back the reserved quota.

2. When deleting resources, you need to reserve a quota in site-quota first. If the deletion is successful, submit the reserved configuration. If it fails, roll back the reserved quota.

3. In order to ensure the final consistency of the quota, the message of resource creation and deletion needs to be additionally sent to the Message Queue to compensate for the quota.

7.4.2.2 Tier 2 Internal Zone Scheduler

After Tier 1 global scheduling, users have allocated the resource to the suitable site. The Tier 2 internal zone scheduler decides which rack or which host will be used for the application. The goals to be achieved at this level of scheduling include:

- Resource Fragmentation Management.
- Scheduling based on workload type.
- User instances should be allocated discretely by default.
- Workload, scheduling, statistics, and resource status visualization.

How It Works

1. The API Server of Scheduler of OneZone instance is currently in response to the active pre-occupation strategy, the asynchronous control unit Garbage Collection (GC) reclaims redundant pre-occupancy, the resource usage delay is consistent, and the working mode of one master and multiple slaves is adopted.

2. The rest of the business is a stateless service model.

3. Supports batch creation, implemented serially by each single machine.

4. The resources include CPU, memory, local disk, cloud storage disk, GPU, NUMA, and other dimensions.

5. Node periodically reports status information containing information such as node activity, actual resource consumption, load, resource utilization, instance images, etc.

Resource Management

1. API-Server (OneZone Schedule)

This module is mainly responsible for the management of fault domain (FD), host group (HG) operation, rack operation (create, read, update, and delete), host tags, reserved resources, resources operation, and dedicated host resources.

2. Schedule-State

This module's capacities include host heartbeat reporting, host resource detail reporting, and host status querying, host run time reporting.

Node Schedule

The following Figure 7-9 presents the node schedule process:

1. Filtering generally includes two categories: label calculation and resources disperse strategy.

2. The scoring framework adopts the chain-based method and hierarchical scheduling.

3. Tag calculation filters candidate nodes through static attributes such as tag matching, host type, service type and availability zone.

4. The resource disperse strategy considers restrictions such as scatter across racks, high-availability group instance distribution FD (physical server group/rack) and so on.

5. Host group scheduling needs to consider the impact of the resource water level in the group on the strategy within the group. For example, the overall resource utilization of the node group reaches the level, empty machines in the group and other allocation strategies.

6. Internal group scheduling can be associated with scoring algorithms such as high priority for hosts with more remaining resources or for hosts with few remaining resources, to support the needs of different business scenarios.

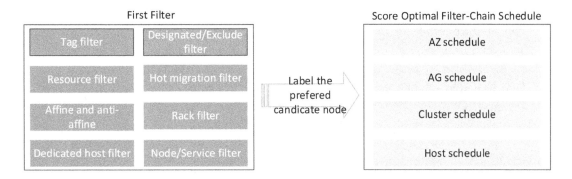

Figure 7-9 Node Schedule

Preemptive Resource Management

The pre-occupation here includes two aspects: when creating resources, it gives priority to using idle even candidate instances; releasing candidate instances gives priority to pre-occupancy; excessive pre-occupation may occur, so asynchronous GC logic needs to be adopted.

GC has two strategies that work at the same time: Periodic GC, which is configurable; GC is triggered by conditions. In the same scheduling space, when the ratio of over-occupied to idle resources exceeds the thread hold (for example, 0.5), GC is triggered immediately.

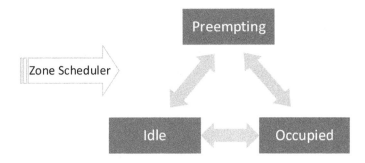

Figure 7-10 Preemptive Resource Management

Below is the Preemptive Resource Management process:

1. Allocate resources from idle, the resource instances are occupied, and the resources are set to the occupied state.

2. Delete non-reserved instances, reclaim occupied resources directly, and then release them to idle.

3. Create a reserved instance, and some resources that exceed the candidate instance are allocated from the idle, but the instance is not bound.

4. Release of preempted resources to idle.

5. First allocate from idle, and then from pre-occupancy when create use the reserved Instances.

6. First release to preemption, and then to idle, when deleting the preemption.

7.5 Resources Layer - Management and Orchestration

After the normalization by the abstraction layer, the tenants or applications can see a standard cloud resource view over the underlying uneven and heterogeneous infrastructure. The Distributed Cloud builds the IaaS over an Abstraction Layer based on edge, data center, 3GPP network enabled site, public, and hybrid clouds. It orchestrates the overlay compute, storage, network, storage, and data resources to provide a uniform management layer for bare metal, virtual machines, and infrastructure containers in a multi-tenant environment to up-layer tenants or applications.

7.5.1 OneZone

OneZone instance is a workload orchestration and manager that is responsible for orchestrating the cloud resources (such as cluster, hosts, computing, networking, and storage) and managing the life cycle of the operation system and application instances running on the infrastructure of the sites belonging to a zone at the Resource Layer.

- **OneZone Daemon**: The OneZone Daemon is the core service of the cloud management platform. It manages the cluster nodes, virtual networks and storages, groups, users and their instances, and provides the API to other services.

- **Database**: OneZone persists the state of the cloud into the selected database.

- **Scheduler**: The OneZone Scheduler is responsible for the planning of the pending Bare Metals, Virtual Machines and Containers on available Nodes.

- **Site Provision**: This component creates fully functional OneZone Clusters on public cloud or on-premises site providers. The Provision module integrates site clusters into the OneZone cloud by utilizing these three core technologies: Terraform, Ansible and the OneZone Services.

7.5.1.1 Clusters Management

Clusters group together hosts, image data stores, and virtual networks that are configured to work together. A cluster is used to:

- Ensure that bare metal, virtual machine, or container use resources that are compatible.

- Assign resources to user groups by creating GVPC.

Clusters should contain homogeneous resources. Note that some operations, like live migrations, are allowed to host within the same cluster.

The Instance Datastore for a Cluster

In order to create a complete environment where the scheduler can allocate VMs, by default, the Instance Datastore is shared across clusters within a zone in a Max site or Pro site.

Managing Clusters in OneUI

The OneUI interface of OneCenter can offer an easy way to manage clusters and the resources within them. You can find the cluster sub-menu under the infrastructure menu. From there, you will be able to:

- Create new clusters, selecting the resources, including hosts, networking, and storage, that you want to include in this cluster.

- Show the list of existing clusters, from which you can update the template of existing ones and modify or delete them.

Typically, if there are multiple clusters in a Max or Pro site, these clusters can share a Datastore instance and SDN-Controller within the site. Whereas the Distributed Cloud can support the clusters using separate Datastore and SDN-Controller.

7.5.1.2 Host Management

Site nodes are managed as the Distributed Cloud hosts. These hosts are distributed across different networks and accessed across a WAN or through the public internet and unreliable connections. This model deviates from the classic data center that is based on on-premises resources interconnected through private, high-band networks. In order to support such a scenario, the following enhancements are necessary:

- Secure communication in the control plane. Every operation on the site nodes needs to be initiated through a secure, authenticated channel.

- Monitor information needs to be sent encrypted to the OneCenter.

- The monitor channel needs to include some reliability mechanisms to control connection errors, at both the transport and application layers.

The use of site infrastructures will potentially increase the number of managed entities by OneZone/OneCenter. In order to preserve its current performance levels, it is required to decouple the processing of the monitor messages from the main workflow of the OneZone/OneCenter daemon.

Note that, in any case, the site resources should be able to operate independently in the event of losing a connection. OneCenter will provide the mechanisms to monitor the health, status trigger alert alarms, and perform recovery actions in such situations.

The hosts include the CPU host, IPU hosts, and the hosts from the vCenter clusters, all being managed, controlled, and monitored by the OneZone and OneCenter instances.

7.5.1.3 Compute Infrastructure

Each on-premises site location consists of a set of bare-metal servers and the public cloud site may contain a Virtual Machine, PAAS, storage, and other resources besides bare-metal servers. Each bare-metal server has some advanced hardware features that may be exposed to the application instances, e.g., PCI-passthrough, SR-IOV of GPU or network devices and Infrastructure Processing Unit (IPU) integration and so on, about the acceleration of hardware, the site design section [6.4 Max Site] gives more description of this, you can refer to it.

In particular, the following different technologies should be considered when using these bare-metal servers:

Virtual Machines are fully isolated application environments running on full virtualization hypervisors such as KVM. VMs provide the most secure environment for multi-tenant applications running at the site with the cost of some overhead. However, for certain application domains (e.g., serverless, functions-as-a-services-Faas, and so on) that still require full resource isolation, the VMs can be simplified to concise such overhead. In particular, the Distributed Cloud can support two VM types:

1. **Traditional VMs** with full control to custom the characteristics of the virtual server (e.g., number of network interfaces, specify the operating system, virtual NUMA nodes, etc.)

2. **Micro-VMs** with a concise feature and hardware set which provides a lightweight and fast provision application instance. The Distributed Cloud feature support for AWS's

Firecracker hypervisor in order to support scenarios where light micro-VMs are needed. About the introduction of Firecracker, you can refer to [5.3 Infrastructure Virtualization].

Containers offer a less resource-consuming solution compared to virtual machines while providing a full operation at the infrastructure level (e.g., network models). The performance gains come at the cost of a lower degree of isolation and Operation System (OS) flexibility since they all share the same kernel space.

Bare Metal Servers can be directly offered to special application scenarios that require high performance, security, dependability, etc. Such as for HPC (High-performance Computing), Big Data Platforms, Databases, and so on.

7.5.1.4 Network Management

In Distributed Cloud, the GVPC can be stretched worldwide across geo-distributed sites. That means the arbitrary two hosts can communicate with each other wherever they are located.

Although the Distributed Cloud is SD-WAN based, you can allocate your workload in a private Subnet to protect the data and resources. The Distributed Cloud hosts get IP addresses from the global IPAM of Beacon Deamon in the OneCenter, including the underlay and overlay network.

7.5.1.5 Storage Management

The Distributed Cloud Architecture combines a 3-Tier architecture for image distribution with an enhanced datastore with replica caching, snapshotting, and backups within each distributed site. Along with the global marketplace and local marketplace cooperation, providing a plat and unified view of storage space to systems and applications.

The OneZone core issue abstracts storage operations that are implemented by specific programs that can be replaced or modified to interface special storage backend and file systems.

The site image datastores will be able to synchronize the image repository in the OneCenter or the site edge to the site nodes of the cluster, so it is completely transparent for the user where the application is being deployed. The synchronization may occur through public networks, so secure transfer distribution mechanisms should be applied.

The synchronization will be guided by the administrator of the site infrastructure by selecting the operation system and application images that should be available at site locations.

7.5.2   OneX

In the Resource Layer, the word "OneX" is an umbrella term and generally refers to OneContainer, OneData, and OneStorage. The design aims of OneX are to provide a global unified point of view regarding container management (Kubernetes Cluster Manager), Big Data platform, and unified storage system.

OneContainer

OneContainer can also be termed Container Infrastructure Management (CIM). It is responsible for the Kubernetes cluster management and control. CIM include Kubernetes Cluster Management and Docker Machine client tool.

Kubernetes Cluster Management includes the Kubernetes Cluster Manager and multiple Kubernetes Clusters that are managed by the Kubernetes Cluster Manager. As shown ❺ in Figure 5-15 of section [5.4.3.3 Kubernetes Clusters Manager Components Architecture], the Kubernetes Cluster Manager and other components of OneCenter is based on the local Kubernetes Cluster.

Docker Machine is a client and management tool in the CIM for the Docker daemons on remote distributed systems. OneCenter provides its users with a custom Docker Machine driver which enables functionality like automated creation of a ready Dockized host without the need to instantiate VM beforehand.

OneData

The Distributed Cloud has some natural native characteristics and features that fit the Data Fabric and Data Mesh architecture, OneData integrates the Data Fabric with data virtualization and the Hybrid Data Mesh to meet the various business requirements of organizations. OneData is shown in Figure 11-3 with Data Mesh and Data Fabric. They are introduced in section [11.2 Flexible Modern Data Architecture].

OneStorage

OneStorage, shown in Figure 7-1, consists of a global marketplace and oneFile, the local marketplace resides along with the OneZone, and it may not collocate with the OneCenter instance. The oneFile is the unified global object storage platform, the OneFile is not described in details. It is backed by Ceph object storage, HDFS storage system, Ozone, and S3 compatible cloud object storage system.

Marketplace

Marketplaces provide the best convenience and experience to deploy your image and application. Integrating with the Distributed Cloud, it is easy to automate the running of your application anytime and anywhere. You can think of a marketplace as an external data store, like a local image data store.

A Marketplace stores Marketplace Appliances. A Marketplace Appliance includes one or more Images and, possibly, some associated metadata like VM boot parameters or templates or multi-VM service definitions information. The Marketplaces component aggregates all the sources of virtual machines, containers, and application images with the needed metadata. A Marketplace can be a Global Marketplace or a Local Marketplace:

1. Global Marketplace

Global Marketplace is accessible universally by all the Distributed Cloud installations. It can include an enterprise scope repository, integrated public online Linux Containers, and a public online Docker Hub repository. The global marketplace serves the whole enterprise scope of the Distributed Cloud and resides in the OneCenter location as a central marketplace with internet or WAN access.

2. Local Marketplaces

In addition to the global marketplaces (leveraging various remote public repositories with existing Appliances and accessible universally by all global site instances), the local ones are local within an organization and specific for a single zone or shared by a federation (a collection of zones) and allow the cloud administrators to create the private marketplaces within a single organization in a specific site where an OneZone instance lives - single zone or shared by a federation (collection of zones). Local Marketplaces provide their users with an easy way of privately publishing, downloading, and sharing their own custom appliances.

A Local Marketplace is a repository of Marketplace Appliances. Generally, Local Marketplace contains images, virtual machine templates, and service templates.

Using private local marketplaces is very convenient, as it will allow you to move images across different kinds of data stores (using the marketplace as an exchange station). It is a way to share the Distributed Cloud images in a federation, as these resources are federated. In a Distributed Cloud deployment where the different VDCs don't share any resources, a local Marketplace will act like a shared datastore for all the users.

7.6 Workload and Consuming Layer

This section introduces some common facilities, cloud tools, storage solutions and data solutions that are important for cloud maintenance, operation, the services offered, etc.

7.6.1 OneUI

The Distributed Cloud comes with a User Interface intended for applications, end users and administrators to easily manage all cloud resources and perform operations. The visual user Interfaces include the tenant console, platform portal, administrator management console, etc.

RESTful API is the primary interface for the Distributed Cloud, through which you can control and manage any Distributed Cloud resources, including Bare Metal, Virtual Machines, Virtual Networks, Images, Users, Hosts, Sites and Clusters, and so on. At the same time, the OneUI also provide SDK and CLI for developer and users.

7.6.2 Cloud Operation

Cloud Tools

Managing and controlling the various heterogeneous underlying public cloud resources is an extremely complex task. To provide a normalized view to upper users and applications, the Distributed Cloud leverages the Terraform and Ansible to communicate to and operate the different geo-distributed cloud providers.

Terraform is used to create, manage, and manipulate infrastructure resources (e.g., physical servers, virtual machines, network devices such as switches and routers, containers, etc.). Almost any infrastructure noun can be represented as a resource in Terraform.

The Distributed Cloud interacts with underlying cloud resources through Terraform. The provider allows users to manage the Distributed Cloud site resources. It needs to be configured with proper credentials before it can be used.

Ansible is another important cloud tool that allows managing common Distributed Cloud resources, e.g., Virtual machines, images, or hosts, with Ansible playbooks. At the same time, you can use Ansible to deploy applications across the distributed sites over different cloud providers.

Docker Machine allows users to create Docker hosts on an any edge site, public cloud providers, or inside an on-premises data center. Section [5.4.2 Manipulate Global Containers with Docker Machine] described some detailed information about it.

DevOps

Distributed Cloud provides both the cloud deployment, monitoring, and maintenance tools of DevOps and the DevOps facilities for the end-users. For the cloud DevOps, section [7.2 ScaleMaker] described more information. This book omitted details of DevOps for the users.

OneMotion

No matter what kind of cloud it is, it must at least have the characteristics of on-demand use, security, stability, and elasticity. Only in this way the cloud computing model and its services can produce real social benefits. In addition to these features, the Distributed Cloud has some compromises in terms of on-demand usage, cost, and security. The infrastructure of the Distributed Cloud will have a certain number of on-premises resources according to business needs. Therefore, the Distributed Cloud has several aspects, such as data migration, backup, disaster recovery, and elastic scaling, which are more complex than hybrid and multi-cloud.

One of the design goals of the Distributed Cloud is to enable migration, backup, disaster recovery, and on-demand elastic scaling across any geo-distributed heterogeneous infrastructures, which may be on-premises to on-premise, Hybrid, heterogeneous multi-cloud (for example, from AWS to Azure), edge to cloud and so on.

All these actions are triggered by abnormal events or business requirements, which means that such operations need to be executed automatically, for example, the resource migration and site scale up and scale down for a Distributed Cloud-based video conference. The following general migration and backup capabilities are prerequisites for building the Distributed Cloud to support more complex businesses:

Host Migration can be a Physical Machine to Virtual Machine(P2V) or Virtual Machine to Virtual Machine(V2V) migration service that helps users migrate physical servers or virtual machines from one site to another, thereby assisting users to easily migrate applications and data on servers to where they need to be used. The requirement includes full and incremental online live migration of Linux and Windows applications and data.

Database Migration needs to support batch data migration between homogeneous data sources to implement the free movement of data. Supports both full and incremental database migration.

Object Storage Migration service supports replication, copying, backup, and recovery between any heterogeneous object storage sites with S3-compatible interfaces and enables data to move automatically, safely, efficiently, and smoothly across the Distributed Cloud sites.

7.6.3   Cloud Consumer

Telco Edge Computing

Generally, Telco Edge includes three types of models. The first model is built on the Communication Service Provider owned Public Land Mobile Network (PLMN) infrastructures, the second model is built on the enterprise owned Non-Public Network infrastructures (termed as NPN), and the third model is integrated with the Communication Service provider-owned PLMN infrastructures within the provider's data center location (this model also be termed as PNI-MEC like AWS Wavelength). This book mainly focuses on the 3GPP NPN and 3GPP PNI-MEC models. For detailed information on those two models, refer to section [9.3 Telcos Cloud Design].

As the central controller of the Distributed Cloud, the OneCenter provides the control plane function of Telco Edge, such as UDM, Slice Analysis &Operation, E2E Service & Slice Orchestration, MEC Platform Manager, MEC Orchestrator, and so on.

Big Data

The OneData component in the OneCenter provides common facilities to build a data platform for an organization. This layer offers tenant isolation, data sharing, and transformation for multiple tenants and data applications.

Database

Distributed Cloud should offer some frequently used data base especially   the well known RDS (Oracle, MySQL, etc.) and MPP (sucha as Greenplum, Teradata etc.).

NOTE: *Distributed Cloud provides a mechanism that can directly leverage the Paas and Saas supplied by the public cloud and adopt the numerous applications that can be brought from the native marketplace and third-party cloud.*

Chapter 8 Hybrid Multi-Cloud in Distributed Cloud

Nowadays, more and more organizations are adopting hybrid and multi-cloud strategies to achieve greater flexibility, cost savings, and performance optimization. This chapter explains how Hybrid, Multi-cloud, WANaaS, and Disaster Recovery can be leveraged in the Distributed Cloud and the multi-site architecture design of hybrid multi-cloud to enhance the Distributed Cloud capacities. In a certain real environment, a solution may contain both Hybrid cloud and multi-cloud architecture simultaneously; we term this kind of scenario a Hybrid Multi-Cloud.

Hybrid Multi-cloud greatly expands the Distributed Cloud capacities to obtain unlimited infrastructure resources, extend the GVPC with the VPC of the public cloud, spread edge computing, etc.

8.1 Hybrid and Multi-Cloud

"Hybrid cloud" refers to the mixing of two or more distinct types of infrastructure. it combines on-premises infrastructures with public cloud, for example, combining an on-premise data center with AWS Cloud infrastructure through a dedicated connection or internet VPN connection to build a hybrid architecture, and multi-Cloud means several different public clouds being provisioned simultaneously for purposes from multiple public cloud providers.

Each architecture has its own intention, and Hybrid architecture can be used for high availability, backup, and restore disasters. At the same time, multi-cloud helps enterprises avoid the pitfalls of single-vendor binding. Spreading workloads across multiple cloud providers gives enterprises the flexibility to switch to use (or offline to stop using) a specific public cloud service whenever they want to avoid lock-in or cost optimization.

Sometimes, hybrid and multi-cloud are mutually exchangeable and overlapping. Often, you need to strike a hybrid architecture, and at the same time, it is a multi-cloud architecture. For instance, your on-premises data center connects to AWS cloud and Azure for WANaas simultaneously (refer to section [8.2.4 WAN as a Service - WANaaS] for details about WANaas).

The Distributed Cloud is not equivalent to hybrid and multi-cloud; it combines hybrid and multi-cloud capacity, and the Distributed Cloud provides central controller, which is independent of only other public cloud providers, while the hybrid and multi-cloud architecture cannot.

8.1.1   Benefits of Hybrid and Multi-Cloud

With the Distributed Cloud, you can get the agility, scalability, and simplicity benefits of the pay-per-use public cloud, with the greater levels of flexibility, performance, and security of a dedicated on-premises environment based on a geo-distributed multi-cloud infrastructure.

Financial reasons are one of the most important driving to increase the Hybrid Multi-cloud demand. Many users try to optimize their infrastructure costs to make sure that they only use as many resources as needed and pay less for them. Using a multi-cloud architecture, based on combining public cloud resources with a cost-effective private data center, is essential to achieve infrastructure cost optimization.

Mitigating Vendor Locking-in is another important driving for Hybrid multi-cloud demand. By meticulously evaluating the expectations and potential pitfalls and having a strong negotiating position that makes it easy to switch from one cloud to another, companies can harness the power of the public cloud and get the most value out of their partnership with any cloud service provider. Enjoy workload portability between any cloud provider and you're on-premises resources.

In addition, Hybrid Multi-cloud provides great Flexibility and Scalability. Multi-cloud allows businesses to scale their storage up or down according to an ongoing demand. Ideally, multi-cloud providers work seamlessly together so companies are able to invest in any level of capacity, security, and protection based on the needs of each data segment.

8.1.2   The True Hybrid Multi-Cloud

In fact, managing and supporting Hybrid Multi-Cloud is not an easy task. In an ideal world, application workloads - whatever their heritage - should be able to move seamlessly between or be shared among cloud service providers and be deployed wherever the optimal combination of performance, functionality, cost, security, compliance, availability, resilience, and so on, is to be found - while avoiding the dreaded 'vendor lock-in.' The following introduces the main features and goals that a solution must meet for Hybrid Multi-cloud adoption:

Combine On-premises and Public Cloud Resources

In the current cloud era, although multi-cloud will become the norm, the on-premises data center still has its necessity, either as part of a hybrid cloud strategy or to host legacy applications that, for whatever reason, are not suitable for migration to the cloud. Some main reasons to keep resources on-premises to host workloads include cost, control, security regulation, traits, and performance.

The Distributed Cloud allows you to leverage your on-premises infrastructure by deploying a normal zone site (Max site) with a OneZone instance, Pro site, Mini site, or Lite site locally. These on-premises sites can be hosted and automatically configured in your enterprise data center in the same way that they would be deployed on a public cloud or at the edge, offering a uniform control plane layer for your enterprise cloud and isolating your corporate users from the underlying heterogeneity.

Manage Workload Across Every Cloud and On-premise from a Single Pane of Glass

The most important thing to managing the Hybrid Multi-cloud complexity is interoperability (that is, the ability to manage your workload across every cloud from a single pane of glass) and portability (that is, the execution of your workloads with the same images and templates on any infrastructure and their mobility across multiple public clouds and on-premises infrastructure).

The Distributed Cloud implements a multi-cloud architecture based on a single OneCenter that controls multiple interconnected sites that can run in different geographically distributed enterprise data locations, Telcos Data Centers (CORD), and on public cloud or other edge infrastructure. This approach offers a complete end-to-end solution that leverages proven open-source technologies in order to provide uniform operation, configuration management, network automation, performance optimization, and capacity and cost management. A Distributed Cloud Hybrid Multi-cloud architecture enables:

Interoperability - offers a unified view of underlying infrastructure and resources of any infrastructure - on-premise, in public clouds, 3GPP, and non-3GPP edge - with a single central user interface console, OneUI.

Portability - by using sites based on a common hyper-converged architecture that has been designed to be deployed on any resource - from bare-metal, hypervisor virtualized to containerized - enabling workload portability and mobility across clouds and on-premises with absolutely without code changing.

Automate Resource Allocation and Align the Right Workloads with the Right Cloud

How to place applications in the right location is also not easy to work. Orchestrators should consider multiple aspects, such as costs, data fees, performance, uptime, latency, etc.

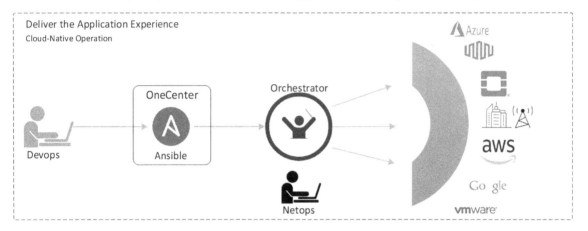

Figure 8-1 Allocation and Align the Workloads with the Multi-Cloud

The site in the Distributed Cloud can be added and removed dynamically in order to meet peaks in demand or to implement fault tolerance strategies or latency requirements. Once the new site becomes a part of the cloud infrastructure, the Distributed Cloud offers advanced capacity planning features to fine tune workload allocation, including:

- Application-level scheduling and placement constraints based on arbitrary site metrics or properties.

- Scheduling for multi-component applications that often require specific affinity (place in the same node or site) or anti-affinity (place in a different node or site) rules to improve their latency, fault-tolerance, or performance.

- And admins need resource isolation or a quota system to limit resource usage in order to implement the capacity plan in a multi-tenant environment.

Those features above can be archived by appropriated scheduler algorithms offered by the Unified Resources Manager in the OneCenter.

Submit Any Workload on Any Cloud

Due to its complexity and dynamic nature, the multi-cloud environment brings challenges in assessing the suitability of on-premises applications for migrating to the cloud.

The Distributed Cloud combines application containers, Virtual Machines (standard VM and MicroVMs), and bare metal nodes on a single platform and integrates with those bare metal nodes, Virtual Machine and container image hubs and marketplaces. An application can be deployed anywhere on the multi-cloud infrastructure without performing any additional configuration or setup. Although new workloads based on containers, microservices, and functions (serverless) should generally be stateless and ephemeral, almost all business applications and High-Performance Computing (HPC)-like software require data persistence in some form. This is why the Distributed Cloud architecture provides support for both non-persistent and persistent VMs and containerized applications and has the capacity to handle the bare metal like a virtual machine without sacrificing performance.

8.2   Hybrid Multi-Cloud Design

This section introduces the network design Hybrid Multi-Clou with SD-WAN and MBGP-EVPN VXLAN Multi-site architecture. Section 3.2 describes the MBGP-EVPN VXLAN Multi-site architecture.

Hybrid Multi-Cloud architecture typically consists of the data center in the public cloud and the on-premises. The on-premises generally contain the SD-WAN-connected data center, branches, campuses, and even the colocation places, which with a hardware device or software of WAN Edge Router.

8.2.1   Hybrid Multi-Cloud Architecture

The following Figure 8-2 illustrates a comprehensive architecture with multi-site data centers, hybrid, SDN, and SD-WAN-enabled sites. Those components are orchestrated and controlled by OneCenter instance through WAN via SD-WAN fabric connections.

As shown in Figure 8-2, a Max site as a Distributed Cloud zone running in an Azure data center and a Max site as a Distributed Cloud zone running in an AWS data center connected by direct link can be paired with Active-Active disaster recovery model, those two sites execute backup and recovery each other. The on-premises site with data center connects with Azure and AWS sites by direct link too and form a hybrid for disaster recovery or a multi-cloud architecture for complex high availability application.

Those three sites can be a separate zone like AWS available zone to compose a logical Zonegroup like AWS region. When taking the three Max type of sites as Zonegroup, the zone external connection to WAN and reach SD-WAN enabled sites such as branch and campus can be independently or from only one site BGW.

The Hongkong Edge site, Singapore Campus site, Tokyo Branch site, OneCenter, zone enabled New York WEST site, zone enabled London site, and zone enabled New York EAST site to connect each other passthrough SD-WAN fabric (5G network, internet or MPLS network) via IPSec or GRE VPN connections.

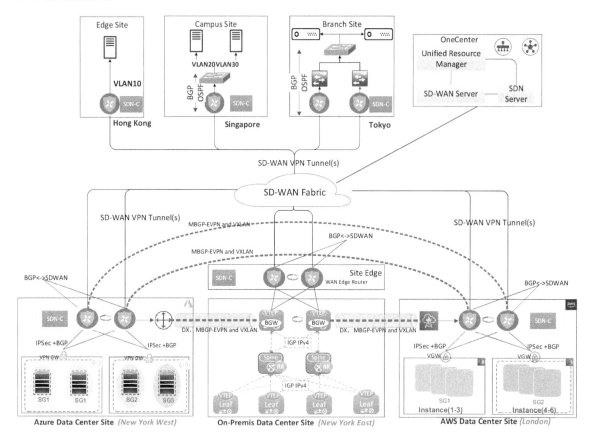

Figure 8-2 Hybrid Multi-Cloud Architecture

8.2.2   Cloud onRamp for IaaS from Public Cloud-AWS

This design is to extend the SD-WAN fabric out to AWS through a transit VPC. A transit VPC is a VPC in AWS that has the single purpose of transporting traffic between other VPCs as well as edge, campus, and branch locations. AWS host VPCs are then connected to the transit VPC through AWS Site-to-Site VPN connections.

This design implemented obtaining IaaS for connecting AWS host VPCs to the SD-WAN network. It should be automated and managed through the OneCenter web-based graphical user interface (OneUI). An example of architecture is shown in the following Figure 8-3.

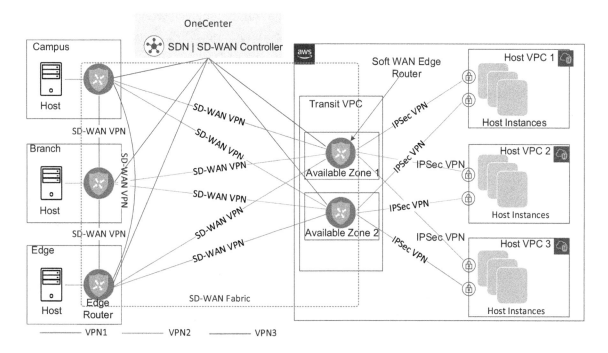

Figure 8-3 Cloud onRamp for IaaS Transit VPC Design with AWS

The Cloud OnRamp for IaaS feature within the SD-WAN solution first provisions a transit VPC of AWS with one or more redundant pairs of SD-WAN edge routers (software WAN edge router). AWS Site-to-Site VPN Connections are then established between AWS Virtual Private Gateways (VGWs) at the host VPCs and the SD-WAN edge routers within the AWS transit VPC. Because each AWS Site-to-Site VPN Connection consists of a pair of redundant IPsec tunnels, a total of six IPsec tunnels are established from each AWS host VPC to the transit VPC.

Traffic between AWS host VPCs flows through the dedicated transit VPC. Traffic from edge, campus, and branch sites to the host VPCs also passes through the transit VPC via the SD-WAN fabric (VPN connections established between SD-WAN routers resided in the edge, campus, and branch sites, and each of the SD-WAN edge routers resided in the transit VPC in AWS).

In the high-level view for this design, a single transit VPC is created by Cloud OnRamp for IaaS within an AWS region. Three host VPCs created in the same AWS region are then mapped to the transit VPC using Cloud OnRamp for IaaS. Because Cloud OnRamp for IaaS is used to map the host VPCs, they connect to the SD-WAN edge routers within the transit VPC through AWS Site-to-Site VPN Connections.

In above Figure 8-3, host VPC 1 is mapped to service VPN 1 within the transit VPC. Service VPN 1 is also configured on the LAN side of the SD-WAN edge router deployed within the Campus site. The host VPC 2 is mapped to service VPN 2 within the shared transit VPC. Service VPN 2 is also configured on the LAN side of the SD-WAN edge router deployed within the Branch site. Similarly, the host VPC 3 is mapped to service VPN 3 within the shared transit VPC. Service VPN 3 is also configured on the LAN side of the SD-WAN edge router deployed within the edge site.

This configuration allows devices within the campus site to access applications running within AWS Elastic Compute Cloud (EC2) instances within the host VPC 1. It also allows communication between applications running on AWS EC2 instances deployed within the host VPC 1. Likewise, this configuration allows devices within the branch site to access applications running within AWS EC2 instances within the host VPC2. However, devices within the campus site cannot access applications running on AWS EC2 instances deployed within the host VPC 2, nor can devices within the Branch site access applications running on the AWS EC2 instances deployed within the host VPC 1.

This design provides segmentation through SD-WAN and, therefore, traffic isolation between the different host VPCs. This demonstrates the use case where different entities within an organization require access only to specific public IaaS cloud resources.

NOTE: In onRamp for the IaaS from AWS, there are multiple options for connecting AWS host VPCs to the SD-WAN. The following three options can be applied to the current AWS.

The first design option is to extend the SD-WAN fabric out to AWS through a transit VPC. A transit VPC is a VPC that has the single purpose of transporting traffic between other VPCs as well as HQ, campus, and branch locations. AWS host VPCs are then connected to the transit VPC through AWS Site-to-Site VPN connections.

The second design option extends the SD-WAN fabric to AWS through a transit VPC, too. However, AWS host VPCs are not directly connected to the transit VPC. Instead, host VPCs are connected to an AWS Transit Gateway (TGW) through VPC attachments.

The third design option is to connect host VPCs to an AWS Transit Gateway and then again connect SD-WAN Edge routers at campus branch and edge locations directly to the AWS Transit Gateway.

8.2.3   Branch Site

The word "branch" is an umbrella term in this section and generally refers to not solely the branch, and it actually also includes enterprise data center, headquarter, branch, or campus location. The integration with the data center and SD-WAN is complete in section [8.2 Hybrid Multi-Cloud Design], and the branch site design of SD-WAN begins.

8.2.3.1 Single WAN Router Site

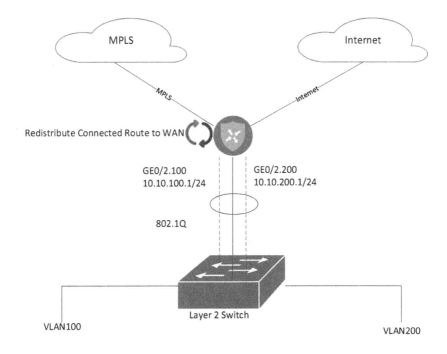

Figure 8-4 Single WAN Router Site-Layer 2 Design

Designing for SD-WAN branch sites can be a bit tricky compared to data centers. Because branch sites come in many scenarios and scales, with different topologies, types of WAN connectivity, high-availability designs, and additional features such as security, all need to be taken into account.

Full Migration of a Single Router Site

If there is only one WAN edge router at the branch site, connect the service end of the SD-WAN router to the core and connect the transmission to the carrier equipment. The transmission does not need to configure a routing protocol if the default route is used to forward the traffic to the next-hop IP address of the operator. The server side of the SD-WAN router supports Layer 2 and Layer 3 connections and can access the LAN through the 802.1q sub-interface, acting as a Layer 3 gateway for all VLANs on the server side. It is also possible to establish a peer-to-peer connection with the layer-3 core through BGP and OSPF, depending on the hardware platform of the device. In the layer 2 design, the subnet of the server will be automatically redistributed to the WMP to achieve end-to-end reachability. Following Figure 8-5 shows the network design of the Layer 2 connection of the server.

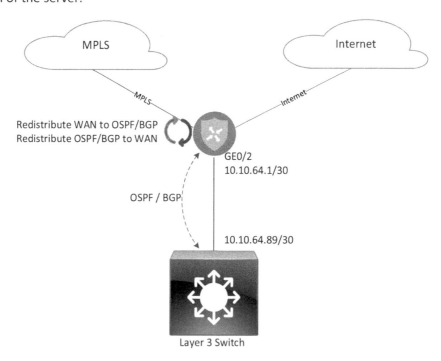

Figure 8-5 Single WAN Router Site - Layer 3 Design

In the single WAN router site with layer 3 design, the routes learned by the server must be redistributed to the WAN. Similarly, the routes of the WAN must also be explicitly assigned to the routing protocol of the server.

8.2.3.2 Double WAN Routers Site

In the double WAN Router sites with Layer 3 design, the branch sites with high availability requirements may need to connect two WAN edge routers. On the server side, users can choose to use VRRP as below in Figure 8-6 for the Layer 2 Design.

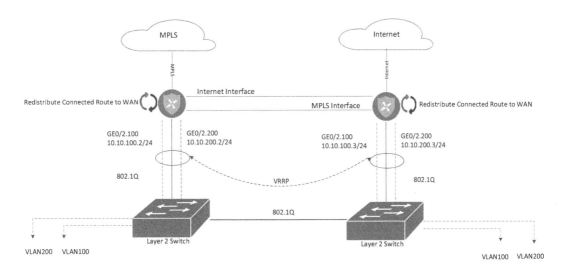

Figure 8-6 Double WAN Router Site-Layer 2 Design

In the double WAN Router sites with Layer 3 design, the branch sites with high availability requirements may need to connect two WAN edge routers. The dynamic (typically OSPF and BGP) or static routing protocol can be applied as Figure 8-7 to integrate the LAN network:

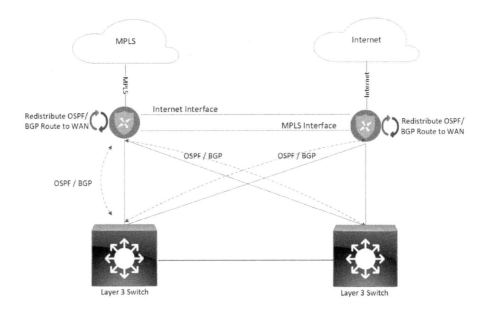

Figure 8-7 Double WAN Router Site-Layer 3 Design

8.2.4 WAN as a Service - WANaaS

WANaaS is an innovative public cloud network service that can help enterprises easily build enterprise backbone networks. Customers do not need to actually own, build, and maintain their own network infrastructure, including switches, routers, and transmission equipment. Not only that, but customers can also quickly deploy network services and flexibly expand the network coverage of enterprises as their business needs change, helping customers reduce hardware expenditure costs while increasing flexibility and scalability.

Leveraging the capacity of global connection and central control of the Distributed Cloud, not only the compute infrastructure but also the high-speed backbone network infrastructure can be utilized to build a modern WANaaS, which is a Distributed Cloud Networking service that can help enterprises easily build enterprise backbone networks. Customers do not need to actually own, build, and maintain their own network infrastructure, including switches, routers, and transmission equipment. Take the Amazon public cloud as an example, as shown in Figure 8-8:

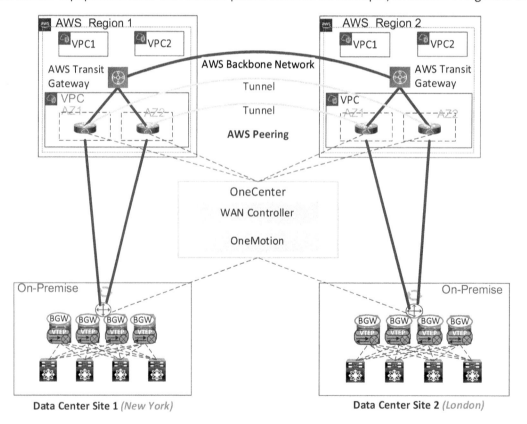

Figure 8-8 WANaaS Service in Multi-Cloud

The on-premises data centers are in the cities where the two Zonegroup are located. The customer does not have its own enterprise backbone network. Locally, the two local data center resources can be connected to the public cloud (such as Amazon Cloud AWS), and then through the routing configuration to allow the traffic to pass through the public cloud backbone network so that the local data center traffic can be forwarded through the public cloud backbone network. The public cloud backbone network serves as the backbone network of the customer's enterprise to carry the traffic between the customer's two data centers. The customer only needs to pay for the backbone network according to usage, and there is no need to spend a lot of money to build the enterprise backbone network.

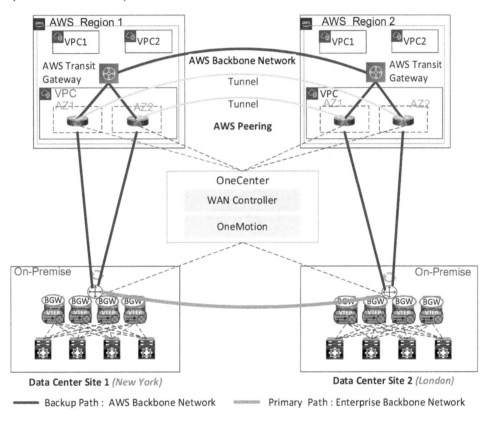

Figure 8-9 WANaaS Service Backbone Network High Availability

If the customer has already deployed their own enterprise backbone network, they can also use the above method to build a backup backbone network line. As shown in Figure 8-9, once the customer's enterprise backbone network (green line in Figure 8-9) breaks down, the traffic can be immediately switched to the AWS cloud backbone network (the deep gray line in Figure 8-9), so that the enterprise network will never be disconnected. Another advantage of using this solution is that the backbone network of the public cloud is charged according to traffic. If the customer's enterprise backbone network does not fail, the public cloud backbone network line is the customer's free backup channel.

8.3   Disaster Recovery in Hybrid

This section introduces a user case of Hybrid Multi-Cloud in the Distributed Cloud. Commonly, enterprises can combine the cloud-native and on-premises deployments into hybrid scenarios where the workload environment has on-premises and public cloud (AWS, Azure, etc.) infrastructure components. Resources, including big data, web servers, application servers, monitoring servers, databases, and so on, are hosted either in the customer's local data center or on the public cloud (AWS, Azure). Applications that are running on-premises are connected to applications that are running on the public cloud, and versa.

When enterprises own their private data center and utilize public cloud such as AWS to augment capacity, these local data centers are often connected to the public cloud network by high-speed network links. For example, with AWS Direct Connect, you can establish private, dedicated connectivity from your on-premises data center to AWS. This provides the bandwidth and consistent latency to upload data to the cloud for the purposes of data protection. It also provides consistent high performance and low latency for dispersed hybrid workloads. The following section will introduce a hybrid disaster recovery case of this kind of environment.

In this book, we use AWS as a public cloud example to design the Hybrid Architecture of Disaster Recovery. Other public clouds such as Azure or GCP can do the same thing.

8.3.1   Strategies for Disaster Recovery

This section describes the basic concepts of disaster recovery and several strategies for this disaster recovery. This book only focuses on introducing the first two types of Strategies, Backup Restore and Pilot Light.

Any disaster can cause asset loss, obviously, the time related to system down time is a key import aspect for DR, so we take the following aspects as disaster recovery:

Recovery Time Objective (RTO) - The maximum acceptable delay between the interruption of service and restoration of service. This determines an acceptable length of time for service downtime.

Recovery Point Objective (RPO) - The maximum acceptable amount of time since the last data recovery point. This determines what is considered an acceptable loss of data.

For both the RTO and RPO, lower numbers represent less downtime and data loss. But with the lower RTO and RPO, you will spend more expense to build such a DR infrastructure. So, you must choose appropriate RTO and RPO objectives according to your business need and budget.

8.3.1.1 Disaster Recovery Objectives

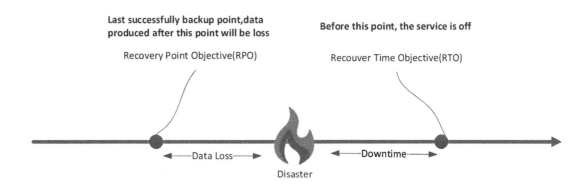

Figure 8-10 Recovery objectives: RTO and RPO

8.3.1.2 DR strategies

AWS offers resources and services with the on-premises Data Center resources to build a Hybrid Disaster Recovery strategy that meets your business needs.

Figure 8-11 shows the typical strategies from left to right. The picture shows how Disaster Recovery strategies incur differing RTO and RPO. The first three are active-passive, and the last one is multi-site active-active mode.

In the real world, we have four classic Disaster Recovery strategy options to choose from: backup and restore, pilot light, warn standby, and active/active. This book only introduces the first two Disaster Recovery strategies to illustrate how the Distributed Cloud architecture supports hybrid disaster recovery. To select the best strategy in your actual conditions, you must rebalance benefits and risks with the business owner of a workload, as informed by engineering and IT. Determine what RTO and RPO are fit for the special workload, cost, project duration, and effort that you are willing to make.

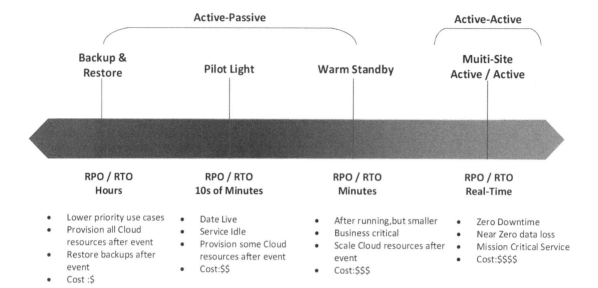

Figure 8-11 DR Strategies-Trade-offs between RTO/RPO and Costs

8.3.2   Backup and Restore in Hybrid Architecture

In this section, you will learn about active/passive strategies that enable your workload to recover from disaster events such as natural disasters, technical failures, or human wrong actions. Now let's learn about the Backups and recovery strategies.

8.3.2.1 DR strategies: Choosing Backup and Restore DR Strategies

As shown in the following Figure 8-12, in the backup and restore strategy, the RTO and RPO are relatively higher. That means longer downtimes and greater loss of data between when the disaster event occurs and recovery. Even so, the backup and restore strategy can still be the right strategy for your workload when you cannot afford too much because it is the easiest and least expensive strategy to implement. Additionally, some workloads do not require RTO and RPO in minutes or less.

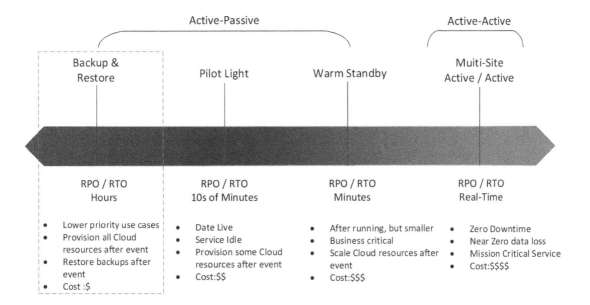

Figure 8-12 DR Strategies-Backup and Restore

8.3.2.2 Implementing Backup and Restore

Like AWS Backup tools, the Distributed Cloud architecture provides a centralized view where you can configure, schedule, and monitor backups for these resources by Cloud Motion. The Cloud Motion can operate backup and restore actions between the public cloud and on-premises.

Figure 8-13 shows backups of various on-premises data resources. Backups are created in the same on-premises Zonegroup as their source and are also copied to the remote AWS Region. This gives you the most effective protection from disasters of any scope of impact. For site failover, in addition to data recovery from cloud backup, you must also be able to restore all infrastructure on the recovery side.

The backup and recovery strategy are considered the least efficient for RTO and often be used. However, you can use OneCenter native tools or AWS resources to build serverless automation, which will reduce RTO by improving detection and recovery.

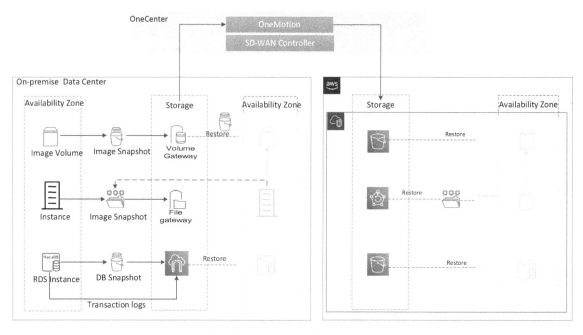

Figure 8-13 DR Strategies - Backup and Restore

8.3.2.3 Getting the Most Out of Backup and Restore

When a disaster at the live site occurs, you will accomplish your DR strategy by these steps:

Detect the impact of the disaster event on your workload automatically.

Restore infrastructure, and data, and re-integrate these to enable your service can be obtained and all workloads to operate.

Fail over will re-routing requests to the recovery target region or zonegroup.

1. Detect

Recovery time is often thought of as the time that it takes to restore the workload and fail over. But as shown in Figure 8-14, the whole recovery time consists of three partitions: disaster detection time, time for escalation/declaration, and restoration/failover. So you must automate the detection time to reduce the recovery time.

Do not wait until your operators notice the problem, and never wait until your customers know about it.

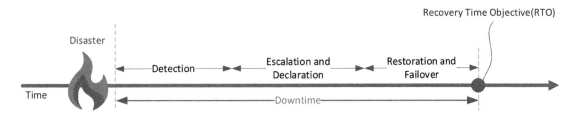

Figure 8-14 Contributors to Recovery Time after a Disaster Event

2. Restore

Restoring data from backup creates resources for that data, such as EBS volumes and Rational Database (RDS) instances when in the AWS case. You can use AWS Backup tools to restore data on the recovery side. Rebuilding the infrastructure includes creating resources like EC2 instances and the Amazon VPC, subnets, and security groups that are required by the application.

In some cases, you will need to re-integrate your infrastructure and data. For example, if you have recovered stateful data in an EBS volume, re-attach that volume to an EC2 instance. And you should have some ways to automate it.

3. Fail Over

Failover re-directs production traffic from the primary site (where the disaster occurs. and the services no longer run) to the recovery site.

8.3.3 Pilot Light in Hybrid Architecture

This section will discuss active/passive strategies that enable your workload to recover from disaster events such as natural disasters, technical failures, or human wrong actions. The following will introduce the pilot light strategies.

8.3.3.1 DR strategies - Pilot Light

When choosing a DR strategy, you must balance the benefits of lower RTO and RPO vs the costs of implementing and operating a strategy.

The pilot light offers a good balance of benefits and cost; the warm standby strategy has some similarities with the pilot light strategy, as shown in Figure 8-15. This book will omit to introduce the warm standby and active-active strategy.

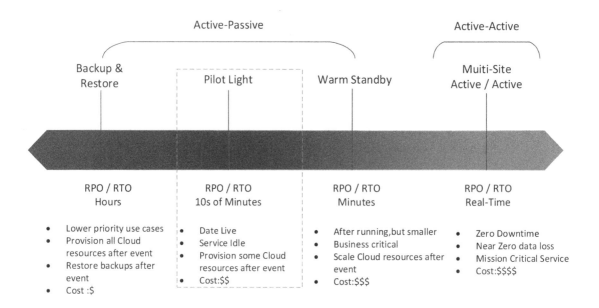

Figure 8-15 DR strategies - Pilot Light

8.3.3.2 Implementing Pilot Light

Figure 8-16 shows how to implement the pilot light strategies. This is a Hybrid cloud active/passive strategy. The left side on-premises site is the primary Zonegroup that is active, and the right-side AWS region is the recovery region that is passive before failover.

With the pilot light strategy, all the data in both sites is live, but the services are idle in the recovery site. Live data means the data stores and databases are up to date (or nearly up to date) with the active site (Region/ Zonegroup and ready to service read operations). In Figure 8-16, the MariaDB database replicates data to a local read-only cluster in the recovery site. But as with all DR strategies, backups (like the DB cluster snapshot) are also necessary. In the case of disaster events that wipe out or destroy your data, these backups let you restore to the last known correct state.

When applying the pilot light strategy, some basic infrastructure elements are in place, like Elastic Load Balancing and Amazon EC2 Auto Scaling in the public cloud site. But other functional elements (like compute machine) are "shut off." In the AWS cloud environment, the best way to shut off an Amazon EC2 instance is not to deploy it, and Figure 8-16 shows no instance deployed. To "turn on" these instances, the user can use an AMI that is specially built for this and copied to the needed site. This AMI can create instances quickly with exactly the operating system and software we need. Like a pilot light in a furnace that cannot heat your house until triggered by an event, a pilot light strategy cannot provide any services and process requests until it is triggered to deploy the remaining infrastructure and get ready state.

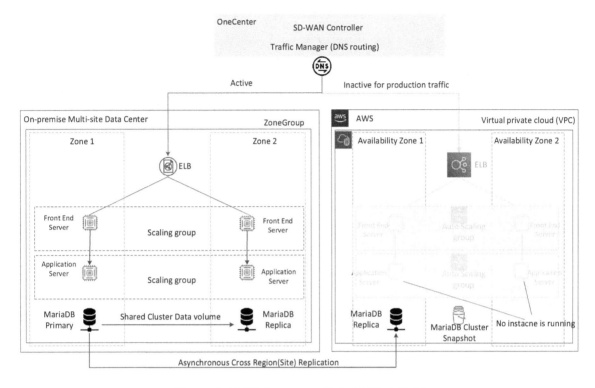

Figure 8-16 DR Strategy - Hybrid Pilot Light

8.3.3.3 Recovery with Pilot Light

In case of disaster, successful recovery depends on the detection of the disaster event, restoration of the workload in the recovery region/zone group, and failover to send correct traffic to the recovery region/zone group.

1. Detect

To detect the problem status of the system，you should determine your workload health based on metrics such as:

Server Liveness Metrics (such as a ping) - Insufficient to inform your DR decision.

Service API Metrics - Error rates and response latencies are a good way to understand your workload health.

Service Validation Metrics - This gives excellent insight into your workload health.

Workload Key Performance Indicators (KPIs) - KPIs indicate whether the workload is performing as intended and meeting customer needs.

2. Restore

Scaling up the desired count for resources such as concurrency for AWS Lambda functions by the AWS Command Line Interface (AWS CLI) or AWS SDK, such as the number of Amazon Elastic Container Service tasks, or desired EC2 capacity in your EC2 Auto Scaling groups.

3. Fail over

After restoring activities, Failover re-directs production traffic from the original site (where you have determined the workload is down and can no longer run) to the recovery site. If you are using the Distributed Cloud native DNS, you can set up both your original site and recovery site endpoints under one domain name. Then, choose a routing policy that determines which endpoint receives traffic for that domain name. Failover routing should automatically send traffic to the recovery site if the original site is unhealthy based on health checks that have been configured before. When a disaster occurs, a pilot light strategy can offer the capability to limit data loss (RPO). Give a sufficient RTO performance that enables you to limit downtime.

Chapter 9   Telco Edge in Distributed Cloud

In the past, the telecommunication network system was mainly based on physical telco infrastructure with dedicated network devices, telecommunication data centers, and physical servers. With the great rapid development of cloud and container technology, the Telcos companies throng to restructure their telco infrastructure with a large scale of investment. Many Telco companies have not only completed the virtualization and containerization of Network Function Virtualization (NFV) but also embraced distributed Hybrid and Multi-Cloud in great strides. From this point of view, the Distributed Cloud architecture is the best choice for most Communication Service Providers.

The Telco Edge infrastructures can be divided into three scenarios. The first is the well-known CORD (Central Office Re-architected as a Data Center) for the Public Network Infrastructure and PLMN, such as public RAN, public Core Data center, etc. It is owned and operated by the carrier to provide mobile network services for the public community. The second is Non-Public Networking (NPN), also termed as private 5G or 3GPP NPN for non-carrier enterprises, and the last one is the Public Networking Integrated MEC (3GPP PNI-MEC) solution extending and embedding the Distributed Cloud computing and storage infrastructures onto the carrier 's CORD to archive low latency for customers. In this book, the last two scenarios are part of Distributed Cloud architecture and will be described more carefully and deeply.

9.1   3GPP 5G Network Introduction

The Telco Edge owned by the carrier operator (based on CSP CORD) is different from the Telco Edge in enterprise owned Distributed Cloud (in the Distributed Cloud, the architecture mainly focuses on the 3GPP NPN, 3GPP PNI-MEC solution mainly), but both are based on the 3GPP network (current 5G or future 6G) and its architecture. The Distributed Cloud mainly focuses on the Private 5G network that is standardized by the 3GPP (The 3rd Generation Partnership Project is an umbrella term for a number of standards organizations that develop protocols for mobile telecommunications).

9.1.1 Deployment Architecture

In the case that the service with tolerance for a 10 ms roundtrip delay for mobile broadband, the Macro Cells deployment model shown of ❶ in Figure 9-1 may be optimal. In this case, the RAN Centralized Unit (CU) and the User Plane Function (UPF) are collocated at the site like a central office, while the Distributed Unit (DU) may be distributed to an aggregation site or to the cell site itself (or be located close by, in a cabinet or shelter). The user case for this mode can be the Mobile Broadband.

The Small Cells deployment model ❷ in Figure 9-1 illustrates the UPF is deployed closer to the edge site, to give around 5 ms roundtrip latency. The multi-access edge computing (MEC) platform also resides at the edge site to host and run latency sensitive MEC applications. The user case for this mode can be used for the automated guided vehicle (AGV) product.

The in buildings deployment model ❸ in Figure 9-1 describes the CU and DU are collocated with the RU, or even integrated into a single unit, at the cell site. Because very low latency is required, the core network (UPF) and MEC server may also be deployed at the cell site to enable applications to run locally. The user case may be Industrial Automation which uses 5G network for robotic motion control in an industrial production line.

The private 5G (Non-Public Network) network deployment model ❹ in Figure 9-1 shows that all of the RU, DU, CU, UPF, and MEC servers collocate together at the edge, 5G Core(5GC) along with RAN elements. This mode is like the previous mode; it can be used for robotic motion control in an industrial production line in industrial 4.0.

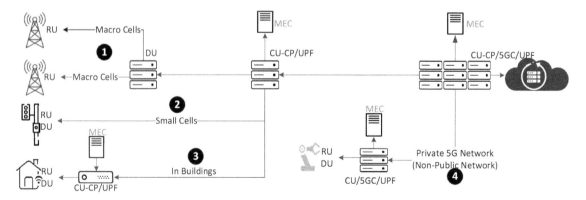

Figure 9-1 5G Network Deployment Scenarios

The private 5G network deployment model is one of the NPN cases, a standalone NPN. For detailed information, please refer to section [9.3.2.1 Standalone NPN - SNPN].

9.1.2   Core Service-Based Architecture

5G network was designed from the ground up, and network functions are split up by different services. That is why this architecture is also called 5G core Service Based Architecture (SBA). The following 5G network topology diagram shows the key components of a 5G core network:

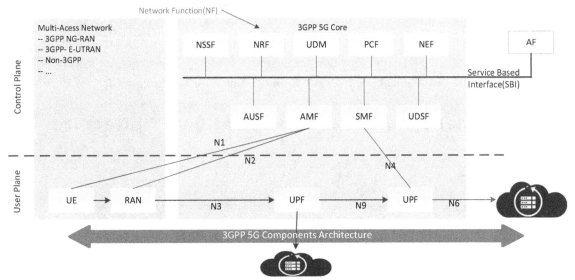

Figure 9-2 5G Service Based Architecture Model

Following Introduce the element function and how they work:

User Equipment (UE) refers to 5G smartphones or 5G cellular devices connected over the 5G New Radio Access Network to the 5G core and further to Data Networks (DN), like the Internet.

Access and Mobility Management Function (AMF) acts as a single entry point for the UE connection. Handles mobility related procedures.

UPF transports the IP data traffic (user plane) between the User Equipment (UE) and the external networks. UPF has a key role in an integrated MEC deployment in a 5G network. UPFs can be seen as a distributed and configurable data plane from the MEC system perspective.

Application Function (AF) is a MEC system functional entity.

Session Management Function (SMF) is based on the service requested by the UE, and the AMF selects the respective SMF for managing the user session. The SMF exposes service operations to allow MEC as a 5G AF to manage the Protocol Data Unit (PDU) sessions, control the policy settings and traffic rules as well as subscribe to notifications on session management events. The SMF can also configure the UPF with different options for traffic steering. The Policy Control Function (PCF), Application Function (AF), and Unified Data Management (UDM) function provide the policy control framework, applying policy decisions and accessing subscription information, to govern the network behavior.

Authentication Server Function (AUSF) allows the AMF to authenticate the UE and access services of the 5G core.

Network Resource Function (NRF) is one of the network functions of the 5G core network. NRF acts as a centralized point for service exposure and has a key role in authorizing all access requests originating from outside of the system. While 5G Service Based SBA Architecture also enables direct access to a Network Function for an authorized AF, there are many cases when services and capabilities are exposed over the Network Exposure Function (**NEF**).

9.1.3   Management & Orchestration Architecture

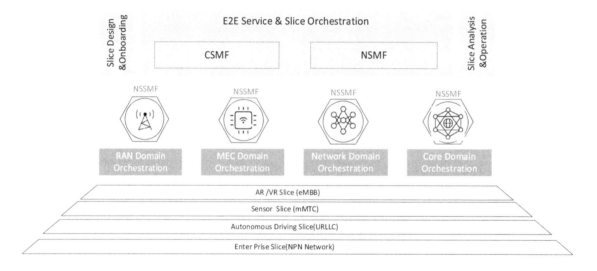

Figure 9-3 5G Network Management & Orchestration Architecture

Network slicing is one of the most important feathers of the 5G system. It drastically enhances the power of 5G networks, enabling operators to guarantee all kinds of applications and services to meet customer needs across a shared network infrastructure. Operators can use flexible network slicing to increase new business value, especially in high-growth vertical business markets.

Management & Orchestration Architecture provides a 5G Operations Automation solution, and This solution should:

- Automates the complete lifecycle of network slices within and across domains, including design, rapid slice creation, real-time delivery, assurance, and optimization, to meet all strict SLAs requirements.

- Provide cross-domain network slicing with the Customer Service Management Function (CSMF) and Network Service Management Function (NSMF) in End-to-End Service Orchestration.

- Provides domain-level slicing capacity with the Network Slice Subnet Management Function (NSSMF).

- Contain a facility of dynamic slice service models for the full lifecycle and all closed-loop control events to maximize automation.

9.2 Multi-Access Edge Computing

5G network features enhance its capacity to support edge computing, this not only spreads its service scope but also promotes the edge computing technology. It also plays an essential role in the transformation of the telecommunications business, where telecommunications networks are turning into versatile service platforms for industry and other specific customer segments.

9.2.1 MEC Deployment Model

UPF is a component network element of the 5G network and MEC system. The MEC system includes the MEC platform, MEC platform management, MEC service, MEC value-added application, infrastructure, and MEC orchestration. UPF is responsible for distributing and diverting edge network traffic to the MEC business system. Logically, the UPF network element and the MEC service system are separated and loosely coupled. In actual implementation, there are the following options for the MEC deployment with UPF.

9.2.1.1 Separated Deployment Between MEC and UPF

The MEC service platform and UPF are deployed separately to support multi-vendor construction, and IT vendors are introduced to provide their own MEC infrastructure and service systems. As a 5G core network element, UPF is physically isolated from third-party MEC service systems, which also brings benefits to the security of 5G networks. However, if the MEC application system under this type of deployment provides network traffic business chain processing services, it cannot share network processing resources with UPF, and there is a certain amount of duplicated investment.

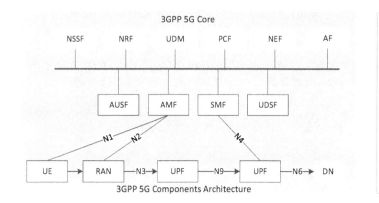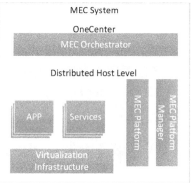

Figure 9-4 MEC Seperatellly Deployed with UPF

9.2.1.2 MEC and UPF Integration Deployment

UDF and MEC are integrated to deploy, and unified by Information and communication technology (ICT)-based infrastructure to bear the UDF and MEC workload. The MEC service system and UPF share the NFV communication infrastructure and are managed by the carrier operator, which can save construction costs.

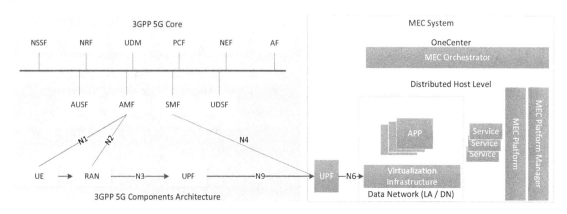

Figure 9-5 Integration Deployment between MEC and UPF

In addition, because the edge access point resources in close proximity to the base station are more limited, this kind of integrated deployment facilitates the reuse of resources. However, this deployment has high requirements on the forwarding performance of NFV networks such as UPF. It needs to support containerized and orchestration management of IT business applications, acceleration of edge AI and GPU/FPGA of video business applications, and heterogeneous computing processing. The NFV communication infrastructure oriented to network communication processing needs to be expanded into an ICT comprehensive edge data center.

9.2.1.3 MEC and UPF Partial Shared Deployment

The MEC business system is divided into two categories of services: CT-type VNF and IT-type applications. CT-type VNF and UPF are unified and integrated for deployment, and IT-type applications are independently deployed. For CT business services sharing NFV infrastructure, operators are still responsible for unified operation and management. At the same time, the IT infrastructure is built independently to meet the flexibility of IT-type edge services. This part of the IT infrastructure can be operated by operators in a unified manner. This model increases the unified management complexity of edge infrastructure.

9.2.2   MEC Location Cases

Logically, the MEC host/cluster is deployed at the RAN edge or central data center, and the UPF is in charge of steering the user plane traffic toward the targeted MEC host where the application resides. Telcos can decide where to place the physical computing resources based on technical and business parameters such as available site facilities, supported applications and their requirements, measured or estimated user load, etc. The MEC management system, which has the role of orchestrating the operation of MEC hosts and applications, may decide dynamically where to deploy the MEC applications.

In terms of physical deployment locations of MEC hosts or clusters, there are multiple options based on various operational, latency, or security related requirements. Figure 9-6 gives an outline of some of the feasible options for the physical location of MECs.

1. MEC and the local UPF collocated with the Base Station (Next Generation Node B - gNB at the edge).

2. MEC collocated with a transmission node with a local UPF.

3. MEC and the local UPF collocated with a network aggregation data center.

4. MEC collocated with the Core Network functions in the data center.

The four options presented above show that MEC can be flexibly deployed in different locations from near the gNB to the core central Data Center. Common for all deployments is the UPF that is deployed and used to steer the traffic toward the targeted MEC applications and toward the network.

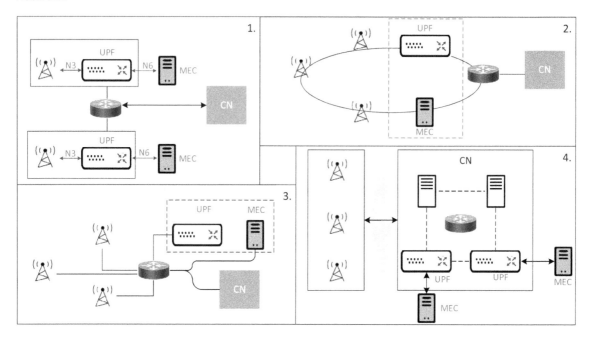

Figure 9-6 MEC Locations Cases of The Physical Deployment

9.3 Telco Edge Design

Traditionally, Telecommunications/Communications Service Providers (also termed Telcos or CSPs) use pure physical infrastructure to build telecommunication network systems. As hardware becomes more and more powerful, virtualization and programming can bring great achievement to CSPs.

Telco Edge is a new-generation network architecture that combines software-defined networking (SDN), network functions virtualization (NFV), and cloud native technology into a distributed computing network. That allows CSP to add services more quickly, respond faster to changes in network demand, and manage central and decentralized resources more efficiently. Since the network and the computing resources are distributed across sites and clouds, automation and orchestration are required.

In the early years, CSPs applied virtual machine virtualization technology from cloud data centers to telecommunications network systems. At the beginning of 5G, NFV was used.

In the Distributed Cloud era, cloud native such as containers and microservices, edge computing, multi-cloud, and hybrid cloud architectures should be considered. At the same time, containers and microservices (CNFs) still have to coexist with older virtualized network functions (VNFs).

9.3.1 Telco Edge Architecture

The hybrid and multi-cloud era for telecommunications Cloud may be a private cloud or public cloud, has brought so many advantages to enterprises. When more and more workloads move to the cloud, cloud resources are being mixed between legacy VNFs and containerized CNFs for running disaggregated network functions (with additional OSS, BSS, and IT workloads). Telcos use more than one cloud infrastructure to maximize flexibility and workload portability.

The main trend shows the telco edge is one that runs natively and efficiently in both multi-cloud and hybrid cloud environments. Therefore, a key approach for success in building a telco edge includes tools, platforms, and services that are built for the hybrid cloud and run in a consistent manner wherever they are implemented.

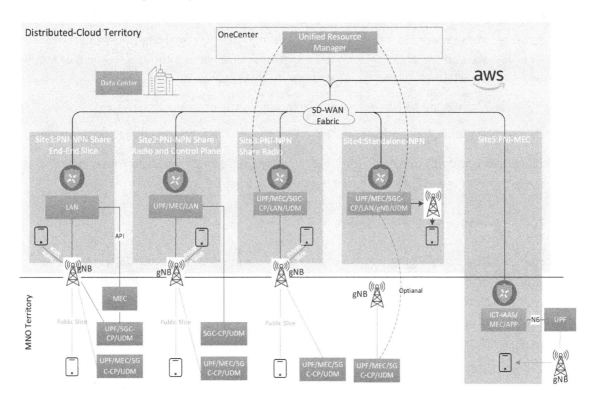

Figure 9-7 Telco Edge Architecture Overview

Almost all telcos have many physical devices and traditional VNF environments. With the Distributed Cloud architecture, the telecommunication cloud can merge those bare metal, VNFs with newer Container Network Functions (CNF) to meet new special requirements, and this can largely optimize the enterprise investment cost.

More specifically, a telecommunication cloud focuses on the creation of a common virtualized infrastructure to manage various network functions required to deliver communications services. Each function is now disaggregated from the hardware to be operated from a horizontal platform as a VNF or cloud-native network function (CNF). This function is designed to execute a specific network function such as a virtual router, load balancing, or firewalls.

From the deployment and architecture points of view, the Distributed Cloud leverages the 3GPP network and related infrastructures with 3GPP NPN and 3GPP PNI-MEC.

9.3.2   Non-Public Network -NPN

In contrast to a network that offers standard mobile network services to the public, in the 3GPP specifications, a Non-Public Network (NPN), also termed as a private 5G, can be defined to provide 5G network services to a clearly defined user organization or group of organizations. The 5G NPN is deployed on the organization's defined premises, such as a campus, branch, or factory location. At the top level, NPN can be divided into two categories:

1. **SNPNs (Standalone NPN)** deployed as isolated, standalone networks, and

2. **PNI-NPNs (Public Network** Integration NPN) deployed integrated with a public network.

The first category has only one deployment case, while the second comprises three, each differing in terms of the degree of interaction and infrastructure sharing with the PLMN.

9.3.2.1 Standalone NPN - SNPN

As shown in the following Figure 9-8, enterprises can build their own private 5G using local private dedicated 5G frequencies independent of the operator's public network. The ultra-low latency and large connection scale of 5G technology can create new enterprise applications or optimize existing applications.

The enterprise dedicated network is physically isolated from the public network (shown as the vertical solid red line of Figure 9-8), providing complete data security. The data flow generated from the private network device, the subscription information, and operation information of the private network device are only stored and managed within the enterprise (enterprise Distributed Cloud scope), ensuring that the enterprise's Internal private data is not be leaked.

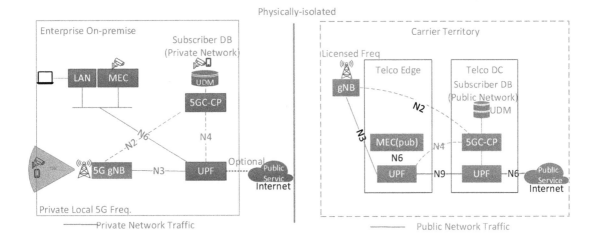

Figure 9-8 5G SNPN Deployment Architecture

The baseline 5G SNPN consists of a private 5GS with an NG-RAN and a lightweight 5GC. The NG-RAN includes a set of gNBs providing indoor 5GNR coverage. The 5GC is in accordance with an SBA with control and user plane separation, i.e., it is designed with a 5G Core Control Plane (5GC-CP) decoupled from UPFs that build up the user plane data path. UPFs are typically deployed on-premises with edge computing. The 5GC-CP (5G core control plane) can be co-located with NG-RAN, on-site on-premises data centers, or hosted off-premises by 3rd party hyperscale public cloud providers such as AWS or Azure. Wherever the 5GC-CP is located, they, along with UPF and edge computing applications, all belong to the enterprise Distributed Cloud.

In SNPNs, the enterprise or a delegating company that operates the Distributed Cloud takes the role of NPN operator, thereby acting as a μ Operator.

At the bottom strata of Figure 9-9, the infrastructure layer represents the on-premises physical network substrate that hosts the SNPN. It includes a set of wireless access devices and a clustered NFV Infrastructure (NFVI), with a transport network providing Time-Sensitive Networking (TSN) connectivity along the entire data path. The wireless access nodes contain gNBs providing small cell 5G New Radio (5GNR) connectivity and Wi-Fi access points. Note that the hardware and software of NFVI should be accelerated to real time processing of the virtualized gNB functions. At the upper strata of Figure 9-9, the network function stratum represents the different functional components constructing the SNPN. Note that the SNPN contains four different network segments: 5GS (divided into NG-RAN, UPF, 5GC-CP), Wi-Fi Access Point (AP), TSN, and the local data network.

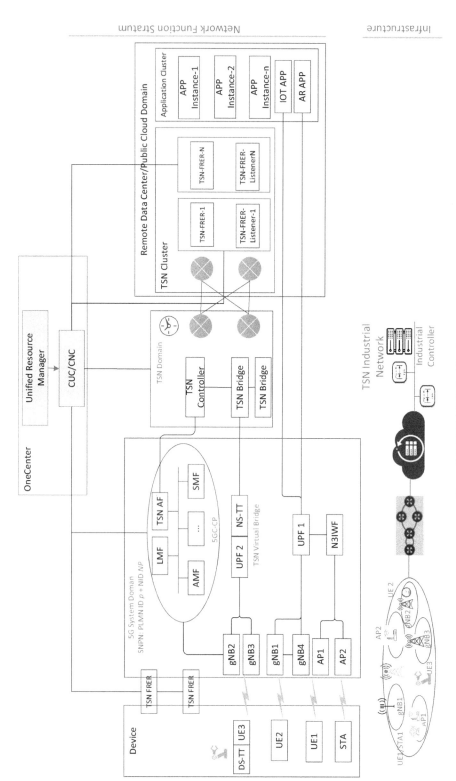

Figure 9-9 3GPP SNPN Architecture

In the 5GS, UPFs and 5GC-CP are executed as VNFs or CNFs in the site node/cluster, while NG-RAN consists of gNBs deployed as physical network functions (PNF). The Wi-Fi segment, with technology features provided by underlay Wi-Fi access points, integrated with the non-3GPP Inter Working Function (N3IWF), archives the 5GNR connectivity capabilities provided by gNBs. This Wi-Fi segment allows for increasing the reliability and throughput at the access side by leveraging multi-access connectivity features (such as traffic offloading, and bandwidth aggregation), as well as enabling the integration with the legacy network. The TSN domain (segment) allows providing deterministic QoS wired access in the SNPN, which is critical for typical Ultra-Reliable Low Latency Communications (URLLC) industry 4.0 services where a wireless device (e.g., industrial 4.0 robot) is operated by an industrial controller (IC) connected to the TSN industrial network. In this scenario, the 5GS behaves as a set of TSN bridges (one per UPF). The combination of 5GS and TSN requires the use of TSN translation components (e.g., Device-Side TSN Translator (DS-TT) and Network-Side TSN Translator (NS-TT)) at the 5G entities interfacing with the TSN network, for example, UE and UPF. The TSN controller transparently configures the 5GS as if it is a classic TSN bridge through the TSN AF. Finally, the local data network (LDN) allows the hosting of applications (such as Augmented Reality/Virtual Reality (AR/VR) applications) that provide the service logic.

Another important thing is slicing can be used in SNPN to differentiate traffic from different industry 4.0 services, although not captured in the above Figure 9-9.

9.3.2.2 Public Networks Integrate NPN - PNI-NPN

These deployments need to combine the Non-Public network and carrier-owned PLMN networks. Some organizations want their NPN infrastructure to be operated by carriers and they can be supported entirely by the public network (They don't want too much capital and manpower investment), whereas others require a dedicated NPN thus they can have full control over the network. Consequently, both public and non-public networks exist with slices allocated respectively and traffic assigned to the appropriate side.

9.3.2.2.1 Shared Radio Access Network

In this mode, UPF, 5GC CP, UDM, and MEC are deployed on the enterprise side and physically isolated from the 3GPP public network. Only 5G gNBs within the enterprise are shared between private and public networks (RAN sharing).

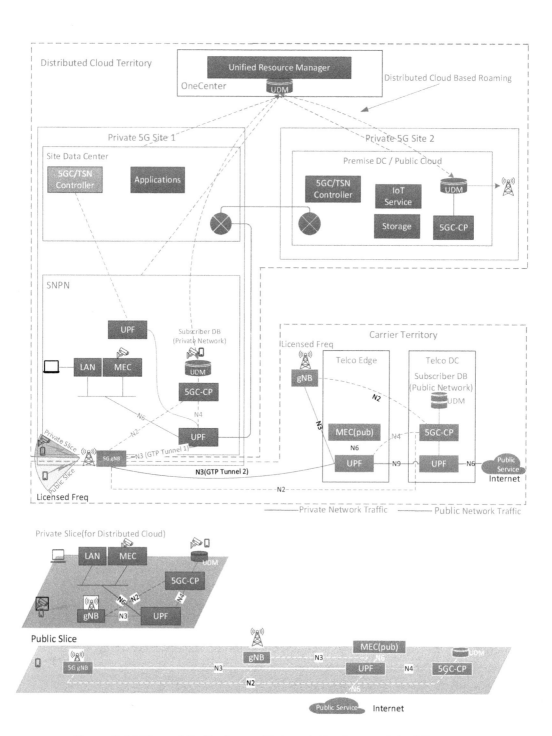

Figure 9-10 Shared Radio Access Network Deployment Architecture

The data traffic belonging to the devices of the dedicated network slice is delivered to the private UPF in the enterprise, and the data traffic of the devices belonging to the public slice (public network) is delivered to the mobile operator edge UPF. In other words, private network traffic like internal device-controlled data, internal video data, etc., remains within the enterprise, while public network service traffic like voice and internet is routed to the mobile operator's network. Although base stations are not separated physically but logically, it is almost impossible to collect data information in private networks at the RAN level, so the security of private network data traffic in enterprises is guaranteed. The enterprise-specific 5GC-CP and UDM are controlled by the enterprise, so the subscription information and operation information of the private network equipment in the enterprise can be stored and managed internally to avoid leakage to the outside of the enterprise.

For the sake of simplicity, Figure 9-10 only captures a single shared base station for the RAN on the defined premises. It is possible to configure additional base stations that are only accessible to NPN users. The NPN is based on 3GPP-defined technologies and has its own dedicated NPN ID. However, there is a RAN sharing agreement with a public network operator. it is possible to have an optional connection between the NPN and the public network via a firewall (not depicted in Figure 9-10).

UPF and MEC are in the enterprise to provide ultra-low latency communication among devices, gNB, UPF, and MEC, and this approach is very suitable for URLLC applications such as autonomous driving, real-time robotics, drone control, etc.

The fully controlled UDM and 5GC-CP information can be leveraged by OneCenter to implement the across sites roaming within the Distributed Cloud scope of the enterprise.

9.3.2.2.2 Shared Radio Access Network and Control Plane

Enterprise dedicated UPF and MEC is built within enterprise sites. 5G base stations (gNB) in enterprises and 5GC CP, UDM of mobile operators are shared between private and public networks (RAN and control plane sharing). gNB, 5GCP, and UDM are logically separated between the private network and public network, and UPF and MEC are physically separated.

Data traffic of devices belonging to a private slice (dedicated network) is delivered to a private UPF in the enterprise, and data traffic of devices belonging to a public slice (public mobile network) is delivered to a UPF at the edge of the mobile operator. As in RAN sharing in Figure 9-10 in the previous section, private network traffic, such as internal device control data, internal video data, etc., remains in the corporate site, while public mobile network services traffic like voice and internet is transmitted to mobile operators. The security of the internal data traffic of the enterprise is also very definite.

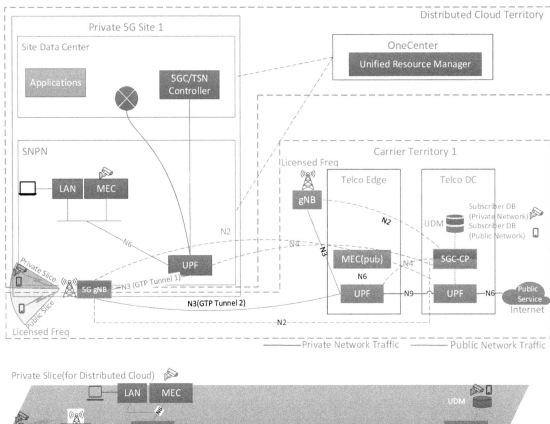

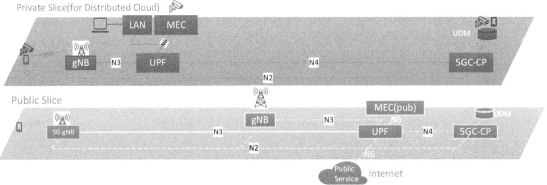

Figure 9-11 Shared Radio Access Network and Control Plane

The control plane functions (authentication, mobility, etc.) of private network devices and public mobile network devices are operated by 5GC-CP and UDM in the mobile operator network. That is to say, the dedicated network equipment, gNB, and UPF in the enterprise communicate with and are managed by the mobile operator's network (via N2 and N4 interfaces). A possible problem is that the operating information and subscription information of the private network device are stored in the mobile operator's servers instead of the enterprise internally.

This mode makes the contractual relationship between the NPN and the public network operator more straightforward. It allows NPN devices to connect directly to the public network and its services, including roaming.

As in the previous case of Shared Radio Access Network, since UPF and MEC are located within the enterprise, it provides ultra-low latency communication between devices, gNB, UPF, and MEC, and it is suitable for URLLC applications.

This deployment case does not support across sites roaming within the Distributed Cloud scope of the enterprise wide because the operating information and subscription information of the private network device are stored in the mobile operator's servers instead of the enterprise internally.

9.3.2.2.3 NPN Hosted by The Public Network

When gNB is deployed inside the enterprise, and UPF and MEC are only located in the mobile network operator's edge cloud, enterprise private network and telco public network share "logically separated 5G RAN and core" (gNB, UPF, 5GC, MEC, UDM), this case also be called as end-to-end network slicing.

Unlike the previous two PNI-NPN schemes, UPF and MEC are located within the enterprise. In this case, there is only gNB in the enterprise. There is no local traffic path between the private 5G device and the intranet (LAN) device (local intranet Server), so all traffic must reach the UPF in the public network operator's edge cloud and then return to the enterprise through a dedicated line to communicate with the enterprise site device.

This architecture has the lowest cost compared to other options that require UPF or 5GC-CP to be deployed on-premises. This mode provides the ability to roam and can be implemented easily in accordance with the agreement between the NPN and the public network operator. However, this model suffers from security (data traffic generated from enterprise private network terminals, subscription information, and operation information of enterprise private network devices) and network latency (RTT [the Round-trip time] between enterprise private 5G devices and MEC application servers and between private 5G devices and intranet/LAN devices) are obvious drawbacks. Since the traffic of the dedicated network equipment is transmitted from the enterprise site to the data center of the mobile network operator, there is a risk of data traffic security. The Distributed Cloud -based roaming cannot be implemented in this deployment case.

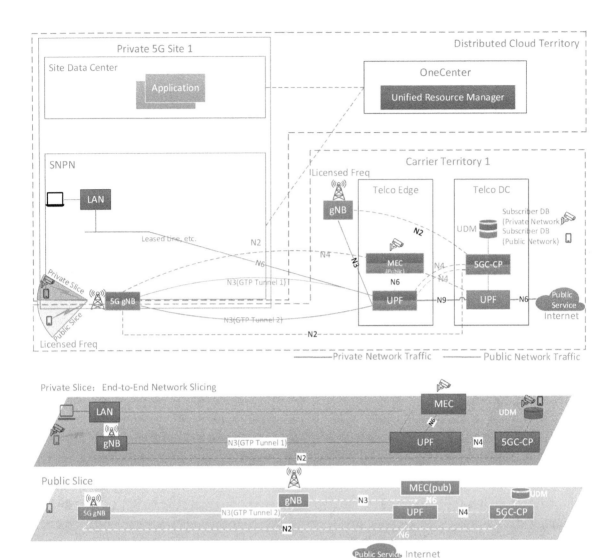

Figure 9-12 NPN Hosted by The Public Network

9.3.3   3GPP Public Network Integrated MEC - 3GPP PNI-MEC

Normally, to reach Distributed Cloud computing environments (may be an on-premise site or public cloud or other infrastructure), traffic must traverse from a base station, through the backhaul network, anchor to a mobile IP address in the core center, and then egress the cellular access network to the internet widely. Leading to each of these mobile traffic incurs a latency penalty through each hop in a mobile packet journey, amounting to more than 80 to 100 ms in round-trip delay.

By cooperating with a public Communications Service Provider, the Distributed Cloud extends and integrates the cloud infrastructure with UPF through the N6 interface of 5G networks to achieve substantially lower latency to mobile devices (user equipment or UEs) than any external site on the WAN or Internet. This UPF entity can be located in transmission nodes, cell aggregation sites, or Core Data Centers of communications providers. For more information on the MEC possible deployment location cases, you can see section [9.2.2 MEC Location Cases].

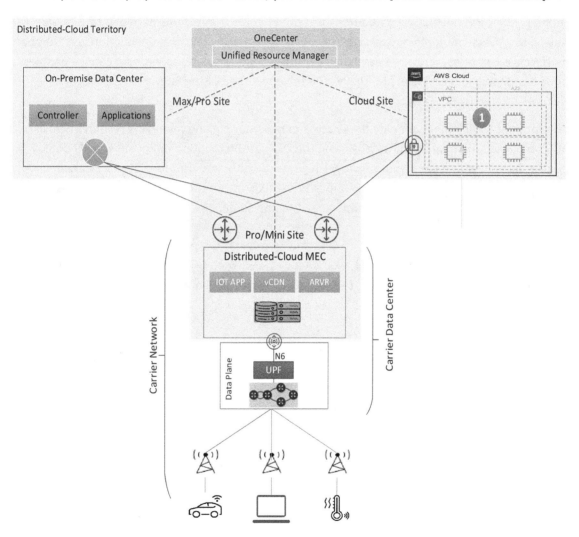

Figure 9-13 Public Network Integrated MEC - PNI-MEC

The MEC infrastructure that extends to the CSP Data Center can be multiple racks of servers belonging to the Distributed Cloud site, a Mini site with an HCI system architecture, or even a Lite site with a single MEC host.

3GPP NPN site brings the Distributed Cloud computing, storage capabilities, and services to the edge of existing 5G networks, embedding the Distributed Cloud hardware and software. This enables developers to innovate and build a new class of edge applications that can exploit high bandwidth and ultra-low latencies as offered by the 5G networks provided by CSPs.

Thanks to 3GPP PNI-MEC solution, application traffic from 5G end devices can reach the servers running in 3GPP PNI-MEC Site without leaving the telecommunications network, thus avoiding having to traverse multiple hops across the internet to reach their final destination, as it happens with a classic normal approach based on a centralized cloud solution. This new service enables both developers and end-users to finally take full advantage of the latency and bandwidth benefits offered by 5G networks.

This integration will really simplify the process of provisioning and managing resources close to 5G end devices, helping organizations using the Distributed Cloud to build and quickly deploy edge applications that can benefit from 5G high bandwidth and ultra-low latency, including machine learning, video streaming, multiplayer gaming, Internet of Things (IoT), augmented reality, virtual CDN (vCDN) and real-time analytics and so on.

NOTE: *The extension to AWS shown* ❶ *in Figure 9-13 is only for onRamp the public cloud IaaS infrastructures to build cloud sites that belong to the Distributed Cloud scope. It has no relationship with the AWS Wavelength product.*

Chapter 10 Approach Edge Computing to The Venue

The Distributed Cloud brings new innovative edge features to enable enterprises to build their own private, light, and nimble edge computing environments based on highly dispersed edge locations in close proximity to their end-users, devices, and sources of data. In a Distributed Cloud environment, not only are companies able to easily create their own edge infrastructure and manage it with utmost simplicity, but they are also able to create these environments from third-party cloud providers (including the carrier infrastructure [CORD data center]) and without needing to provide or to own those underlying resources at all.

10.1 Distributed Edge Model

With the mutual promotion of multiple technologies such as telecommunication, the Internet of Things (IoT), and big data, emerge many hard requirements for real time event responding and being able to provide innovative services and capabilities with absolute immediacy for their customers. The Figure 10-1 shows different use cases that meet different response time.

10.1.1   Architecture

With the rapid development of communication, network, and cloud computing, edge computing technology has been widely and further developed from centralized processing to processing as close as possible to mobile devices, sensors, and end users. However, the current edge computing technologies are all isolated and separated and there is no unified, centralized, and constantly adaptable global platform. Now, edge computing become one of the core parts of the Distributed Cloud. The advanced architecture of the Distributed Cloud will further promote the development of edge computing.

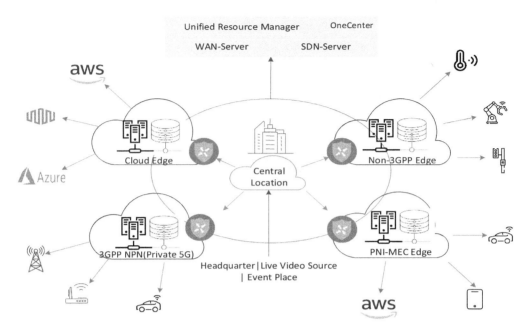

Figure 10-1 Architecture for Disaggregated Edge Scenarios

In the Distributed Cloud architecture, the disaggregated edge architecture is composed of a Central Location, Cloud site, 3GPP NPN (divided into SNPN and PNI-NPN) site, PNI-MEC site, and non-3GPP edge site.

Central Location is a new special concept of application level in the Distributed Cloud world, and the edge is a relatively logical concept from a global view. For an enterprise headquarter, the branch or SoHo site is its edge site; When creating an online meeting, the present location of the live video source is the central location, and the video/audio receiver is look at as the edge, and so on. During the whole Distributed Cloud life cycle, the Central Location for one organization can change to fit the requirements of enterprise business. In a typical scenario, the central location of the edge and application have the same locale as OneCenter.

Cloud Edge is the public cloud infrastructure that is located far away from the Central Location. It is introduced in section [10.2 Cloud Edge].

3GPP Edge contains 3GPP NPN and 3GPP PNI-MEC. Section [10.3 3GPP Edge] describes the detailed information, and you can refer to it.

Non-3GPP Edge mainly refers to LoRa WAN based IoT gateway, LoRa WAN Network Server or wired monitoring device converge server, etc. It is introduced in section [10.4 Non-3GPP Edge - Internet of Things (IoT)].

10.1.2   Containerize the Edge

By using the Distributed Cloud's provisioning system, besides on-premises data center, branch, campus, non-3GPP edge, 3GPP edge, cloud admins can now expand their clouds in an incredibly flexible way using resources offered by third-party cloud providers like AWS, Azure and Equinix Metal, incorporating, when necessary, the distributed dedicated infrastructure they need to satisfy their users' requirements for fault tolerance, capacity, traits regulation or low latency.

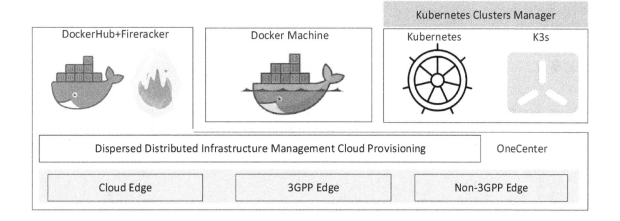

Figure 10-2 Edge Computing with Containers

The Distributed Cloud also offers a simple, but powerful approach for running containerized applications and workflows - both on-premises and on public cloud or edge locations - by using Docker images and running them as lightweight Firecracker micro-VMs. In case Kubernetes is necessary or is the best fit, the Distributed Cloud, At the same time, deploying a lighter Kubernetes solution based on K3s cluster at the edge is recommended.

10.2 Cloud Edge

By using the Distributed Cloud's provisioning module, cloud admins can now expand their clouds in an incredibly flexible way using resources offered by public cloud providers like AWS and Equinix Metal, incorporating, when necessary, the distributed dedicated infrastructure they need to satisfy their users' requirements for fault tolerance, capacity, traits, regulation or low latency. We regard the node or site provisioned by a public cloud vendor worldwide at geo-distributed locations in close proximity to end-users for special purposes (fault tolerance, capacity, regulation, or low latency) as cloud edge.

An AWS instance (EC2) in an AWS region (available zone) can be looked at as an edge host to the central location (for example, in the OneCenter) of an edge application, although the cloud regional location may be a central place in other most cases.

10.3 3GPP Edge

3GPP edge can also be termed as Telco edge, and it contains 3GPP NPN and PNI-MEC cases. Along with the non-3GPP edge, those three types of edge belong to the Distributed Cloud infrastructure mainly discussed in the book.

10.3.1   3GPP Edge Computing - Converged SNPN Site

This solution focuses on the context of the section 'Standalone Non-Public Network' (SNPN), targeted to describe the overview architecture and how the 3GPP SNPN scenario (one of private 5G cases described in section [9.3.2.1 Standalone NPN - SNPN]) works in an actual implementation.

10.3.1.1 Architecture

With the development of multi-access edge computing (MEC) technology, edge computing SNPN environment gives a network architecture that reduces backhaul network traffic and delivers low-latency applications through the Distributed Cloud.

Converged SNPN Edge Computing (CSEC) offers a compute, storage, and networking specification that unifies and converges Internet of Things (IoT), 5G SNPN wireless infrastructure to simplify workload convergence at the edge site while densifying wireless networks.

With the expected proliferation of edge site nodes, one aspect of particular importance is connectivity management. As the number of connected sites number grows, network connectivity becomes more important to ensure workers have the tools to be productive. This requires delivering network performance, security, and uptime while minimizing the cost of maintaining the network. With these requirements in mind, the SD-WAN solution provides a highly scalable, automated, access-independent platform to serve the networking requirements of the private 5G (3GPP NPN) site.

This solution introduces a scenario to illustrate how retailers like grocery stores can monitor storefront events and take immediate actions to optimize cost, promote the service, and improve customer experience. In this architecture, 5G-enabled internet protocol (IP) smart cameras capture real-time video of shelf inventory, curbside pickup, cashier queues, and so on.

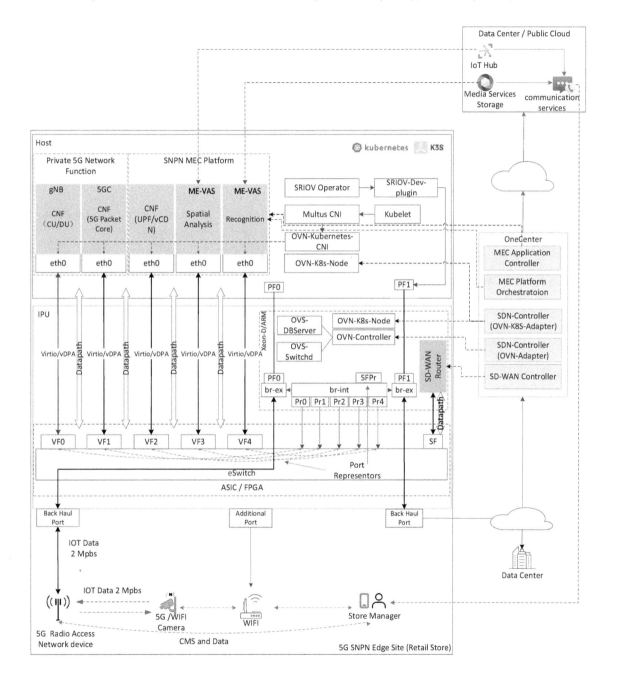

Figure 10-3 Converged SNPN Edge Computing Architecture

10.3.1.2 Components

This solution contains the following key components:

- 5G SNPN MEC host is a private 5G edge portfolio of devices that bring compute, storage, network, and intelligence to the edge for low-latency, local data processing and residency—allowing your business to support emerging and innovative applications, Co-locating on-premises with the Telco Network. This edge solution has a typical use case that acts as a cloud storage gateway that enables data transfers to remote data centers or public cloud locations while retaining local access to files.

- Web Apps creates and deploys mission-critical web applications that scale with your business.

- IoT Hub is a Distributed Cloud native or third-party public cloud based managed service for bidirectional communication between edge devices and the cloud.

- Media Services Storage uses the Distributed Cloud or third-party Cloud Object Storage such as Ceph with S3 API or AWS S3 to store massive media files.

- SD-WAN Edge Router enables the deployment of network functions to the Edge using consistent cloud tools and interfaces.

- Private 5G Network Function provides the private high bandwidth with the predictable and secure coverage needed to support new latency-sensitive applications and an ever-increasing volume of devices.

- The data of End Devices from a variety of devices (such as 5G Camera) is captured and transmitted to the MEC applications in the MEC platform via the Private 5G Network.

- SNPN MEC Platform provides video processing related applications such as vCDN, Spatial Analysis, and Cognitive Services with the integration of UPF.

10.3.1.3 Solution and Scenario

This CSEC solution describes how a retailer, like a grocery store, can monitor storefront events and take immediate actions to improve customer experience. In this solution, 5G-enabled Internet Protocol (IP) cameras capture real-time video of shelf inventory, curbside pickup, and cashier queues. Edge devices analyze the video data in real time to detect the number of people in checkout queues, empty shelf space, or carts in the parking lot.

Metrics analysis can trigger anomaly events to alert the store manager or stock supervisors to take corrective actions in case of abnormal situations. This solution can store summary video clips or events in the public cloud or on-premises data centers for long-term trend analysis.

Dataflow

1. SNPN enabled IP cameras to capture video in real time and send the video feed to a 5G Radio Access Network (RAN) equipment.

2. The 5G radios in the stores forward the data to the private 5G packet core running on the edge site host.

3. The 5G packet core authenticates the devices, applies Quality of Service (QoS) policies, and routes the video traffic to the target MEC application (for recognition).

4. The custom Edge module co-locates on the edge host with 5G network functions, which provides the low latency necessary for transporting and processing the video feeds.

5. The custom module simplifies setting up a video streaming pipeline and pre-processing the video for the spatial analysis module of the MEC application.

6. The Spatial Analysis module on the edge host anonymously counts cars, goods on a shelf, or people in line. The module sends these event notifications to the IoT Hub module which can reside in the on-premise data center or public cloud.

7. The IoT Hub module records the event notifications in an application, and alerts store managers or stock keepers if certain thresholds are reached, or a special event arises.

8. A Media Services Storage located in the data center or public cloud stores the events for long-term trend analysis to help with resource planning.

5G Network Reference Solution

Figure 10-3 presents the architecture of the 5G network reference solution. The architecture contains the following 5G network related components:

- 5G access network and core network (AN and CN) components (RAN L1, L2, and L3 and 5G Core) that deliver a 3GPP-compliant solution that services remote radio heads (RRHs) at the front haul and provide an N6 interface connectivity onto the platform.

- UPF VNF/CNF that bridges MEC applications and 5G network.

- MEC platform that directs traffic to edge services co-located on platforms and manages the lifecycle of these services.

- SD-WAN to provide more secure IPsec-enabled backhaul functionality.

This solution implements the data plane segmentation, which is a key foundation of this architecture. With this data plane, all wireless 5G, wireless LAN, and wired LAN data traffic is decapsulated on the edge site host. For 5G network, the N6 interface steering data traffic from it presents itself on the edge site.

In an enterprise or Telecommunication WAN environment, it is expected that the converged platform is replicated across hundreds or even thousands of edge sites or branch offices. The SD-WAN function and applications hosted on the converged platform are also deployed at a similar scale.

In addition to centrally hosted applications, the MEC host might host enterprise applications that need communication between the enterprise's branch servers or data center, or third-party, public cloud, and it is necessary for privacy and security between the different application data flows.

WAN Connection

In this Distributed Cloud edge environment, the network transition from a site-to-site context to a client-to-cloud context with the goal of delivering the best application user quality of experience (QoE). This shift has driven many enterprises to re-architect their Wide Area Network (WAN) and security architecture.

WAN Edge router at the edge site enables this transition with its innovative SD-Edge solution that combines routing, networking, SD-WAN, and security features in a unified solution that simplifies and automates site network operations and WAN edge services while helping secure the distributed enterprise. The main elements of the SD-WAN include the following:

- **VNF / CNF** is intelligent multiservice and multi-tenant edge software that delivers scalable, segmented, programmable, and automated SD-Infrastructure (SD- Routing, SD-WAN, SD-Security, and SD-Branch, SD-Edge) at the edge site.

- **WAN-Server** provides centralized control and management for both connectivity, WAN Edge router, and services, this server located in OneCenter location.

- **WAN-Controller** is the network-wide controller with data security features that manage the distributed control plane across the SD-WAN fabric.

SD-WAN Networks enable organizations to simplify the WAN and edge site networks by consolidating networking, SD-WAN, and security features into a single platform instead of deploying siloed hardware or virtual appliances from multiple vendors. Main remarkable features and functionality of the solution contain the following:

Integrated Security Features enable enterprises to deploy a more secure SD-WAN fabric for their branch/multi-cloud networks, with deep contextual visibility, enabling better WAN cost management.

Multi-cloud and Hybrid Extensibility enables multi-cloud topologies with cloud-to-cloud interoperability for workload migration, additional security, management, analytics, and monitoring.

SD-WAN provides an elastic, application-aware, access-agnostic networking solution with integrated security features. SD-WAN integrates with the Converged SNPN with MEC platform to create multiple virtual private networks for helping secure the communication of each VNF or CNF hosted on a Converged SNPN with MEC platform.

10.3.1.4 use cases

This solution is ideal for the retail, automotive, and facilities/real-estate industries. It includes the following scenarios:

- Monitor and maintain occupancy limits in an establishment.
- Stop unauthorized users from tailgating others into an office building.
- Prevent fraud at grocery store self-checkout stations.

This solution can be expanded to support other relative scenarios as shown in the table:

Table 10-1 CSEC Extended User Cases

Fields	Potential User Cases	Fields	Potential User Cases
DSS	POI	**Industrial**	Manufacturing
	Security		Automation
	Surveillance		Worker Safety
Retail	Digital Signage	**Advertising**	Traffic Management
	Advertising		Intersection Safety
Monitoring	Air Quality Monitoring	**Streetlights /Traffic Lights**	Small Cells
	Flood Warnings		Street lights Traffic Lights

10.3.2 3GPP Edge Computing - Containerized PNI-MEC Site

Like AWS Wavelength, in collaboration with 5G telecommunication providers such as Verizon, Vodafone, and others, has presented 3GPP PNI-MEC edge computing, this new Telco Edge Service brings the Distributed Cloud computing, storage capabilities, and services to the edge of existing 5G networks, embedding the Distributed Cloud hardware and software within the telecommunication data centers. This enables developers to innovate and build a new class of edge applications that can exploit high bandwidth and ultra-low latencies as offered by the current 5G or future new 6G networks.

Thanks to PNI-MEC edge computing, application traffic from 5G devices can reach the servers running in the PNI-MEC edge computing host without leaving the telecommunications network, thus avoiding having to traverse multiple hops across the internet to reach their final destination, as it happens with a traditional approach based on a centralized cloud solution. This new service enables both developers and end-users to finally take full advantage of the latency and bandwidth benefits offered by 5G networks.

10.3.2.1 The PNI-MEC Architecture

Most companies want to deploy a multi-container application at the edge (i.e., a Machine Learning solution), closer to the 5G devices of their end-users. The following architecture illustrates how this would be implemented based on the features provided by the Distributed Cloud and on the new resources made available by PNI-MEC services:

PNI-MEC edge service is designed to provide access to services and applications that require low latency, but it's important to remember that you don't need to deploy your entire application in the edge host. You only need to deploy those latency-sensitive parts of your application that are really going to benefit from being deployed at the PNI-MEC edge. In this architecture, the API server and MEC Apps (inference engine and vCDN) are located on the edge host because one of the design goals of the application is the low-latency processing of the inference requests. On the other hand, given that the MEC manager and web server don't have those latency requirements, it can be located on-site as a zone with a data center, even at the OneCenter location, and doesn't really need to be hosted on the edge host.

A PNI-MEC edge host/cluster can belong to a specific Max type site in a data center, known as the "parent site" where the OneZone instance along with its scheduler resides. Also, PNI-MEC edge instances are only accessible from 5G devices on a specific Telcos provider network.

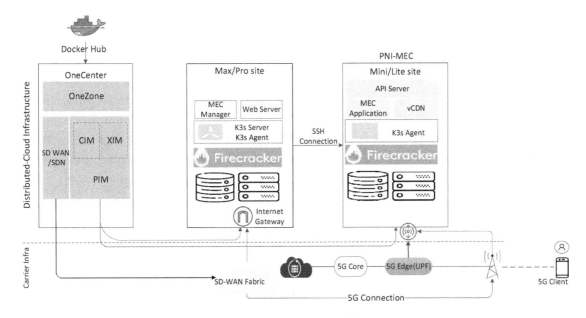

Figure 10-4 3GPP PNI-MEC Architecture

For the deployment of a multi-container application that benefits from this approach, some well-known open-source technologies can be used, such as K3s, a certified Kubernetes distribution now hosted by the CNCF. K3s is a lightweight, production-grade distribution designed for organizations looking to run Kubernetes in resource-constrained environments, which makes it ideal for deployments at the edge. The company is able to deploy a K3s cluster by simply using its public Docker image in a bare-metal environment. For magic, a company can also integrate with Firecracker. Firecracker is a new open-source virtualization technology -popularly used by AWS as part of its Faregate and Lambda services - especially for serverless services. With Firecracker integration and running application containers (e.g., the K3s Docker image) as Firecracker microVMs, users can obtain enhanced security and workload isolation of a traditional VM without undermining the speed and resource efficiency of a container.

In this solution architecture, we assume that the PNI-MEC edge host has bare-metal instances. If bare-metal instances are not available in the current PNI-MEC edge host, we can use Ubuntu's LXC system containers to deploy K3s agents on the edge resources.

As shown in Figure 10-4, in order to deploy a containerized application composed of different function components, the Distributed Cloud allows you to instantiate a K3s cluster across multiple hosts with mixed hypervisors and then let the customer deploy the application (e.g. using a helm chart or kubectl) by scheduling the components on the right resources, typically deploying the latency-sensitive module (i.e. The API server) on the PNI-MEC edge host and the other components (i.e. Web Server) on the parent site.

10.3.2.2 Integration of PNI-MEC Edge with The Distributed Cloud

The first thing to set up PNI-MEC edge resources is the deployment of two subnets: the pubic subnet is related to the associated parent site location, and the private subnet is related to the PNI-MEC site. We have then to associate to an Internet Gateway that is used to assign public IPs to resources that are deployed within the public subnet, plus a Carrier Gateway that is used to assign carrier public IPs to the resources deployed on the PNI-MEC edge host. That means The public subnet in the parent site will be associated with the Internet Gateway to get public IPs, whereas the private subnet in the PNI-MEC edge host will be associated with the Carrier Gateway to get public IPs from the 5G carrier network. The parent site can be managed by OneZone instance. The PNI-MEC Edge host belongs to the zone/cluster under the parent site.

The Carrier Gateway in a PNI-MEC edge host only allows access from the carrier's 5G network. So, since the private subnet resources cannot be accessed by using the internet, it is not possible to provision, configure, and set up those resources by directly accessing them. In order to integrate PNI-MEC Edge resources with the Distributed Cloud, we can use the public subnet's servers as "bastion hosts" to access PNI-MEC Edge resources via SSH, since they are only reachable through the private subnet. Resources in the public subnet in the parent site can also be used to deploy those parts of our application that are not latency-sensitive or require high bandwidth.

Using the standard provisioning function of OneCenter, the user can provision resources on a regular parent site, by using a bastion host and customized SSH configuration files, and it is then possible to provision and configure instances on the PNI-MEC site host and to add them as hosts to the OneZone instance. Since OneCenter can use SSH to perform any operation on the hosts, once bastion and PNI-MEC site resources are set up, it is possible to deploy containerized applications (i.e., a K3s cluster) both on the parent site and on the PNI-MEC site instances.

The final goal is to allow organizations using OneCenter to easily provision PNI-MEC site resources and quickly deploy Kubernetes clusters and containerized applications on the edge.

10.4 Non-3GPP Edge - Internet of Things

In the IoT Edge case, several scenarios should be considered: LoRa WAN, WIFI 6 connected edge device Bluetooth, etc. This section describes one of the IoT edge cases LoRa WAN.

The Distributed Cloud and its seamless integration with Firecracker make it a clear-cut and agile platform to be able to deploy containerized applications on resources at the edge, utilizing bare-metal infrastructure providers at on-premises or public cloud.

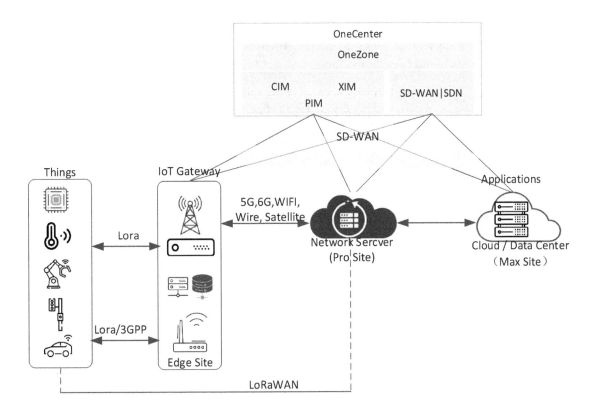

Figure 10-5 Non-3GPP IoT Edge Architecture

LoRa is the signal of physical end devices that transmit data to gateways. The Long-Range Wide Area Network (LoRa WAN) is a continually evolving solution developed by the LoRa Alliance.

LoRa WAN is a wireless communication standard and software architecture that piggybacks off the physical layer of LoRa. That means LoRa WAN is a cloud-based middleware layer that listens for LoRa signals from hardware and controls their interaction with the network before relaying information onto application servers.

LoRa WAN Gateways collect and consolidate packets of LoRa data from end-node technology such as (Industrial) Internet of Things (IIoT/IoT) sensors. They then upload these data sets to the Network Server using the LoRa Basics Station protocol which enables remote updates and configuration for the edge device.

The Network Server implements and terminates the LoRa WAN protocol, validates the authenticity and integrity of IoT edge devices, deduplicates uplinks, selects the gateways used for downlinks, and sends commands to optimize the data rate of edge devices. The LoRa WAN Network Server plays the brain and the controller role of a LoRa WAN network.

The Application Server is responsible for decrypting the data received from the edge sensors and encrypting the data sent to the end devices. The data can be integrated into existing data management systems in the Distributed Cloud.

OneCenter takes the cloud-level control plane role to automate, control, operate, and orchestrate the whole LoRa WAN network and data flow.

10.5 Distributed Cloud Based Conferencing Platform

A growing number of businesses, small and large, rely on video conference services every day. Video conference services offer multiple connection paths utilizing various protocols across a geographically distributed infrastructure to ensure a successful connection for all participants.

This section designs a video conferencing system that is based on an easy, reliable Distributed Cloud and profits from the Distributed Cloud's architecture benefits. We term this system as a Distributed Cloud Conferencing Platform (DCP).

The DCP provides a video conferencing platform for collaborations, education, commercial and misc. It integrates with other services, such as voice and messaging, into one easy-to-use, reliable, and high-quality system.

10.5.1   DCP Architecture

The key components in DCP include the DCP Client, Distributed Cloud Native Infrastructure, and the Web infrastructure.

10.5.1.1 DCP Client

The DCP client is the main way for terminals to access the DCP Server. Although it can be compatible with multiple operating systems (macOS, Windows, Linux, Android, iOS, Chrome OS, etc.) and a range of context-aware applications (mobile, desktop, DCP Meeting Room), its mode of interaction with DCP Server works in all configurations remain consistent. This DCP Client is the software on computers or devices to perform the video content processing, encoding, and decoding. It also provides network Quality of Service (QoS).

10.5.1.2 The Distributed Cloud Native Infrastructures

The Distributed Cloud comprises the on-premises (data center, branch, campus), multi-cloud, and edge location infrastructure. Those geo-distributed infrastructures connect together through private links to support worldwide video conference system connection and workload.

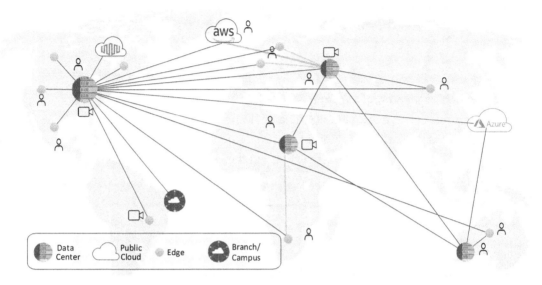

Figure 10-6 Geo-distributed Architecture of DCP

DCP is built from a Distributed Cloud-native infrastructure. The Distributed Cloud Native means the system is architected using the Distributed Cloud technology from the ground up. Of course, the Distributed Cloud Native contains the full capacity of traditional Cloud Native and extends some of its special features. The microservices allow developers to seamlessly grow capacity.

Public Cloud

The public cloud is provided by third-party cloud providers and is the place where the DCP servers (can be bare metal or virtual machines) hold the meetings. DCP can be built geographically in a distributed public cloud worldwide. The cloud controllers (OneCenter) inside the Distributed Cloud are for syncing meetings between the public cloud and other types of locations. Public Cloud real-time traffic can be served for DCP also you can expand to build a multi-cloud architecture among AWS, Azure GCP, and so on.

Data Center

The Data Center is typically the enterprise's private infrastructure and is the place where the DCP servers (can be bare metal or virtual machines) hold the meetings. DCP can be built geographically in distributed data centers worldwide. They use a network of private links to connect multiple others. The users can connect to the data center closest to their locations. Data centers serve real-time video-conferencing in their data centers or inside corporate networks.

Branch

The word "branch" is an umbrella term that is a branch office, which also refers to a Campus, enterprise headquarter, or even a Small Office or Home Office (SOHO) location and the data center. Colocation is similar to Data Center, but this kind of infrastructure is typically provided by third-party cloud infrastructure vendors such as Equinix, which can cover all over the world and help with the key business.

Edge

The edge typically can be the 3GPP NPN, 3GPP PNI-MEC edge with vCDN application, Campus, or non-3GPP edge site. The Campus can also be a logistic edge site, industrial factory site, etc.

NOTE: *Local Data Centers, branches, campus, and edge belong to the on-premises, while the public cloud is the third-party provider. Both the on-premise and public cloud can be managed through a unified, consistent, end-to-end, enterprise-scope network space. By integrating into the corporate network, any kind of client, DCP server, MMR, cluster controller, eCDN server, the staff terminals inside the corporate network, etc., can be reachable and routable to each other. This is convenient for routing and connecting for the DCP.*

10.5.1.3 Meeting Center

This meeting center hosts a website that links all things about a conference for conference operation, user management, and participant access. This center also provides Web Infrastructure, for example, developing environment and extensive API facilities for external developers and other useful components of the DCP infrastructure.

10.5.2 Networking Architecture

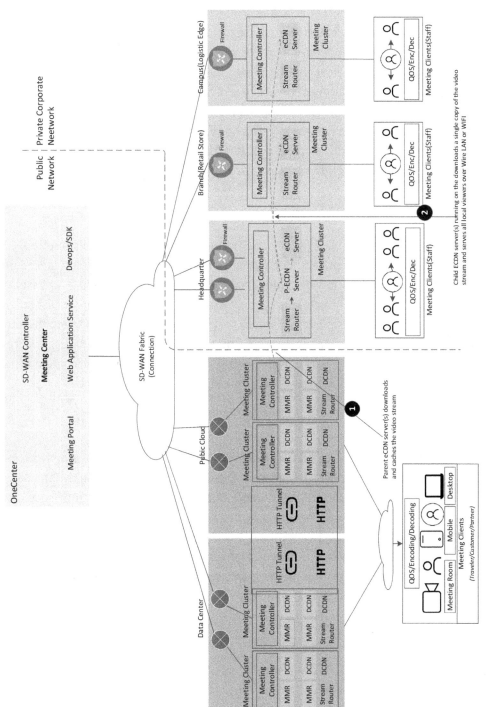

Figure 10-7 Networking Architecture in DCP

Distributed Cloud networking provides global connectivity, allowing worldwide users using different types of networks to meet reliably and ensuring the highest user experience.

Video and audio conferencing, collaboration, messaging, and webinars on mobile devices, desktops, smart mobile phones, and meeting room systems on an easy and reliable Distributed Cloud platform. One of the key factors that facilitates the ease of use and reliability of the Distributed Cloud platform is the connection process of the DCP. DCP's connection process ensures that whenever someone tries to access the platform, there is an optimized path to DCP's geographically diverse but highly available infrastructure. To meet the demanding real-time requirements of streaming data, there are several key features that differentiate the backend technology and the Distributed Cloud native infrastructures:

1. General Process Architecture

The Distributed Cloud has the characteristics of no fixed central point, global distribution, dynamic site and resource allocation, and deployment of distributed infrastructure based on SD-WAN, SDN and OVN to build a worldwide, unified, consistent, end-to-end, secure, private network system based on this architecture and apply GeoDNS, Anycast, and other technologies, DCP enables clients or viewers to seamlessly access secure private network connections and obtain resources and services through the nearest cloud site. This makes DCP global, secure, flexible, and scalable, hence letting tens of thousands of clients in any physical location around the world simultaneously access it without affecting a reliable video experience.

2. Multimedia Router

DCP uses video-first client/server architecture to separate video content processing from video stream routing. The video processing takes place at the meeting client side and dynamically encodes and decodes the stream based on the network topology, network performance, and bandwidth. Several network protocols are used, such as UDP, TCP TLS, and HTTPS. When only two participants are in a conference, peer-to-peer will be used to simplify the flow and accelerate the process performance. On the cloud (at the server) side, the Multimedia Router provides optimized paths to connect the meeting participants. Under this method, multimedia routing can carry more participants in each meeting by reducing computing, which is shared by multiple clients.

3. Meeting Cluster

A Meeting Cluster is a logical association of server infrastructures that are typically physically co-located and can host a meeting session. A Meeting Cluster can be located in the edge, on-premises, with a corporate network or public cloud locations running DCP. Multimedia Routers and Meeting Cluster Controllers are the two critical components in Meeting Cluster.

4. Meeting Cluster Controllers

Meeting Cluster Controllers are responsible for managing and orchestrating all activities that occur within a given conference zone. These systems are deployed in a high-availability infrastructure that tracks the load of all servers in the cluster and helps broker requests for new connections into the meeting Cluster.

5. HTTP Tunnels

The HTTP tunnels work as connection points to some clients who cannot connect DCP through other network channels. The HTTP tunnel service enhances the reliability of the DCP network. These services are located in various public clouds and data centers to provide connection points for clients that cannot connect to the DCP platform through normal network channels. After a tunnel is established between the client and the DCP HTTP tunnel, the client can access conference areas across data centers.

6. Corporate Network

Some DCP servers are located inside the corporate network (on-premises deployment). There is a firewall between the internal network and the public cloud. The internal staff connect to the internal DCP servers directly to avoid public traffic and have a higher degree of security and performance.

7. eCDN and SD-WAN

Enterprise Content Delivery Network(eCDN) improves transformation performance for live video/audio streaming and distribution within an enterprise network environment. eCDN can allow millions of enterprise users(staff) around the world to communicate face-to-face efficiently and reliably. With the eCDN and SD-WAN Edge Router, companies can remove network bottlenecks associated with using streaming video. This enables robust, highly scalable video delivery from a company's headquarters all the way down to remote offices.

As shown with❶ and ❷ in Figure 10-7, the parent eCDN(P-eCDN) server(s) pull the video stream from the public DCDN server and child eCDN server(s) running on the branch (Retail store) or Campus (Logistic edge) pull or downloads a single copy of the video stream and feed all local client participants over private 5G network, wire LAN or Wi-Fi. With SD-WAN Edge Router, organizations can support any branch office location, removing network strain out to the edge site without requiring smaller branches to run additional appliances or servers. In this way, eCDN can support large-scale viewership of live and on-demand streaming video within enterprises and empowers massive simultaneous user scale while reducing WAN strain by delivering a single copy of a video stream no matter how many viewers.

8. Multiple Bitrate Encoding

When transportation, video and audio files in the same video stream are converted into digital data, encoded, and compressed at a bit rate. In theory, The higher the bitrate, the less the compression rate, and the better the audio or video quality. DCP's multi-bitrate encoding uses single stream multiple layers, in which each stream has every separate resolution and bitrate that is needed, and then the stream by itself can adjust to multiple resolutions. In this method, the action to encode and decode the multiple streams for each endpoint is eliminated to provide higher quality and transportation reliability for various network conditions and for different endpoint devices.

9. Application layer quality of service

Quality of service (QoS) primarily manages the traffic and ensures the quality of critical applications. QoS measures several related aspects of the network, such as packet loss, bit rate, throughput, transmission delay, availability, jitter, etc. Normal QoS solutions are deployed in the network layer. Here QoS is applied on the application layer at the client side. They use proprietary algorithms to optimize video/audio and prioritize the factors that are more important for the particular type of device.

10.5.3   Connection Process Flow

The process of connecting to a DCP session is mainly divided into the following several stages:

Meeting Creation

The system will pre-prepare some resources for the conference based on the historical information of the conference creator, the location distribution of historical clients, the scale of historical clients, and the client behavior preferences. This process may trigger the building up of new Distributed Cloud sites at appropriate locations to meet the distribution requirements of DCP infrastructure, create conference areas and Multimedia Routers (MMRs) in existing or newly created sites, configure link attributes, etc. After the meeting is created, the meeting invitation information can be sent to the participants by SMS message or email.

Meeting Searching

Participants receive a meeting invitation, and then they join a given meeting at the expected time. The client first contacts the network infrastructure (Distributed Cloud infrastructure) to obtain the applicable metadata needed to access the video conference. By connecting using HTTPS, participants can better gather the current network environment. At the other end of the connection, the network infrastructure prepares a packet optimized for that client. Based on the enterprise's global overlay network and by using Geo DNS, Anycast, and other technologies, the list of the best available conference area and related area controllers will be returned to the participants together with the conference details so that the participants can enter the next step of the connection process stage.

Meeting Cluster Selection

Once the list of meeting Clusters that can serve the client session is obtained, the connection process moves to the next stage of the workflow. To ensure the optimized connection is used, the client attempts to connect to each Meeting Cluster controller in the meeting cluster provided in the previous phase and then executes a testing of network performance. By comparing the test results, the client can confirm that there are connection paths for each conference area and choose the one with the best performance. This connection uses HTTPS and attempts to communicate over Secure Sockets Layer (SSL).

MMR Selection

After obtaining the optimal meeting cluster selection from the previous stage, the DCP client requests the Meeting Cluster controller for the details of the optimal MMR. After confirmation, the client will directly contact MMR to establish a control channel for the session. This connection is via secure SSL communication.

Media Routing

After successfully connecting to the best multimedia router for a session, the client prioritizes creating connections for each type of media that will be transported, such as video, audio, and content. Try to connect using UDP first. If that UDP connection cannot be established, the DCP will also try to connect using TCP and then SSL. Utilizing separate connections for each type of media, deep network optimization techniques can be applied to ensure the most important media is accelerated across the network.

End Up a Meeting

When a video meeting is finished, the meeting center releases related sessions and web infrastructure resources. If new sites are closed to the end user, delete the site immediately.

10.5.4   Survivability

There are special cases where methods are needed to help ensure reliable sessions, even in complex networks.

Proxy Server

During the meeting lookup phase of the connection process flow, the client can determine whether a proxy server is used as part of the network connection path point. If usage is detected, the client will immediately utilize the proxy server and attempt to establish an associated connection to the Meeting Cluster controller and multimedia router using SSL during the meeting cluster and multimedia router selection phases of the connection process.

HTTP Tunnel

If no response from any Meeting Cluster controller is received after a long time, the DCP client will try to connect using HTTP tunneling. To ensure multiple paths to a successful connection, these servers are located both in the public cloud and in the on-premises data center. This connection was attempted over SSL. The client will ping multiple HTTP tunnels and use the first one that responds.

Web Client

If the DCP client is unable to connect via any of the methods listed above, it will instruct the user to connect to the meeting via the web client in their browser without downloading any plugins and software. Web clients will attempt to connect over SSL.

Chapter 11   The Distributed Cloud Based
Data Platform Architecture

The architecture of the data platform is closely related to the IT infrastructure. The infrastructure of the Distributed Cloud has its special characteristics of distribution, heterogeneity, diversity, and centralized management. This data platform is based on the Distributed Cloud and takes advantage of these characteristics and advantages to build a Distributed Cloud Native Data Platform.

At the same time, standalone open-source big data frameworks such as Flink and Data Government can also leverage the benefits of innovative Distributed Cloud architecture.

11.1 Data Architecture Evolution

In the past, storage was on-prem (physical) and extremely limited. Data warehouses have been used to store data in a format ideal for analytic purposes (queries and BI) since the invention of the database. But now, the modern data stack is about more than storing analytic data - it's about understanding data origins, tracking lineage, managing access and permissions, and maintaining flexibility in modeling.

11.1.1   Lakehouse

Before understanding the Lakehouse, we first introduce the Data Warehouse and Data Lake.

Data Warehouses have a long history in decision support and business intelligence applications. In the last about 40 years, the data warehouse has evolved from single machine systems to massively parallel processing (MPP) architectures to handle larger scale data in near real time. Even more in recent years, cloud native data warehouses such as AWS Redshift have become more powerful and convenient. But while those warehouses were great for structured data, a lot of modern enterprises also have to deal with unstructured data, semi-structured data, and data with high variety, velocity, and volume. For many of these use cases, data warehouses are incapable and cost more.

Data Lake is a single store for all kinds of data—whether it be raw, unstructured, semi-structured, static, stream, etc. This data is taken from multiple sources and lacks a predefined schema/meta data. The idea is that a central repository holds every bit of this raw data, which can then be leveraged for downstream data needs.

Storing mass scale of data of any source and format is data lake's main merit, but data lake also has some fatal drawbacks: no transaction capacity, not good data quality, lack of consistency/isolation, and so on. Therefore, some promise of the data lake becomes empty. And more, in many cases, leading to a loss of many of the benefits of data warehouses.

Companies need a system that can handle diverse data applications, including SQL analytics, real-time monitoring, data science, and machine learning. Most of the recent advances in AI have been in better models to process unstructured data (text, file, images, video, audio), but these are precisely the types of data that a data warehouse is not capable or optimized for.

Lakehouse is a new system that is beginning to emerge that addresses the limitations of data lakes. it is an open architecture that combines the best elements of data lakes and data warehouses.

Lakehouse uses a new system design approach. Over low-cost cloud storage in open formats, the data warehouse data structures and data management features, which are warehouse applied, can be leveraged in the Lakehouse.

With the development of cloud technology. The public cloud storage (mainly referring to the objects stores) become faster and faster, cheaper, and highly reliable. These help to enhance the Lakehouse performance.

11.1.2   Data Mesh

Data Products

Data is an asset that drives business insights and decisions. A Data Product refers to a valuable, processed, organized, and structured dataset created from raw data, packaged for consumption either internally (by different department teams within an organization) or externally (by clients or other stakeholders).

Data Products can be in various forms: simple datasets, data feeds such as SQL, CSV, FTP, etc., Restful APIs, or even complex analytics dashboards and machine learning (ML) models. The critical factor is that they are consumable, providing actionable information, and driving value for other Data Products or the end-users.

Data Mesh

The Data Mesh is a data architecture that aims to address the data duplication, team cooperation, and scaling issues associated with traditional monolithic data platforms. As organizations grow, it becomes challenging to manage vast amounts of data from various organizations and sources effectively.

The Four Characteristics of the Data Mesh

Distributed Data Mesh addresses this concern with a new architecture that is marked by four primary characteristics:

1. Domain-Oriented Decentralized Data Ownership and Architecture.

2. Data as a Product.

3. Self-Serve Data Infrastructure as a Platform.

4. Federated Computational Governance.

Each characteristic represents an essential aspect of the approach that collectively ensures the successful implementation of a data mesh.

These four characteristics form the backbone of the data mesh approach. By decentralizing data ownership, treating data as a product, enabling self-serve data infrastructure, and implementing federated governance, organizations can harness the full potential of their data assets while maintaining scalability and agility. Data mesh architecture mainly addresses the four issues:

1. Data scattered among sites, and at times hundreds, of legacy and cloud systems, making it a big challenge to achieve a single source of truth.

2. Speed and volume of data, that data-centric enterprises have to face with.

3. Data is hard to fetch and put together when access often requires data engineering.

4. Lack of communication among business analysts, operational data consumers, data engineers, and data scientists.

Less Decentralization Architecture

To avoid duplication, enterprises often choose one central data distribution data platform over many deployed logical components that are managed by all their individual teams. A reference model describing such an architecture with a single platform instance and data product ownership is shown in the following Figure 11-1.

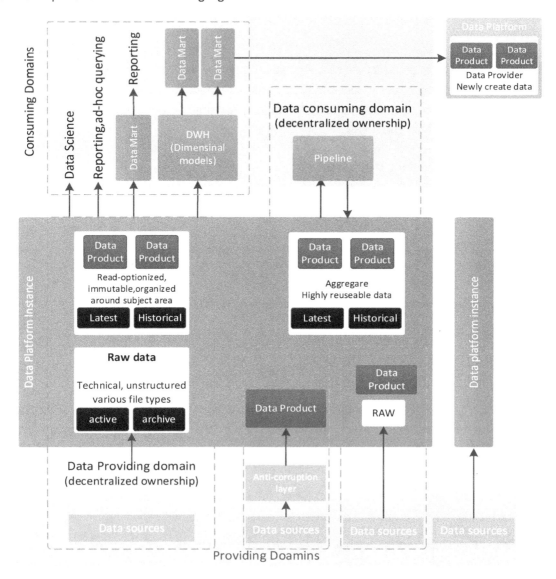

Figure 11-1 Less Decentralization Architecture

This design is still a domain-oriented architecture. Although a shared platform instance is used, either the data-providing or consuming domain takes ownership of the data. The data ownership also holds true for data products that are derived from newly created or aggregated data. There's no central or shared integration layer that merges or moves all data.

This solution is the optimized Data Mesh architecture, and it merges with some ideas of Data Fabric. This architecture can be used as a standalone data mesh implementation. At the same time, this Data Mesh idea can also co-work with the Hybrid Data Mesh architecture that will be presented in the next section [11.1.3 Data Fabric].

11.1.3   Data Fabric

A centralized data architecture implies that every domain (e.g., IT, finance, human resources etc.) is duplicated to one area (for example, a data lake under one use space). It likewise means centralized responsibility for data.

Gartner defined the data fabric as "*A data fabric is an emerging data management design for attaining flexible, reusable and augmented data integration pipelines, services and semantics. A data fabric supports both operational and analytics use cases delivered across multiple deployment and orchestration platforms and processes. Data fabrics support a combination of different data integration styles and leverage active metadata, knowledge graphs, semantics and ML to augment data integration design and delivery.*".

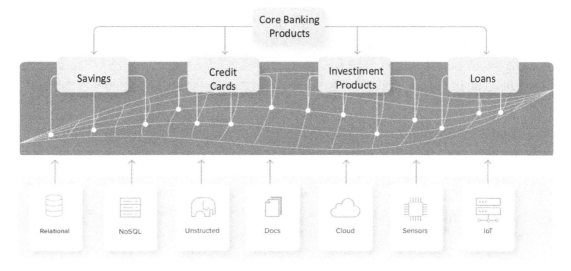

Figure 11-2 Data Fabric Architecture

A data fabric is an architecture and suit of data services/tools that provide consistent capabilities across a choice of data endpoints spanning edge, hybrid, and multi-cloud environments. It is a powerful architecture that standardizes data management practices and practicalities across cloud, data center, and edge sites. Among the many advantages that a data fabric affords, seamless data connectivity, the elimination of data copies/moving, avoiding data duplications/overlaps, data visibility and insights, data access/control, data protection, and security quickly rise to the top.

From the top view, data fabric can be thanked of an enterprise virtual data-access layer in which different heterogeneous data sources can be connected to provide data services to various consumers with consistent data management, security, and governance capabilities while abstracting all data consumers from the complexities of access, including where and how the data is stored, what format the data is.

A data fabric stitches together integrated data from many different sources and delivers it to various data consumers.

Data fabric has its special benefits, and it can address some challenges of data mesh, but data fabric does not aim to replace the data mesh because data mesh has its special user cases and necessity. We typically use data mesh in a small business scenario or start-up with data mesh and parallelly construct with data fabric, finally reaching the architecture of the Hybrid Data Mesh with Data Fabric.

11.2 Flexible Modern Data Architecture

The Distributed Cloud is the new cloud system with some innovative features, and the modern data architecture should utilize its benefits points and match the new architecture features. To achieve this goal, the Distributed Cloud Based Modern Data Architecture should meet at least the following requirements and preconditions:

A distributed hybrid architecture is a key requirement of modern data architecture. It is composed of on-premises, cloud, and edge. Most enterprises have existing on-premises infrastructure investments that need to work seamlessly with your new investments in edge, on-premises, and cloud. It takes much time and significant financial investment to migrate legacy IT systems. Therefore, you need to have a consistent architecture that can make edge, on-premises, and cloud applications coexist in the Distributed Cloud.

11.2.1   Architecture

Before diving into the architecture detail design, we first see some criteria and goals of a new modern data architecture:

- Capture, store, and process your data anywhere, in any format.
- Enable edge site Connectivity.

- Establish a single pane of glass.

- Apply consistent security and governance.

- Track data lineage and provenance.

- Enable easy data discovery for self-service analytics.

- Run Ephemeral Workloads in the Public Cloud to Optimize Costs.

- Leverage Shared Metadata Services for Ephemeral Workloads.

- Implement a Consistent Hybrid Architecture for Containerized Workloads.

In the later of this section, you can find out how the Data Architecture meets those criteria and achieve the goals that are described.

The Distributed Cloud is the new reality, which requires a versatile enterprise data platform based on a modern data architecture. As you embark on a journey to construct an enterprise data platform, view your enterprise data assets at a global scale - spanning multiple edges, on-premises, hybrid, and multi-cloud environments, forming a data fabric. To truly obtain the potential of enterprise data and turn it into a strategic asset, build a modern data platform that provides a single pane of glass for all of your enterprise data assets, regardless of where the data lives and comes from, with consistent security and governance as one of the key tenets.

Whereas a data management platform is organized around a single data repository and is deployed for each repository, a data fabric combines data management platforms for one global view of data. Only connect, map, and control from one data module of OneCenter, the data merge, join, move, and process operation occur in seperate remote sites where data lives in.

As a result, the Distributed Cloud Data Platform is perfectly placed to implement modern data architectures with:

- A Data Lakehouse that enables data processing and multi-function analytics on both dynamic streaming and static stored data in a nimble storage system at the edge and a cloud-native object store among hybrid and multi-cloud environments.

- A unified Data Fabric that centrally orchestrates disparate data sources sophisticated and securely among edges, multiple public clouds, and on-premises.

- A Hybrid Flexible Data Mesh that helps eliminate data silos by distributing ownership to cross-functional teams/departments.

The Distributed Cloud Data Architecture offers a multi-location architecture for on-premises, multi-cloud, hybrid, and edge scenarios without sacrificing performance, security, and governance. It has been specifically designed to provide location transparency, minimizing expensive data movement between different locations. The multi-layered architecture allows a hierarchy of the Distributed Cloud Data Platform instances that can be co-located close to data sources, carrying out local data processing in the dispersed remote locations (including at edge, data center, and cloud) and therefore greatly reducing the data transfer cost over the network. Data caches at the data gateway of the separate remote site can keep recently calculated data that can be leveraged in subsequent queries in the local location.

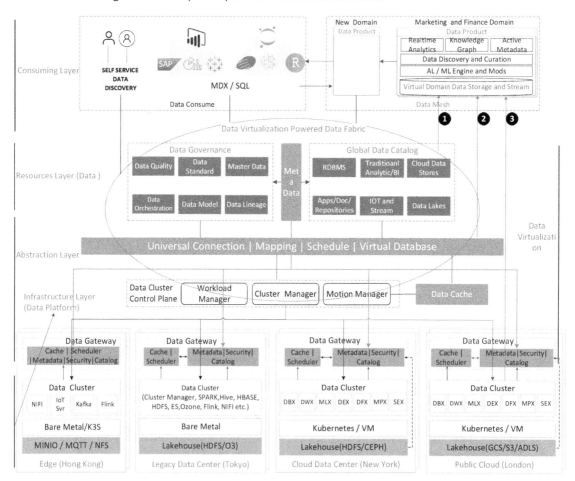

Figure 11-3 Modern Data Architecture in The Distributed Cloud

The control plane of the infrastructure layer plays an important role in supporting multi-location architectures as it automatically adapts the metadata from remote data fabric instances to point to the relevant data sources in every node of the hierarchy, and the metadata of data fabric instances at a higher level in the hierarchy to the right fabric instances in lower nodes.

The data fabric can be the data virtualization platform on the public cloud, such as AWS, Azure, GCP, and Docker container with Kubernetes, offering a dynamic and elastic infrastructure that enables users to start small and scale. For this purpose, the data fabric can support AWS and Azure auto-scaling to dynamically add new instances to a site according to workload.

11.2.2   Data Fabric - Infrastructure Layer

The Distributed Cloud Data Platform has been built from the ground up to support hybrid, multi-cloud data management in support of a Data Fabric architecture. In this section, we focus on the data process and management capabilities that enable the Data Fabric.

The Distributed Cloud Data Platform is designed to provide the freedom to choose any location, any analytics, and any data. The Distributed Cloud Data Platform delivers faster and easier data management and data analytics for data anywhere, with optimal performance, scalability, and security.

The Distributed Cloud Data Platform provides the freedom to securely move applications, data, and users' information bi-directionally across any kind of site, such as edge, data center, public cloud, and multiple data clouds, wherever the data lives.

11.2.2.1 Control Plane

The Control Plane in the Distributed Cloud Data Platform provides a ubiquitous service that is consistent and spans an organization's deployment instances. Figure 11-3 shows how OneCenter shares components and services such as governance with the cloud infrastructure provider such as public cloud, data center, or edge. It goes further in supporting dispersed edge, multiple cloud, and multiple on-premises deployments. The Control Plane is a federated service that enables the metadata, schema, security, encryption, and governance to be managed as a central but federated service. The Control Plane at the OneCenter location can interface with the separate remote edge, legacy data center, and data center in the cloud to support full Distributed Cloud architecture deployments.

Cluster Manager

Cluster Manager is a general service used by the Distributed Cloud Data Platform administrators to manage, monitor, and orchestrate all of the Distributed Cloud Data Platform services or data clusters from a single pane of glass across all sites' scope. If you have deployments in your edge or on-premises as well as in multiple public clouds, you can manage them all in one central place - creating, monitoring, provisioning, and destroying data services or data clusters.

Workload Manager

Workload Manager in data fabric is responsible for optimizing performance and resource utilization across platform workloads.

Delivering great end-user experience while ensuring critical analytics needs and SLAs are met requires in-depth process visibility. Workload Manager offers a full visual workload for performance tuning and migration, data model optimization insight, and other facilities for performance improvements and supporting platforms.

Observability

Observability is a function that continuously discovers and collects platform performance telemetry across applications and infrastructure components running in the Distributed Cloud data platform environments. It creates a granular single source of truth for collecting and maintaining metrics, logs, dependencies, and traces.

Observability performs real-time correlations that indicate existing and potential problems and includes prescriptive guidance and recommendations to resolve them. Observability typically contains main aspects, including Observability, Monitoring, and Insights Recommendations.

Motion Manager

The Motion Manager is designed to serve a number of use cases around cross-fabric data orchestration and migration, such as workload migration, cloud bursting, backup and disaster recovery, and replication. It supports full and incremental replication for all data storage types available in the data fabric.

Motion Manager is used by administrators and data stewards to move, copy, migrate, snapshot, backup, replicate, and restore data in or between sites with data gateway and data clusters.

11.2.2.2 Data Clusters

Data Process Engineering (DEX) is a full data engineering toolkit based on open-source Apache Spark that enables orchestration automation with Apache Airflow, advanced pipeline monitoring, visual troubleshooting, and a comprehensive management toolset to streamline ETL processes across enterprise analytics teams.

Dataflow (DFX) is a cloud-native universal data distribution service building on open-source Apache NiFi that allows developers to connect to any data source anywhere with any structure, process it, and deliver it forward to any destination.

Data Warehouse (DWX) is a service for creating and managing data warehouses for data analyst teams. This service makes it easy for an enterprise to provision a new data warehouse and share a subset of the data with a specific department or team. The service is ephemeral, letting you quickly create data warehouses and terminate them once the job at hand is finished.

Machine Learning (MLX) is a service for creating and managing self-service Machine Learning workspaces (Integrated Development Environment - IDE). This enables teams of data scientists to develop, verify, train, and ultimately deploy result models for building predictive applications all on the data under management within the enterprise data platform.

An Operational Database (DBX) is a service of an operational database. DBX is a scale-out, autonomous database based on Apache HBase (Cassandra is an alternative option for implementation) and Apache Phoenix. These types of databases offer low-latency and high-throughput use cases with the same storage and access layers.

A massively Parallel Processing Database (MPX) is a database that is optimized to be processed in parallel for many operations to be performed. Typical products include Greenplum, Vertica, and Teradata, which can be used in the Distributed Cloud.

Search Engine (SEX) provides easy, natural language access to data stored in or ingested into HDFS, Hadoop, HBase, or cloud storage such as Ceph and S3. End users and other web services can use full-text queries and faceted drill-downs to explore text, semi-structured, and structured data, as well as quickly filter and aggregate it to gain business insight.

11.2.2.3 Data Gateway

The modern data architecture in the Distributed Cloud applies a multiple-tier architecture with higher Tier 1 and lower Tier 2. In Tier 2, there is an agent role of component, termed as Data Gateway residing in site edge locations of separate sites.

As shown in Figure 11-3. several Tier 2 components be hosted in the Data Gateway, such as local Data Caching, local Meta data, local scheduler, and local Data Catalog, etc.

The Data Gateway is also a security gate offering a complete audit log of all access and modifications made to data sets located anywhere in the data fabric, typically with Knox and similar components.

In addition, the Data Gateway also has the capacity for data job interpreting, transforming, and offering the workplace to process and analyze data.

The Data Gateway can be deployed with single or multiple nodes as a cluster depending on the scale of data and the organization's business needs.

11.2.3   Data Fabric - Abstraction Layer

This layer is the most important layer, which leverages some modern data technologies such as data virtualization, data caching, smart integration, and global data scheduler to abstract the geo-distributed, heterogeneous data courses and data types, whatever type it is and wherever it lives, to a resource layer for serves the data consumers.

11.2.3.1 Data Virtualization

We now live in a world with unprecedented explosion in the volume, variety, and velocity of incoming data. And emerging technologies, such as the cloud and big data systems, which have brought large volumes of disparate data, have only compounded the problem. All kinds of data are still stored in functional silos, separate from other sources of data. Organizations require immediate information for real-time processes and decisions, but this is challenging when the information they need is scattered across multiple location sources. In most cases, moving forward until data from key sources is brought together as a central unified repository is almost impossible and difficult.

Data virtualization is an ideal data integration strategy that is unlike the traditional approach, which physically moves the data to a new, physical location. Data virtualization provides an actual-time view of the consolidated data, leaving the source data exactly where it is when the data is processed or operated.

Data virtualization establishes an enterprise data-access function, providing universal access to all of an organization's key data sources. It abstracts users from complexities such as where the data is stored or what format it is in. Data virtualization places between all data sources on one side, and all data consumers on the other side, be they individuals or applications. Data virtualization normalizes the underlying complexity and heterogeneities for the upper layer.

NOTE: *In the data fabric with Hybrid Data Mesh architecture. You can think of Data Mesh as one kind of data consumer.*

It is important to remember that because data virtualization does not move and replicate any data, the data virtualization is a logical layer. It stores no data actually; instead, it merely requires a reachable secure network and contains the metadata required to access the various data sources.

Data virtualization is a modern data connect and integration strategy that implements enterprise-wide access controls enterprise-wide access controls to provide a central point to which developers can connect the APIs for accommodating different sources, from the most structured to the least structured.

This method performs many of the same transformation and quality-control functions as the conventional data integration approach, but it offers immediate data integration at a lower cost, with faster speeds and enhanced agility. It can either replace classic data integration processes (mainly for real-time data) and their associated data marts and data warehouses or simply augment them, extending their capabilities. As an abstraction layer, data virtualization can be easily leveraged between original and derived data sources, ETL (Extract, transform, and load) processes, enterprise service busses (ESBs), and other middleware, applications, and devices, whether at edge, on-premises, or cloud, to provide flexibility between layers of information and business technology.

NOTE: *In the Distributed Cloud, using data virtualization does not mean to moving and copying anything absolutely. Only means not moving or copying all of the data to a stational central repository. Some archive data without real-time requirements can be moved to a desired central repository.*

11.2.3.2 Data Connectivity

The Data Connectivity is the Data Access function that accesses information from the various repositories and decouples the heterogeneities of the underlying communication protocol and data formats from the upper layers. The user can create "base views" over data sources that represent a normalized schema that is available to upper layers in a uniform structure. This access layer is responsible for performing the data source type conversions and normalization needed to match the user definition of the base view. To the upper layers, all base views appear as relational views of the data, regardless of the underlying data source categories, which can be Hadoop, Databases, Web services, Files, Email, etc.

The Distributed Cloud Data platform uses specialized connectors to access specific data repositories or applications in order to retrieve their schemas and the source data for subsequent processing. Data Connectivity should support the widest range of data sources:

Table 11-1 Data Sources of Data Connectivity

Data Source Category	Contents
Relational Databases	MYSQL, MariaDB, Oracle
Parallel and Distributed Databases	Greenplum, Teradata
Multidimensional Databases	Multidimensional databases
Cloud data Warehouses	Amazon Redshift, Snowflake
Packaged Applications	SAP ECC and Salesforce
Web Services	SOAP, REST, OData
RAW File	Excel spreadsheets, XML, JSON, log files
Web Applications	data from the hidden web
Unstructured	Unstructured repositories and search engines, email servers, mainframes, queues
Streaming	Kafka, NIFI
NoSQL Databases	NoSQL Databases

11.2.3.3 Data Integration

Data Integration lets organizations create virtual data models to expose data to an upper layer, conforming to a pre-defined business canonical model to comply with the business governance policies defined within the organization. The virtual data model can be built using a layered approach with multiple levels to facilitate governance and reuse.

This Data Integration offers data combination and transformation capabilities with logical operators for the seamless creation of composite data views on top of the base data views delivered by the Data Connection. The Data Integration makes use of the abstraction created by the Data Connection to manage all data from a unified schema standpoint, regardless of where the data lives and comes from. In Data Integration, the user will be able to perform complex data transformation, metadata modeling, and data quality and semantic matching operations using SQL and a set relational tool, as we all know.

11.2.3.4 Data Scheduler

The Distributed Cloud provides the Data Scheduler for executing batch jobs (see Figure 11-4). Data Scheduler can be implemented in two-tier modes. The higher Tier 1 is the global Scheduler, which is typically located in the central location of the data fabric (in the OneCenter place), whereas the lower Tier 2 is the site Scheduler residing in the data gateway of separated distributed sites hosting the data workloads.

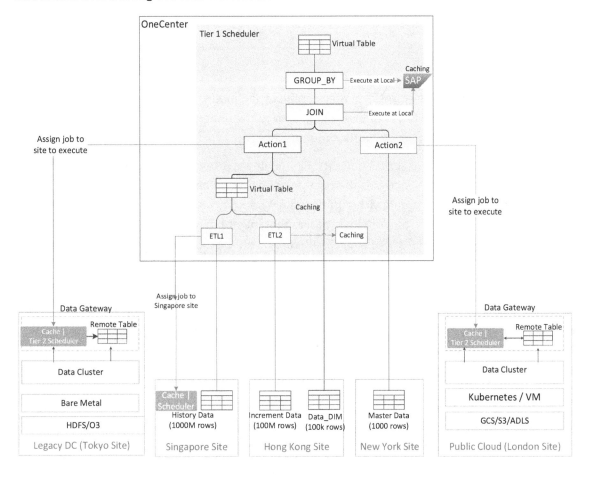

Figure 11-4 Data Scheduler

The data cluster can be an MPP Database, a commercial data platform such as Cloudera Data Platform (CDP), or an open source big data cluster such as Ambari managed Hadoop ecosystem platform.

As shown in Figure 11-4, assume a query contains multiple sub-operations with ETL, JOIN, and GROUP-By. The Tier 1 global Scheduler is responsible for the top-level optimization of execution, calculating the distributed resource status to decide the locations where the jobs/sub-jobs are to be executed. When Tier 1 Scheduler does such work, it also makes decisions based on the source data location, data scale, and current cloud site workload.

When a job is assigned to a certain site, the Tier 2 scheduler in the site interprets the requests, and then it may dispatch this job to an MPP, DEX, DFX, DWX, or DBX to execute, even call the MLX to train a model. If the DEX or DWX receives the job from the Tier 2 Scheduler, it will launch another Directed Acyclic Graph (DAG) job as normal application sending to it. Then, the job executes the actual data process activities.

11.2.3.5 Data Caching

The data caching technology offers multiple configuration modes, providing highly granular configuration and avoiding heavy queries being sent to the underlying data sources (perhaps in remote site locations over poor network conditions).

The data cache provides two critical benefits: First, it improves performance as data is fetched directly from the cache, which avoids the querying of data original sources and the subsequent query processing time in the data virtualization layer. Second, when configured in full cache mode, it avoids hitting data from original sources that might be overloaded at business times. The data cache can be the caching product software or the Distributed Cloud native in-memory cache system.

The Distributed Cloud can provide the widest range of fine-grained cache configuration options to meet various needs. Caching can be defined at any level or sub-component so that a combined view may have a portion of the data coming from the cache and the other portion coming from the original data source in real time.

The Distributed Cloud can be configured with Partial Cache mode (Query-by-query caching), Full Cache mode, and Incremental mode for different scenarios.

 The Distributed Cloud makes use of external storage for data cache materialization, which can be a relational database, a parallel database, or an in-memory database.

The data caching is the role of the data virtualization layer, but it can be located both in the data fabric central location and at distributed separate data gateway belonging to respective sites shown in Figure 11-4.

11.2.4   Data Fabric - Resources Layer

After the abstraction of the unevenly varied data types and data sources from the abstraction layer, the resource layer can see a complete data resource view. Based on the virtualized data resources, these data assets can be processed like standard data type and as it lives locally.

11.2.4.1 Data Labeling

Data labeling, also termed data annotation, is the preprocessing stage before developing a machine learning (ML) model. It requires the identification of raw data (i.e., things items, images, text files, videos) and then the addition of one or more labels to that data to specify its context for the models, allowing the ML model to make accurate predictions. The data labeling module includes label management, label application, and label development.

11.2.4.2 Data Catalog

The Data Catalog is based on the Data Virtualization layer and is a service for searching, organizing, securing, and governing data within the enterprise data cloud. A Data Catalog is used by data stewards to browse, search, and tag the content of a data fabric or a lakehouse.

Comprehensive - Support for all entities that make up the Distributed Cloud ecosystem: Hive database and tables, Kafka topics, Nifi flow, HBase tables, Machine Learning Models, etc. Each asset will be displayed alongside its contextual metadata, such as schema, security policies, labeled tags and classifications, profiles, governance rules and business annotations.

Discoverability - A single central location of the fabric to discover and search for data from all sites and all nodes of the whole data fabric. The client subscribes to a table, and the data catalog can push data after subscription. Ant usage statistics (most frequent datasets, etc.).

Lineage - Automatic capture of lineage information based on meta data to help understand where the data came from, how it is being used, and what impact changes would have. It can further be extended to propagate security policies across the entire Data Fabric, making it safer and easier to use and share data.

Policy - Security, compliance and governance policies can be assigned to any data asset directly from the Catalog. It creates and manages authorization policies (by file, table, column, row, individual API access and so on), identifies what data a user has accessed, and accesses the lineage of a particular data set.

Collaboration - Supports business annotations, curation and collaboration.

NOTE: The Data Catalog is implemented in two Tiers. The higher Tier 1 is a global data catalog with a full, complete catalog. It is typically located in the central location of the data fabric (for example, in the OneCenter). In contrast, the lower Tier 2 is a site data catalog residing in the data gateway of separated distributed sites bearing data workloads. The Tier 2 data catalog can be fully or partially synchronized to the Tier 1 data catalog based on requirements, securities, and regulations.

11.2.4.3 Meta Data

Metadata describes different facets of any data (not only tabular data, the unstructured data such as an image has its Metadata), such as the data's context. It is produced as a byproduct of data moving through enterprise systems. Metadata can be divided into four categories: technical, operational, business, and social metadata. Each of those types can be either "passive" Metadata that organizations collect but do not actively analyze or "active" Metadata that identifies actions across two or more systems utilizing the same data.

Metadata is implemented in two Tiers; Tier 1 resides in the central location (typically in the OneCenter) of fabric with full complete Metadata, and Tier 2 is located in the data gateway of separated distributed sites, and it is synchronized to Tier 1 global Metadata in real time. Metadata components usually include Metadata collecting, Metadata management, and Metadata analysis.

11.2.4.4 Metadata Catalog

Metadata Search - For the collected metadata, the system supports rough query, advanced query, and other operations for lookup, helping users to quickly and accurately find the required metadata.

Metadata Map - Display the full link diagram of metadata between databases in the system from a visual perspective and support drill-down to view specific tables, fields, etc., blood relationship and affects analysis, helping users to have a unified view of the blood relationship in the system from a unified perspective, which is convenient for data deriving and leadership strategic analysis.

Metadata Catalog is implemented in two-tier mode. The high-level Tier 1 is the global Metadata catalog typically placed in the central location of the data fabric with a full Metadata catalog, whereas the lower Tier 2 is the site Metadata catalog residing in the data gateway of separated distributed sites having data workloads. The Tier 2 metadata catalog synchronizes with the Tier 1 metadata catalog.

11.2.4.5 Data Governance

"Data Governance (DG) is defined as the exercise of authority and control (planning, monitoring, and enforcement) over the management of data assets.", this is the definition of Data Governance in the Data Management Association - Data Management Body of Knowledge (DAMA-DMBOK), second edition. From the cloud point of view, the following aspects should be taken into account:

Control move data and workloads between data platform deployments for optimum performance, cost, and resilience, meeting ever changing business needs. For more information, you can refer to section [11.2.2.1 Control Plane] about Observability and migration.

Data Quality mainly includes Quality requirements, quality verification, quality scheduling, problem details, and quality reports.

Metadata is a core part of data governance, and Data Governance deeply depends on metadata. About the metadata-related information, refer to section [11.2.4 Data Fabric - Resources Layer].

Data Catalog and Metadata Catalog also scope data governance; Data Governance deeply depends on the data catalog and metadata catalog. About the two catalogs, you can refer to section [11.2.4.2 Data Catalog] and section [11.2.4.4 Metadata Catalog].

Data Security typically contains:

1. **Data Classification** includes:
   - Data business classification and authorization.
   - Data Sensitivity Classification and Authorization.
   - Data row access label and authorization.
   - Hierarchical and domain authorization.
   - User Resource Access List.

2. **Data Permissions** is about Role and data permission configuration and list of user permissions.

3. **safety rules** include desensitization rule definitions.

4. **Encryption** is about strong cryptography for data in motion and rest, centralized authentication with single sign on.

11.2.5   Data Fabric - Consuming Layer

Fabric consuming applications (e.g., a reporting tool, a web application, or the data mesh, etc.) will access data fabric through the Data Consuming layer, and the Data Platform will receive the queries from the upper client layer and access the underlying physical data sources as needed, in a way that is transparent to the data consumer.

In the Data Consuming layer, the Distributed Cloud can offer the broadest data delivery options to suit customer needs via JDBC, ODBC, SOAP web services, RESTful web services (XML, JSON, and HTML), OData, GraphQL, GeoJSON, exports to Excel/SQL, Tableau, or message queues, etc. Published web services can be secured through OAuth with JSON Web Tokens and OAuth Token introspection, and automatically documented using the Open API specification.

The service catalog of the Resources Layer provides a unified display of data services, and file services published in the background, also provides service search and service subscription operations.

11.2.6   Hybrid Data Mesh

"Data Mesh is a viable option for organizations with incomplete metadata. So long as they have data architects with subject matter expertise, they can start with data mesh and build their active metadata stores in parallel." this is also Gartner's suggestion. Data mesh seems not a perfect approach, but it is often an option that works well in most cases.

Similarly, in the Distributed Cloud, an organization does not need to build a large scale comprehensive full data fabric with a complete Data Virtualization Layer from the start. Another scenario is in a small business company with a single or few domains, and they can start with data mesh. This is as shown ❸ in Figure 11-3. A Data Fabric can be built without adopting Data Mesh architecture. To create data products, data mesh can depend on the data fabric's discovery and data analysis principles. An enterprise starts from a data mesh architecture and has no effect on the constructed data fabric and its infrastructure. This gives the organization full flexibility without only one option exclusively. They can start from data mesh at the beginning and move to over data fabric seamlessly (as shown ❶ in Figure 11-3), build data fabric and data mesh simultaneously, and finally can choose whether to migrate data mesh to over data mesh or not; also, they can only build a standalone data mesh or independent data fabric through all the time. This kind data mesh is termed Hybrid Data Mesh.

11.3 Standalone Flink in Distributed Cloud

The previous section designed a modern Distributed-Cloud-based big data platform, but in some cases, organizations do not need such a comprehensive heavy data platform that requires too much investment and resources. Actually, some open-source big data frameworks can be lightly deployed on the Distributed Cloud environment, leveraging the central and fully distributed feathers. For instance, the Flink solution in the following section will be described.

Flink Running Architecture

Flink is a distributed system and requires effective allocation and management of compute resources in order to execute streaming applications. Except for Hadoop YARN, it can be integrated with Kubernetes as a cluster resource manager but can also be set up to run as a standalone cluster or even as a library. This book focuses on the Kubernetes manager case.

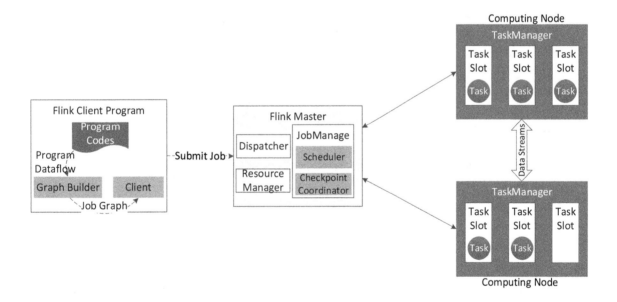

Figure 11-5 Flink Running Architecture

The Flink runtime architecture mainly includes four different core components that work together when running stream processing applications, namely, Job Manager, Resource Manager, Task Manager, and Dispatcher. Because Flink is implemented in Java and Scala, all components will run on the Java virtual machine.

Dispatcher

The Dispatcher is mainly responsible for receiving the JobGraph object submitted by the client. For example, tasks submitted by the CLI client or Flink Web UI will eventually be sent to the Dispatcher component. The Dispatcher component distributes and executes the JobGraph, which includes starting the JobManager service based on the JobGraph object. Used to manage the life cycle of the entire task. The Dispatcher will also launch a Web UI to easily display and monitor job execution information. The Dispatcher may not be required in the architecture, depending on how the application is submitted to run.

ResourceManager

ResourceManager is mainly responsible for managing computing resources in the Flink cluster. The JobManager initiates a SlotRequest to the ResourceManager, and the ResourceManager assigns the TaskManager with free slots to the JobManager. If the ResourceManager does not have enough slots to satisfy the JobManager's request, it will also apply for a Container from the cluster resource manager and start the TaskManager to ensure the normal operation of the task. In addition, ResourceManager is also responsible for terminating idle TaskManager to release computing resources.

JobManager

The dispatcher will create a JobManager service for the task based on the received JobGraph object. The JobManager service manages the life cycle of the entire task and is responsible for converting the JobGraph into an ExecutionGraph structure. The JobManager will request the resources necessary to execute the task from the ResourceManager, that is, the slot on the TaskManager. Once it obtains enough resources, the JobManager will distribute the ExecutionGraph to the TaskManager that actually runs them and monitor the running status of each Task until all the Tasks in the entire job are executed or stopped. In addition, JobManager is also responsible for the coordination of Checkpoint and records task status information by taking snapshots at regular intervals.

TaskManager

TaskManager is responsible for providing slot computing resources to the entire cluster and managing tasks submitted by JobManager. After the TaskManager starts, it will actively register the slot information with the ResourceManager, that is, the slot resources it can provide. When the ResourceManager receives the slot computing resources in the TaskManager, it will immediately send a slot resource application to the TaskManager and allocate the slot computing resources required for submitting tasks to the JobManager service. The JobManager will eventually submit the Task to the TaskManager to run according to the assigned slot computing resources. During execution, a Task Manager can exchange data with other TaskManager running the same application.

Kubernetes Operator

Operators are used to extend the Kubernetes API and specific application controllers, which are used to create, configure, and manage complex stateful applications such as databases, caches, and monitoring systems. Operators are built on top of Kubernetes' concepts of resources and controllers but include application-specific domain knowledge. The key to creating an Operator is the design of Custom Resource Define (CRD).

This feature allows developers to extend and add new features, update existing features, and automate some management tasks. These custom controllers are just like Kubernetes native components. Operators directly use the Kubernetes API for development. That is to say, and they can monitor the cluster, change Pods/Services, and scale running applications based on custom rules written inside these controllers.

Operator Framework

The Operator Framework is also a toolkit for the rapid development of Operators. The framework consists of two main parts:

- **Operator SDK** helps you to build an Operator application based on your own expertise without having to understand complex Kubernetes related features.

- **Operator Lifecycle Manager (OLM)** allows you to install, update, and operate all Operators (and their associated services) running across the Kubernetes clusters.

Workflow

Use the Operator SDK and the following workflow to develop a new Operator:

1. Create a new Operator project using the SDK.

2. Define a new resource API by adding a custom resource (CRD).

3. Specify the resources to watch using the SDK API.

4. Define the operators ' reconcile logic'.

5. Use the Operator SDK to build and generate the Operator deployment manifest file.

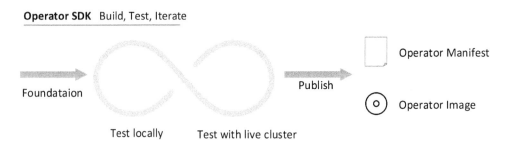

Figure 11-6 Operator SDK

Flink Kubernetes Operator

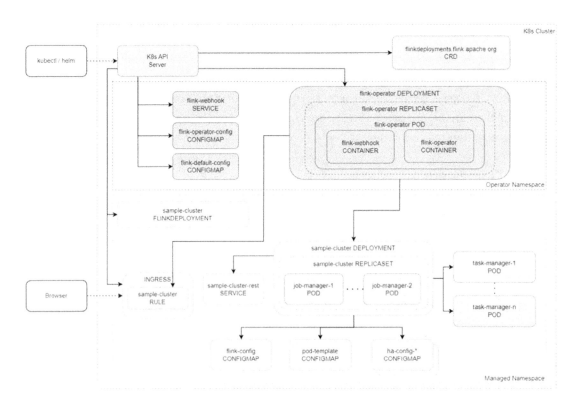

Figure 11-7 Flink Kubernetes Operator (picture from Flink Project on https://apache.org)

Flink Kubernetes Operator is responsible for acting as a control plane to manage the complete deployment lifecycle of Apache Flink applications. The Operator can be installed on a Kubernetes cluster using Helm. In the Distributed Cloud, it can be deployed in a designated namespace and controls Flink deployments in one or more managed namespaces.

The Flink Kubernetes Operator manages Flink applications on the Kubernetes cluster. The operator extends the Kubernetes API with the ability to act as a control plane to manage the complete deployment lifecycle of the Flink Cluster resources:

- Deploy and monitor both Flink application and session deployments.

- Upgrade, suspend and delete deployments.

- Collect log and metrics information.

Flexible Deployments and Native Integration with Original Kubernetes Tooling

For isolation, you should deploy it in a designated namespace and control Flink deployments in single or multiple managed namespaces for production environments. The custom resource definition (CRD) that describes the schema of a Flink Deployment is a cluster-wide resource. For a CRD, the declaration must be registered before any resources of that CRD kind(s) can be used.

There are several benefits to running Flink on Kubernetes, and it becomes more flexible and lighter weight to deploy streaming applications without needing to manage infrastructures. The Flink operator aims to abstract out the complexity of hosting, configuring, managing, and operating Flink clusters from application developers. It achieves these benefits by extending any Kubernetes cluster using custom resources. For detailed information on Kubernetes custom resources, please go to the Kubernetes official website https://kubernetes.io.

As shown in Figure 11-7, The Operator creates Flink clusters dynamically using the specified custom resource. Flink clusters in Kubernetes consist of JobManager Deployment, TaskManager Deployment, JobManager Service, and Ingress for the UI (if it is needed).

Flink Kubernetes Operator Managed Flink Cluster

In addition to the previously introduced Distributed Cloud data architecture, you can deploy any standalone open-source data software on the Distributed Cloud leveraging the advanced features of the Distributed Cloud. Now, here we will introduce the architecture using the Flink operator to steer the Flink cluster based on the Kubernetes environment.

The Tier 1 Scheduler empowered by the Flink Operator at the OneCenter, Flink Operator corresponds to multiple Job Managers located in the distributed site edges. The Task Managers running on the computing node are responsible for the slot schedule and edge devices control (shown as ❶ in Figure 11-8). In the case of a fewer resource edges site, the Flink Task Managers can connect to the Job Manager that is located on the site edge of the parent site or located in the IPU host of the edge node. The data flow is shown as ❷ in the Figure 11-8 travels from the edge site to the data center over the MQTT or HTTP, etc., continuously.

Under the Flink cluster, the Kubernetes cluster provides an elastic cloud environment based on the geo-distributed Distributed Cloud site infrastructures.

For the Flink users and applications, they can think the resources of the Kubernetes Cluster and the Distributed Cloud site infrastructure are elastic and have no scope/volume/location limit to consume.

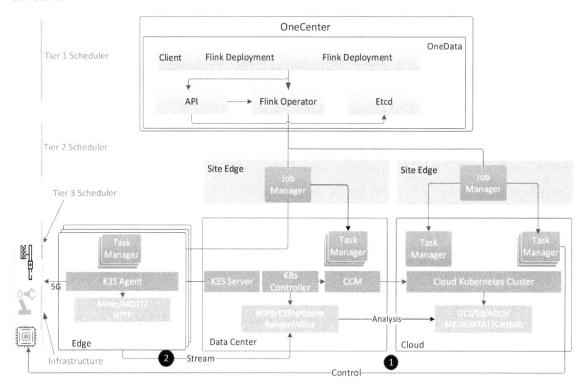

Figure 11-8 Reference Architecture of Flink Kubernetes Operator Managed Flink Cluster

11.4 The Distributed Cloud Based Data Governance

With the development of the scale of the company and the vary the type of business, the type, quantity, and location of the data generated by the business are undergoing tremendous changes, whether the data management, including data storage, data integration, data quality management, data security, and database management, or Data applications have become very complex. Especially when multiple types and multiple data sources are connected, and real-time processing is required.

From the failure of a single infrastructure, public or private cloud, to deliver expected business outcomes comes the era of hybrid and multi-cloud. Changes in data architecture driven by these cloud computing technologies. However, there are still many limitations and challenges.

Although it is said that now is the era of data and artificial intelligence, data governance and data analysis still face many complex challenges, such as isolated data storage impacting seamless data integration due to the rapid increase in data sources, data types, and data volume. Low data quality or lack of data governance policies at the corporate strategic level, etc.

1. Data Governance Pitfalls Based on Hybrid Multi-cloud

In most cases, the business of an enterprise is across multi-nation worldwide, and the data is also distributed widely. These distributed resources may be provided by multiple specific cloud vendors. Resources are shared over the private cloud, hybrid cloud, and multi-cloud environments. However, the heterogeneity of these cloud platforms and the differences in compliance, etc., make data movement and data governance very difficult.

2. Data Governance Challenges Based on Cloud Warehouse

The cloud warehouse seems to be an ideal solution; data governance requires centralized management, but it needs to be executed locally. This effectively means that the actual execution is done by the database and application as close to the data sources rather than being put into another layer, which would become a single point of failure.

In conclusion, enterprises need a technical solution in terms of advanced data management platforms and tools that can solve all the above challenges.

3. The Distributed Cloud is Coming

For the hybrid cloud, one part is designed, owned, controlled, and operated by the customer, and the other part is steered by the public cloud provider. Coordinating with each other brings many challenges. Customers retain responsibility for parts of their operations but have very limited capabilities (e.g., skills, speed of innovation, investment, and technology) to leverage public cloud providers.

The Distributed Cloud facilitates the coexistence of multiple public cloud networks across geographies, combining local data centers, remote public cloud providers' networks, telco edge in the CORD, and other edge locations. Management is centrally controlled from a central single point. The Distributed Cloud is a new generation of cloud computing, which has all the capabilities and advantages of classic cloud computing but at the same time expands the scope, capabilities, flexibility, and use cases of traditional cloud.

In a Distributed Cloud environment, the speed, quality, and performance of business analytics can be greatly improved by providing edge computing that allows applications to execute very close to where the data is generated. More importantly, with the emergence of advanced data related technologies such as big data, IoT, and AI, various edge computing has been greatly promoted. Multi-mode edge computing based on the Distributed Cloud helps to solve the overlooked and hard-to-solve compliance challenges in the Distributed Cloud.

4. Data Fabric Simplifies Data Governance and Security

As data becomes increasingly distributed and complex, it becomes increasingly difficult to effectively manage and secure data across the enterprise. Whether securing data across disparate repositories or monitoring access across disparate business units, the proliferation of data technologies and repositories on-premises and in the cloud is making the task impossible, and the continued pressure to provide business users with self-service access to data will only make the challenge even bigger.

The Data Fabric and Data Virtualization technologies fit with the Distributed Cloud architecture. It not only increases the agility of data delivery but also provides a simple, fast, and cost-effective way to integrate, protect, and govern all enterprise data.

5. The Distributed Cloud Based Data Governance is the Future

The Distributed Cloud has its natural and unique architectural advantages in supporting data governance. With the change in enterprise business, data distribution mode, the diversity of data types, and the rapid growth of data volume, it is impossible for a centralized IT team to manage and govern data across the enterprise to ensure that data access to all of its users is well managed and monitored, enterprises must move to a distributed data management model. In this distributed model, data management roles and responsibilities are shared across the enterprise. This new scenario is architecturally consistent with a Distributed Cloud, where decentralized teams of experts will "manage data access and permissions while eliminating bottlenecks that exist today with centralized IT."

In short, in the future, Distributed Cloud-based data governance technology and architecture will further develop rapidly, promote each other, and accelerate the rapid development of the global digital industry and digital economy.

Appendix: Bibliography

Microsoft; https://learn.microsoft.com/en-us/azure/architecture/solution-ideas/articles/video-analytics; 2023

Jason Gooley, Dana Yanch, et al.; Cisco Software-Defined Wide Area Networks: Designing, Deploying and Securing Your Next Generation WAN with Cisco SD-WAN (Networking Technology); 2020

AWS; AWS Certified Solutions Architect Official Study Guide; Sybex; ISBN:978-1119138556; 2017

Denodo; The Denodo Platform 8.0 Technical Architecture; 2022

Gartner; https://www.gartner.com/en/information-technology/glossary/The Distributed Cloud; 2020

Gartner; https://www.gartner.com/en/data-analytics/topics/data-architecture;2022

DAMA; DAMA-DMBOK, Data Management Body of Knowledge; 2ndEdition; ISBN: 9781634622349; 2017

Zoom Video Communications Inc.; Zoom Connection Process Whitepaper; 2020

Apache;https://apache.org; 2023

3GPP;https://www.3gpp.org/specifications;2023

Appendix: About the Author

Weiqi Tian has worked in Fujitsu, Samsung Electronics, JD.COM, and other listed companies, with extensive work experience in research, development, design, and architecture in 3G to 5G communication technology, networking, Big Data, and Cloud Computing fields. He is good at big data platform architecture design, mobile communication product design, and cloud computing platform architecture and design and has considerable practical experience in related fields. He has earned certifications as an expert Administrator and Professional Architect from Cloudera and AWS, etc.

Hong Lin has many years of working experience in famous publishers, with rich experience in book editing, proofreading cover design, etc.

Appendix: Glossary

Glossary	Description
5GC	5G Core
5GC-CP	5G Core Control Plane
5GNR/NR	5G New Radio/ New Radio
ACL	Access Control List
ADLS	Azure Data Lake Storage
AF	Application Function
AFI	Address Family Identifier
AI	Artificial Intelligence
AMF	Access and Mobility Management Function
AMI	Amazon Machine Image
AR/VR	Augmented Reality/Virtual Reality
ARP	Address Resolution Protocol
AS	Autonomous System
ASM	Any-Source Multicast
AUSF	Authentication Server Function
AGV	Automated Guided Vehicle

Glossary	Description
BDS	Boot Device Selection
BFD	Bidirectional Forwarding Detection
BGP	Border Gateway Protocol
BGW	Border Gateway
BM	Bare Metal
BMC	Board Management Controller
BSS	Business Support Systems
BUM	Unknown, Broadcast, and Multicast
CDP	Cloudera Data Platform
CI/CD	Continuous Integration/Dilevery
CIDR	Classless Inter-Domain Routing
CIM	Container Infrastructure Management
CN	Core network
CNCF	Cloud Native Computing Foundation
CNF	Container Network or Cloud-Native Network Function
CNI	Container Network Interface
CORD	Central Office Re-architected as a Data Center
CRD	Custom Resource Define
CRI-O	Container Runtime Interface - Open Container Initiative

Glossary	Description
CSEC	Converged SNPN Edge Computing
CSI	Container Storage Interface
CSMA	Carrier Sense Multiple Access/Collision Detection
CSMF	Customer Service Management Function
CSP	Communication Service Provider
CU	Centralized Unit
DAG	Directed Acyclic Graph
DAMA	Data Management Association
DBX	Operational Database
DCDN	Dynamic Content Delivery Network
DCI	Data Center Interconnect
DEX	Data Process Engineering
DF	Designated-Forwarder
DFX	DataFlow Engine
DG	Data Governance
DGP	Distributed Gateway Port
DLR	Distributed Logical Router
DMBOK	Data Management Body of Knowledge
DN	Data Networks
DNAT	Destination Network Address Translation

Glossary	Description
DPDK	Data Plane Development Kit
DPU	Data Process Unit
DR	Distributed Router
DSS	Digital Security Surveillance
DTLS	Datagram Transport Layer Security
DU	Distributed Unit
DVR	Distriubted Virtual Router
DWX	Data Warehouse
DXE	Driver Execution Environment
eBGP	Exterior Border Gateway Protocol
EBS	Amazon Elastic Block Store
eCDN	Enterprise Content Delivery Network
ECMP	Equal-Cost Multipath
EIP	Elastice IP
EKS	Amazon Elastic Kubernetes Service
Elastic EP	Elastic Endpoint
ER	External Router
ESB	Enterprise Service Busses
ESI	EVPN Ethernet Segment Identifie
EVPN	Ethernet Virtual Private Network
FC	Fibre Channel

Glossary	Description
FD	Fault Domain
FIP	Floating IP
FPGA	Field Programmable Gate Arrays
FRR	Free Range Routing
GC	Garbage Collection
GCS	Google Cloud Storage
GKE	Google Kubernetes Engine
gNB	Next Generation Node B
GPU	Graphics Processing Unit
gPXE	Open source (GPL) Network Bootloader
GRE	Generic Routing Encapsulation
GRUB	GRUND Unified Bootloader
GTP	GUID Partition Table
GUI	Graphical User Interface
GVPC	Global End-to-End Virtual Private Cloud
HA	High Availability
HCI	Hyperconverged Infrastructure
HG	Host Group
HPC	High-performance Computing
HWOL	Hardware Offloading

Glossary	Description
IAM	Identity and Access Management
iBGP	Internal Border Gateway Protocol
IC	Industrial Controller
ICT	Information and Communication Technology
IDE	Integrated Development environment
IETF	Internet Engineering Task Force
IGP	Interior Gateway Protocol
IGW	Internet Gateway
IIoT	Industrial Internet of Things
IKE	Internet Key Exchange
IOMMU	Input-output Memory Management Unit
IOPS	Input/Output Operations Per Second
IPAM	IP Address Management
IPMI	Intelligent Platform Management Interface
IPU	Infrastructure Processing Units
iPXE	A Leading Open Source Network Boot Firmware
IR	Ingress Replication
IRB	Integrated Routing and Bridging
iSCSI	Internet Small Computer System Interface
KPI	Key Performance Indicators

Glossary	Description
KVM	Kernel-based Virtual Machine
LILO	Linux Loader
LRP	Logical Router Ports
LSP	Logical Switch Ports
LXC	LinuX Containers
MBR	Master Boot Record
MDS	Metadata Server
MEC	Multiple Edge Compting
MLX	Machine Learning
MMR	Multimedia Routers
MBGP	Multiprotocol BGP
MP-BGP	Multiprotocol BGP
MPLS	Multiprotocol Label Switching
MPP	Massively Parallel Processing
MPX	Massively Parallel Processing Database
N3IWF	Non-3GPP InterWorking Function
NAT	Network Address Translation
NBP	Network Bootstrap Program
NEF	Network Exposure Function
NFV/NFVI	Function Virtualization/NFV Infrastructure
NIC	Network Interface Controller

Glossary	Description
NLRI	Network Layer Reachability Information
NPN	Non-public Network
NRF	Network Resource Function
NS-TT	Network-Side TSN Translator
NSMF	Network Service Management Function
NSSMF	Network Slice Subnet Management Function
NUMA	Non-uniform Memory Access
NVE	Network Virtualization Edge
NVMe-oF	NVMe over Fabric
OEM	Original Equipment Manufacturer
OLM	Operator Lifecycle Manager
OSD	Object Storage Daemons
OSPF	Open Shortest Path First
OSS	Operations Support Systems
OU	Organization Unit
OVN	Open Virtual Network
OVS	Open vSwitch
OVSDB	Open vSwitch Database
P2V	Physical Machine to Virtual Machine
PBR	Policy Based Routing
PCF	Policy Control Function

Glossary	Description
PCI	Peripheral Component Interconnect
PDU	Protocol Data Unit
PEI	Pre-EFI Initialization
PF	Physical Function
PG	Place Group
PIM	Protocol-Independent Multicast
PIM	Physical Infrastructure Management
PIP	Private IP
PLMN	Public Land Mobile Network
PNF	Physical Network Functions
PNI	Public Networking Integration
POSIX	Portable Operating System Interface
POST	Power-on Self-test
PV	Physical Volumes
PXE	Pre-boot eXecution Environment
QEMU	Quick Emulator
QoE	Quality of Experience
QOM	Qemu Object Model
RADOS	Reliable Autonomic Distributed Object Store
RAN	Access Network
RBAC	Role-Based Access Control

Glossary	Description
RBD	Ceph's RADOS Block Devices
RD	Route Distinguisher
RDMA	RemoteDirect Memory Access
REST	Representational State Transfer
RGW	RADOS Gateway
RP	Rendezvous-Point
RPO	Recovery Point Objective
RS	Route Server
RT	Route Target / Run Time
RTO	Recovery Time Objective
RTT	Round-trip time
RU	Radio Unit
SAFI	Subsequent Address Family Identifier
SAN	Storage Area Network
SAS	Serial Attached SCSI
SATA	Serial Advanced Technology Attachment
SBA	Service-Based Architecture
SDN	Software-Defined Network
SDPK	Storage Performance Development Kit
SEX	Search Engine
SLA	service-level agreement

Glossary	Description
SMF	Session Management Function
SNAT	Source Network Address Translation
SNPN	Standalone NPN
SOHO	Small Office, Home Office
SQS	Simple Queue Service
SR-IOV	Single root I/O virtualization
SSL	Secure Sockets Layer
STT	Stateless Transport Tunneling
SVI	Switch Virtual Interface
TC-Flower	Traffic Control Flower
TLS	Transport Layer Security
TLV	Type-Length-Value
ToR	Top of Rack
TRM	Tenant Routed Multicast
TSL	Transient System Load
TSN	Time-Sensitive Networking
UDM	Unified Data Management
UE	User Equipment
UEFI	Unified Extensible Firmware Interface
UPF	User Plane Function
URLLC	Ultra-Reliable Low Latency

Glossary	Description
	Communications
UX	User Experience
V2V	Virtual Machine to Virtual Machine
vCDN	Virtual CDN
vDPA	Virtio Data Path Acceleration
VF	Virtual Function
vGPU	Virtual Graphics Processing Unit
VGW	Virtual Private Gateways
VIP	Virtual IP
VMM	Virtual Machine Monitor
VNC	Virtual Network Computing
VNF	Virtual Network Function
VNI	VXLAN Network Identifier
VPC	Virtual Private Cloud
VRF	Virtual Routing and Forwarding
VDC	Virtual Distributed Cloud
VT	Virtualization Technology
VTEP	VXLAN Tunnel End Point
WAN	Wide-Area Network
WMP	WAN Management Protocol